H.D. and Modernist Religious Imagination

Also available from Bloomsbury

Conrad's 'Heart of Darkness' and Contemporary Thought, edited by Nidesh Lawtoo
In the Beginning, She Was, Luce Irigaray
Irigaray, Incarnation and Contemporary Women's Writing, Abigail Rine
Katherine Mansfield and Literary Modernism, edited by Gerri Kimber, Susan Reid, Janet Wilson
T. E. Hulme and Modernism, Oliver Tearle
Reading Mina Loy's Autobiographies, Sandeep Parmar
Virginia Woolf's Late Cultural Criticism, Alice Wood
The Modernist God State: A Literary Study of the Nazis' Christian Reich, Michael Lackey

H.D. and Modernist Religious Imagination

Mysticism and Writing

Elizabeth Anderson

Bloomsbury Academic
An imprint of Bloomsbury Publishing Plc

B L O O M S B U R Y
LONDON • NEW DELHI • NEW YORK • SYDNEY

Bloomsbury Academic
An imprint of Bloomsbury Publishing Plc

50 Bedford Square
London
WC1B 3DP
UK

1385 Broadway
New York
NY 10018
USA

www.bloomsbury.com

BLOOMSBURY and the Diana logo are trademarks of Bloomsbury Publishing Plc

First published 2013
Paperback edition first published 2015

British Library Cataloguing-in-Publication Data
A catalogue record for this book is available from the British Library.

ISBN: HB: 978-1-4411-8597-6
PB: 978-1-4742-2283-9
ePDF: 978-1-4411-3973-3
ePUB: 978-1-4411-9089-5

Library of Congress Cataloging-in-Publication Data
A catalog record for this book is available from the Library of Congress.

Typeset by Newgen Imaging Systems Pvt Ltd, Chennai, India

For David Lynn, who set my feet on this path,
and James Anderson, who travels it with me daily.

Contents

Acknowledgements

This book began its life as a doctoral thesis and my first thanks must go to my supervisors, who showed great care in nurturing this project. Dr Kate McLoughlin supported the early stages of this project and always pushed me towards greater clarity in my thinking and writing. Dr Bryony Randall effortlessly picked up the threads of a project already begun, and I am grateful for her continuing thoughtfulness and nuanced commentary in directing it towards completion. Profound gratitude is due to Dr Heather Walton, who has been a faithful and tireless midwife to this project since its earliest conception. Without her ongoing engagement and support, this book would not have been written.

I wish to gratefully acknowledge the Arts and Humanities Research Council, for providing the Doctoral Award that supported this research. The AHRC, along with the Arts Faculty (now College) at the University of Glasgow, also provided additional funds to conduct research at Yale University. I also wish to add my voice to the chorus of H.D. scholars in thanking the staff at the Beinecke Rare Book and Manuscript Library. Their kindness and professionalism made my two weeks in New Haven a happy and productive time.

I would like to thank David Avital and Laura Murray at Bloomsbury for their support, encouragement and belief in this book. I also wish to thank the Bloomsbury readers whose thoughtful feedback enhanced this project considerably.

Fruitful research is rarely done in a vacuum and I have been extremely fortunate in the support and encouragement offered by the staff and students in Theology and Religious Studies, English Literature and the Graduate School for the Arts and Humanities at the University of Glasgow. The Centre for the Study of Literature, Theology and the Arts provided a welcoming and encouraging environment for my interdisciplinary interests to grow. In particular, I would like to thank several colleagues: Anna Fisk, for asking the questions I don't dare; Jamey Heit, for his linguistic inventiveness and ongoing encouragement; Meg MacDonald, for making things happen and keeping all my ducks in a row; Kate Morris, for her timely French consultations; Jennifer Reek, for tea, Cixous and sympathy; and Alana Vincent, whose rigorous scholarship and creative thinking is a constant inspiration, for helping me think through many problems and rescuing me from numerous quagmires. Thanks are due Professor David Jasper and Professor Morag Shiach for their invaluable feedback. I also wish to thank the members of the Cixous Reading Group, who helped develop my thinking and deepen my enjoyment of Cixous's work. To colleagues across GSAH: Marc Alexander, Ellen Bramwell, Mark Godin, Johanna Green, Ruth Hawthorn, Hannah Little, Erin Riley and Tania Scott – your camaraderie kept me going through endless revisions and ref checking. Tea, cake and gin for everyone!

I was aided by the editorial eyes of several colleagues: Ruth Hawthorn, Jamey Heit, Kate Morris, Bryony Randall and Alana Vincent. I am grateful for their time and effort.

Thanks are due to Kate Reynolds and Kimberly Bohan for their unwavering belief in this project, as well as in me, and for teaching me the meaning of visionary.

Early version of sections of Chapters Four and Five were presented at the International Society for Literature, Religion and Culture (ISRLC) conference in Aarhus, Denmark, in October 2008; at the Modernist Studies Association conference in Montreal, Canada, in November 2009; at the Re-writing the Bible conference in Glasgow in June 2010; and at the ISRLC conference in Oxford in September 2010. I would like to thank the organizers for giving me the opportunity to present my work and the audiences for their supportive and helpful feedback.

Previous versions of portions of Chapters One, Two, Three and Five appeared in the following journals: *Women: a cultural review*, *Christianity and Literature* and *Literature and Theology*. I would like to thank the editors for their permission to republish this material here.

I gratefully acknowledge the permission to quote from the following published and unpublished works of H.D. granted by the directors of her Estate in the UK (Carcanet Press Ltd) and the US (New Directions Publishing Corp).

I wish to thank my first teachers – my parents, my sister and my brother – for early lessons in critical thinking. This book has its roots in my undergraduate years at Kenyon College. I wish to thank Professor Ted Mason for introducing me to Hélène Cixous, Beth Costello Peters for insisting I read *Trilogy*, Professor Sergei Lobanov-Rostovsky for teaching me to write and Professors David Lynn and Wendy Singer who taught me much about life within and beyond the academy.

My son Owen has done everything in his (considerable) power to distract me from the task of finishing this book. I thank him for these lessons in perseverance – and for lessons in the joy and creativity which are the heart of my life both on and off the page. To those adopted aunties – Isobel MacNaughton, Meg MacDonald and Jennifer Reek – whose timely interventions provided urgently needed time to work, heartfelt thanks are due. This book would not have been completed without you.

Finally, always, to James, for providing thoughtful commentary when I wanted it, silence when I asked for it and encouragement when I didn't know I needed it, for endless housework and generous childcare: gratitude unending. You have fed this project, and me, from the beginning. No words are precise enough.

Introduction

Making poetry is a craft that always exceeds the poet – who shares in the process but does not have dominion over it – as language exceeds, escapes, flies.

> Wingéd words, we know, make their own spiral; – caught up in them, we are lost, or found. It is what a poem does, or can do [...]
> This winged victory belongs to the poem, not to the poet. But to share in the making of a poem is the privilege of a poet.[1]

> We must not step right over into the transcendental, we must crouch near the grass and near to the earth that made us.[2]

In these passages H.D. employs images that reappear frequently across her work: spirals and wings, which both indicate dynamism and movement. She suggests that poetic language makes us, as much, if not more, than we make it. She emphasizes that poetry is a craft and a poem an artefact. An insistence on the material marks both passages – the materiality of language and the materiality of the world. The phrase 'Wingéd words' recalls the sacred figures such as angels and bees that populate H.D.'s poetry.[3] 'Wings' also has a more personal meaning for her; it was an important word during her 1940s spiritualist experiments that in turn reminded her of a visionary experience from 1920.[4] 'Wingéd words' brings together poetry, vision and unorthodox spiritual practices. The multilayered inventive delight in language evident in her work is generated by attention to the material world; for H.D., writing is a spiritual practice. In her texts alterity and mystery are located in the intersection of language, the sacred and the material.

This book examines this nexus of H.D.'s religious sensibility and her creative work. In this introduction I outline her idiosyncratic spirituality, consisting of the syncretism of Moravian Christianity, Hermeticism, spiritualism and other occult beliefs and practices, which I define as visionary Hermeticism. I then go on to outline my theoretical framework which draws upon the work of the poststructuralist French theorist Hélène Cixous. I then outline my key texts by H.D. and situate my work in the critical context of H.D. studies' and modernist studies' growing interest in religion, and conclude with a chapter outline.

Visionary Hermeticism

Like many modernists, H.D. was interested in art's potential as a resource for cultural renewal. However, she did not see art as a replacement for religion but as a means to, and expression of, spiritual understanding. Neither atheist nor orthodox, H.D. – like W. B. Yeats, D. H. Lawrence, Rosamond Lehmann and Mary Butts – followed a third way. Her religious syncretism allows her to engage with spiritual concerns in her writing without subordinating it to the demands of doctrine, unlike writers such as T. S. Eliot who ultimately viewed art as subservient to religion.[5] H.D.'s continued interest in the Moravian Christianity of her childhood and her blending of pagan, Hermetic and spiritualist imagery with Moravian rituals and history distinguishes her from writers who express a more straightforward relationship to the occult.[6] Hermeticism as the search for ancient wisdom, and the apprehension of that wisdom through visionary consciousness, are the guiding forces of H.D.'s syncretism. In examining the strains of religious syncretism in her work, the mythic and the visionary are rarely far away. Visions and dreams present opportunities for heightened awareness of the sacred, but for H.D. vision and ordinary reality are not two distinct spheres. Vision provides a dynamic that aligns her poetry with both the past and the future.

In 1919 H.D. travelled to the Scilly Isles with her companion Bryher; the following year the pair went to Greece.[7] During these travels H.D. experienced a number of visions which would preoccupy her for years, proving a creative catalyst for her imaginative, religious and mythological thinking and providing a counterpoint to the war's traumas. They would form a crucial element in her analysis with Freud in the 1930s and inspire works from the prose essay *Notes on Thought and Vision* (written in 1919 and published in 1982), to the memoir *Tribute to Freud* (serialized in 1945 and 1946 and published in book form in 1956) and to her autobiographical novel *The Sword Went Out to Sea* (written in 1947 and published in 2007).[8]

It is difficult to determine the appropriate terminology for discussing H.D.'s experiences and her writings on them. These strange psychic phenomena were not entirely visual: one of H.D.'s experiences was primarily kinaesthetic, yet another had a stronger emotional cast than others. H.D. herself uses a number of different highly idiosyncratic ways of referring to the phenomenon – 'jelly-fish experience', 'a state of transcendental imagination', 'writing-on-the-wall'.[9] For the sake of simplicity I will use 'vision' or 'visionary consciousness' as broad term to include the range of these sorts of events.

H.D. describes the process of seeing visions as simultaneously spontaneous and willed as she indicates that intense concentration was required to maintain the frame of consciousness that allowed the images to appear. Moreover, she describes the process of maintaining this concentration as a high-stakes quest:

> I have the feeling of holding my breath under water. As if I were searching under water for some priceless treasure. […] In a sense, it seems I am drowning. […] I must drown completely and come out on the other side […] with a new set of values, my treasure dredged from the depth. I must be born again or break utterly.[10]

Visionary consciousness becomes a quest for transformation. H.D. combines the language of loss, danger, death and rebirth with that of seeking after treasure. Her treasure is the vision itself, new spiritual consciousness and inspired writing. Her own survival and transformation is the key to this new awareness.

After her illness in 1919 she had declared to Bryher, 'If I could only feel that I could walk the sacred way to Delphi, I know I would get well'.[11] Delphi is aligned with healing and artistic inspiration; H.D. mourns the modern separation of religion, art and medicine and suggests that their unity is represented by the tripod (one of the images in her visionary experience on Corfu in Greece). In *Tribute to Freud* she describes telling her visions as laying down cards in expectation of Freud's analysis of the images.[12] With this reference to Tarot she simultaneously casts Freud in the role of fortune-teller and aligns her visions with esoteric traditions. She connects her writing with her visions and Delphic prophecy, noting that the Priestess of Delphi prophesied in couplets that could be read in many ways.[13] Moreover, by considering the images as writing and referring to them as picture-writing she relates her vision to hieroglyphics.[14] Thus she connects her own visions with psychoanalysis, esoteric traditions, ancient religions and art. Vision becomes a catalyst for writing, while writing gives expression to vision.

This brings my discussion of H.D. as visionary to the question of religion. The religious ideas, images, visions and practices that permeate H.D.'s writing result in a highly creative, idiosyncratic mysticism. H.D.'s syncretist view of religion included spiritualism, Moravian Christianity, astrology and Hermeticism. I would argue that not only is Hermeticism the dominant religious philosophy of perhaps her best known work, the epic poem *Trilogy*, as Timothy Materer claims, but it is also the worldview that frames her entire oeuvre.[15] Furthermore, Hermeticism subsumes the other elements of her religious syncretism, as they can all be understood, in H.D.'s formulations, as enabling a search for hidden wisdom. H.D.'s work expresses a Hermetic Christianity, Hermetic spiritualism, a Hermetic approach to pagan mythologies, etc.

Scholars of Hermeticism are quick to point out the complexities, contradictions, diversity and enigmas of this tradition. The proliferation of texts and myths and the complex dynamics of secrecy and revelation make it difficult to track. It spins off in numerous directions – alchemy, Rosicrucianism, Freemasonry, and other strands of esotericism – and has numerous similarities with systems that are, in fact, fundamentally different, such as Gnosticism and Neoplatonism. I will outline Hermeticism in more detail in Chapter Three. Here let me simply note it is marked by devotion to the Greek god Hermes and the ancient wisdom revealed and concealed in texts ascribed to the ancient Egyptian sage Hermes Trismegistus (the honorific means 'thrice-great' and this figure is sometimes elided with the god); it is 'a form of thought rather than a doctrine'.[16] As well as being a way of thinking, Hermeticism contributes significantly to H.D.'s stylistics. The close association she draws between writing and Hermeticism is revealed not only in terms of content, but also in the form and style of her work. Umberto Eco argues that the interconnectedness the Hermeticist finds in the world enables an interpretative tradition based in reasoning by way of analogy; each interpretation is partial and unfolds into the next.[17] As Antoine Faivre puts it, a Hermetic reading will always be plural.[18] As Materer and Tryphonopoulos argue, H.D.'s associative style is not only a manifestation of her modernism but also an expression of Hermeticism.[19]

H.D. and Cixous: Mysticism in writing

Like many modernists, H.D. has been read psychoanalytically, using a number of theorists including Kristeva and Lacan.[20] While a reading of H.D. and Hélène Cixous could follow this critical trend, I wish to focus on under-researched areas of Cixous's work: her engagements with spirituality and trauma.[21] These aspects of Cixous's writing are particularly helpful for my investigation of H.D.'s religious sensibility and concern with language and creativity. What I find most suggestive about reading H.D. and Cixous together is their interest in language as excessive, mysterious and material.

H.D. and Cixous have a number of stylistic affinities: both employ a complex constellation of allusions within their texts; both bend genre conventions; both use non-realist narration and word-play. Cixous's texts are frequently in dialogue with modernist texts and she can be read as part of the European avant-garde tradition.[22] Their writing style is reiterative. Themes, metaphors, ideas and images continue to circulate across their numerous texts and many of these concepts themselves bleed into one another. These stylistic qualities enable their attention to difference within and between subjectivities, which is the source of much of their writing's energy. Their writing speaks from the other's place on the margins of dominant cultural narratives: as woman, as Jew, as queer. Their writing on subjectivity and alterity engages the relationship between culture, imagination and the body.

In this book I argue that H.D. and Cixous view language as mysterious and sacred yet rooted in the earth, the domestic and the bodily, not a transcendent ideal. Cixous writes:

> But god, I say, is the phantom of writing, it is her pretext and her promise. God is the name of all that has not yet been said. Without the word *Dieu* to shelter the infinite multiplicity of all that could be said the world would be reduced to its shell and I to my skin. [...] God is not the one of religions [...] [but] [t]he force that makes me write, the *always unexpected Messiah* [...] the returning spirit or the spirit of returning.[23]

Here she demonstrates the capacity of language both to make a space for mystery and to celebrate the material. Like one of H.D.'s spirals, this passage is circular but not static; the 'not yet' suggests orientation towards the future and yet the final emphasis on return invokes the past. God is called into being by writing, 'of my making', and yet is other than writing, 'what has not yet been said'. The divine is both the shelter of the writing and the inexplicable unknown beyond the writer's knowledge, an elsewhere that is invoked and explored, but never fully understood or appropriated.

Cixous's concern with writing as such leads to an emphasis on the materiality of language. For Cixous, 'elsewhere' is a mystery within the text, located in the shifting layers of the density of language. Her work is resolutely literary, drawing attention to its textuality by wordplay, apostrophes to the reader and meta-discourse on the nature of language and writing. However, intertwined with these language games is an attention to the world beyond the text. Ordinary objects and experiences are ubiquitous in her oeuvre. She rhapsodizes the pleasures of an orange, the magic of the telephone, the strange and wild love provoked by a cat. She brings the mysterious and material together by de-familiarizing ordinary objects and activities and then presenting them as strange and new: 'I believe that the stone is a diamond [...] What interests me is precisely to enable the celebration of the grain of dust.'[24] In the attention to the materiality of language and the signifying possibilities in objects, her work is concerned with the transformative potential of writing.[25] The stone becomes a diamond – infinitely precious – without losing its stoniness.

Alterity is a crucial concept for understanding Cixous's oeuvre.[26] Her writing is a search for an encounter with alterity and a welcoming gesture towards the other that does not appropriate or annihilate, but recognizes, difference. Her writing approaches alterity through paradox. She alternately describes writing as a place – 'the passageway, the entrance, the exit, the dwelling place of the other in me' – or a movement, which is also a message – 'A poem merely passes, coming from elsewhere then moving on. Signifying to us, in passing, at its passage, this elsewhere.'[27] Cixous's writing provides a way of reading H.D. by way of 'a tradition that [...] allow[s] us to read feminine speech as divine speech, as mystified writing.'[28]

Mystified, mystical, mysterious – these words occupy an uneasy space in academic discourse. They are often used as terms of abuse by scholars to dismiss work as not suitably materially, historically or politically grounded. Alternatively, they are used to demarcate an unknown space beyond or aside (and therefore, irrelevant to) the matter at hand.[29] Using 'mystified' or 'mystical' as a term of dismissal allows one to avoid a more nuanced critique. Alternatively, these terms are used to demarcate a zone into which the argument will not enter. Both of these strategies impoverish academic discourse. I want to recover these terms, while acknowledging their slippery, evasive nature. I am not persuaded that there is a *necessary* link between the mystical/mystified and the a-political, a-historical, immaterial. Moreover, the use of 'mystified' or 'mystical' as a term of dismissal avoids the question of what theorizing about or exploring this terrain might actually involve. In this book I explore how Cixous and H.D. deploy the mystical and mysterious while considering what resources these terms might bring to materialist, historical concerns.

Scholars have found the term 'mysticism' itself notoriously difficult to define and many definitions begin with some sort of disclaimer about the ambiguity of the term.[30] Some definitions are primarily historical, based on particular religious traditions in particular times and places.[31] Others look to the (primarily psychological) trends which characterize mysticism across differing traditions; however, these run the risk of taking instances of mysticism out of context and eliding historical differences.[32] Mystical writing has been described in terms that resonate with visionary poetics: 'the [mystical] experience [...] can only be presented indirectly [...] by a series of verbal strategies in which language is used not so much informationally as transformationally.'[33] Moreover, 'the paradox of mystical language lies here, for it is a discourse predicated on its own impossibility.'[34] For my purposes, a loose definition will suffice. Mysticism involves a passion for the divine. Imagination and affect have primacy over doctrine. This understanding accords with H.D.'s and Cixous's writing; their work is highly affective and involves a passionate attachment to the divine, which remains at most an ambiguous, changeable presence in their writing.

Texts and contexts

This book does not present a survey of religion in H.D.'s writing. I do not discuss the incantatory poems or the religious novel *Pilate's Wife* (2000) of the 1930s. This book focuses primarily on H.D.'s writing from the Second World War because this is where her religious syncretism is most crucial to her writing, where she explores Moravian history most fully and where a number of spiritual themes that appear across her oeuvre have their first full expression. I focus on the novels and poetry of this period because I am primarily interested in the intersection of H.D.'s spirituality and creative practice, i.e. what she *does* with her beliefs and experiences through the medium of literature. Thus, for example, I have chosen to focus on *The Sword Went Out to Sea* as a more complex engagement with the spiritualist episodes detailed in the memoir *Majic Ring*. *Trilogy* is the only text I consider at length that was published in H.D.'s lifetime; a perennial text of H.D. studies, I find it newly resonant when read alongside recently published prose from the same period. The ordering of this book is thematic rather than chronological, with the later chapters taking a wider range of focus. My main texts are from the 1940s but I also draw upon the early poetry of *Sea Garden* (1916) and her essay on aesthetics, *Notes on Thought and Vision*, in Chapters Four and Five while in Chapter Five and the Conclusion I look forward to the late novel *The Mystery* (written 1950/1 and published in 2009) and her late poetic sequence 'Sagesse' (written in 1957 and published in 1972). Before going on to outline the critical context of this study I will briefly summarize my three key texts: *Trilogy*, *The Gift* and *The Sword Went Out to Sea.*

Trilogy

H.D.'s 'war trilogy' was originally published in three separate volumes: *The Walls Do Not Fall* (1944), *Tribute to the Angels* (1945) and *The Flowering of the Rod* (1946).[35] Each of the long poems consists of 43 sections, written in two-line stanzas (except for the first section of *Walls*, whose stanzas have three lines). Although *Trilogy*'s length and theme suggest that it is best classed as an epic, the form and style of its linked sections are closer to lyric, an example of H.D.'s challenge to genre conventions. The poem's theme – a quest for spiritual and cultural renewal for a world shattered by war – is explored through a complex palimpsest of allusions. Egyptian, Greek and Roman gods and goddesses join biblical figures and apocryphal angels to point towards regeneration found in the processes of the natural world, visions, rituals and, most importantly, writing. The first volume, *Walls*, explores personal and creative transformation in the face of London's crumbling buildings. The second, *Angels*, focuses on the presence of angels within the war-torn city; in its central vision, a Lady (the Roman fertility goddess, the Bona Dea) joins the poem's other sacred figures in exhorting the poet and reader to search for renewal, signified by the blank book she carries. The final volume, *Rod*, moves from direct evocation of London to an imagined space where H.D. provides a feminist revision of the Gospel narratives. She focuses on Mary Magdalene and the Arab sage, Kaspar; between them, these two marginalized figures discover and deliver the gift of myrrh to Mary of Nazareth at the Epiphany. Through this narrative H.D. further explores the nexus of sacred materiality and visionary experience. *Trilogy* explores a feminist spirituality that is an ongoing concern in many of her texts.

The Gift

The Gift was written between 1941 and 1943 but it remained unpublished until an abridged version was published by New Directions in 1982. This edition left out much compelling material, and scholars still turned to the archive for the full manuscript. The complete memoir was published by the University Press of Florida in 1998, edited and introduced by Jane Augustine.[36] This autobiographical text oscillates between episodes from H.D.'s childhood in Pennsylvania, narrated by the child, Hilda, and the London Blitz, narrated by the adult writer, H.D. The childhood sections describe experiences that illuminate spiritual and artistic giftedness as rooted in the family and female genealogy. The gift is first presented as characteristic of artists and lacking in Hilda's generation. As the text progresses Hilda challenges this interpretation as she discovers the spiritual meaning of the gift. Hilda's grandmother Mamalie shares memories of her discovery as a young woman of the 'secret' – a peaceful pact made between Moravian Christian colonists and Native Americans in the eighteenth century.[37] A group of Moravians and Algonquians formed a

Hidden Church that recognized the unity of the Moravian Holy Spirit and the Algonquian Great Spirit.[38] However, this peace was broken and the Hidden Church was lost. By the end of the novel, H.D. understands her spiritual and creative vocations as unified: to fulfil the broken promise and lost dream through passing on the message of peace in her own writing.

The Sword Went Out To Sea

This complex two-part novel was written in 1946 and 1947 but, despite H.D.'s efforts, she failed to find a publisher. The text was published in 2007 by the University Press of Florida, edited and introduced by Cynthia Hogue and Julie Vandivere. The protagonist of *The Sword Went Out to Sea* is Delia Alton, a pseudonym frequently used by H.D. in her later writing. I will refer to the author as H.D., for clarity and to emphasize the shared authorship of *Trilogy*, *The Gift* and *The Sword*, and to the character as Delia for textual accuracy and to emphasize the (always slippery) distinction between author and character. *The Sword* is a largely autobiographical account of H.D.'s experience as a medium in the 1940s when she received what she believed to be messages from RAF pilots killed in the Battle of Britain. The first part of the text, 'Wintersleep', describes Delia's attempts to pass on these messages to Lord Howell (a fictional version of Lord Hugh Dowding, the Air Chief Marshal responsible for the victory in the Battle of Britain and himself a spiritualist known to H.D.), her despair at his rejection of the messages and her subsequent mental breakdown. Part II, 'Summerdream', contains a series of linked vignettes, drawn from Delia's life (her youth in Pennsylvania, England in the First World War, European travels in the inter-war years) and earlier historical eras at times of great change or disaster (ancient Athens, imperial Rome, medieval France and Elizabethan London). Throughout these sections a number of characters re-appear in different guises. Delia and Lord Howell are repeatedly re-figured as estranged lovers whose eventual reconciliation will bring in a new era of peace.[39] Written during the post-war era, *The Sword* extends the historical scope of *The Gift*, focusing on the threat of a third world war and the destruction wrought by the atomic bomb.

Critical context: Modernist religious imagination

Certain critical assessments of modernism persist in consigning H.D. to the margins of literary history.[40] However, these judgements were challenged in a series of interventions in the 1970s and 1980s by critics such as Rachel Blau Duplessis, Susan Stanford Friedman, Susan Gubar and Alicia Ostriker.[41] While it may still be a stretch to call H.D. a 'major modernist', she has certainly enjoyed a significant revival in terms of critical attention, revisions of literary history and increased archival research (which has led to greater attention to her substantial prose oeuvre, much of it unpublished in her lifetime).[42] The trickle of posthumous publications emerging from her archive has become a flood; a number of letter collections have appeared recently, four of her novels have been published in scholarly editions by the University Press of Florida (*The Sword Went Out to Sea* in 2007 and *Majic Ring*, *The Mystery* and *The White Rose and the Red* in 2009) and more fiction and prose collections appeared in 2012.[43]

H.D. criticism has developed into a diverse field: psychoanalytic readings took up the theoretical tools of Lacan and Kristeva to consider issues of familial psycho-sexual drama, bisexuality, and creativity while historical readings have considered her work in the context of late nineteenth and early twentieth-century literary and material culture.[44] A particular strand of H.D. criticism is concerned with H.D. as a visionary poet. Susan Stanford Friedman, Alicia Ostriker, Adalaide Morris, Eileen Gregory, Demetres Tryphonopoulos and Timothy Materer analyse the transformative poetics developed in H.D.'s work and make reference to the religious elements in her texts, particularly esotericism.

Robert Duncan's criticism emphasized the importance of H.D.'s work in the face of critics who dismissed her from the modernist canon. His prose opus, *The H.D. Book*, took H.D.'s work as a starting point for a lengthy meditation on modernism and its sources in a quest for a poetics that engaged fully with the occult. Written from 1959 to 1964, sections from *The H.D. Book* were published in little magazines between 1966 and 1985 and quickly became difficult to obtain.[45] The full manuscript was published in 2011 by the University of California Press. The publication of the entirety of the work in a single volume is a welcome contribution to the study of modern and contemporary poetry; it remains to be seen how the availability of this resource will impact readings of H.D. and other modernists. Duncan's reading of H.D. as mystical and Romantic enables his heterodox meditation on the sources and expressions of modernism more broadly. He emphasizes the role of women modernists including, among others, Laura Riding, Jane Harrison, Mary Butts and Edith Sitwell. *The H.D. Book* explores the occult in H.D., intending to 'bring what is hidden to our attention while honouring its hiddenness'.[46] Duncan recognized and embraced H.D.'s Hermeticism, reading her work, especially *Trilogy*, as an attempt 'to keep Hellenistic mysteries alive in the imagination'.[47] *The H.D. Book* is more a meditation than a work of literary criticism or theory. As an aesthetic manifesto, it brings to mind H.D.'s own prose writings on aesthetics and writing. Susan Stanford Friedman's magisterial monograph *Psyche Reborn* (1981) is the cornerstone of contemporary H.D. studies, particularly for any critic interested in H.D. and religion. *Psyche Reborn* focuses primarily on the epic poems *Trilogy* and *Helen in Egypt* (1961), although it also references the prose texts written alongside these epics, particularly *Tribute to Freud*, *The Gift* and *The Sword*. Friedman argues that the two most significant influences on H.D.'s work are psychoanalysis and esotericism. Her contention that the religious experience that drove H.D.'s commitment to working out 'spiritual realism' in her writing 'depend[ed] upon the poet's strong identification with an ongoing mystical tradition' is a claim that I will pick up and explore more fully in this volume.[48] Friedman charts the various elements of H.D.'s syncretist approach to the occult – astrology, alchemy, spiritualism, Hermeticism, Kabbalah – and their relationship to psychoanalysis.[49]

In *Writing Like a Woman* (1983), Alicia Ostriker also turns her attention to H.D.'s mature poems. She uses a strategy common to feminist reclaiming work, arguing simultaneously that H.D.'s long poems belong in the centre of the modernist canon – '[t]hese are works that wrestle with the great modernist issues of faith's collapse and the possibility of reconstruction; self and society; the nature of language and the value of poetry in history; the meaning of the imagination' – and also that they challenge the parameters and values of that tradition.[50] Ostriker finds that elements of H.D.'s early work come to fruition in *Trilogy* (organic imagery, sexuality and war trauma), arguing that the early work itself deconstructs the categories of Imagism. She aligns H.D. with a tradition of visionary poetry that she traces back to William Blake. Ostriker defines the visionary poet as someone 'for whom, behind the flux of secular existence, there exist[s] permanent sacred realities that are both supremely beautiful and supremely forceful'.[51] Ostriker argues that the substance of visionary poetry is located beyond, not within, the poem. Although her reading is supported by the references to complex mythological systems in the text, H.D.'s emphasis on the practice of writing and the significance of language cautions against too transcendent a reading; H.D.'s poetry is resolutely literary.[52]

Like Ostriker and Friedman, Adalaide Morris pays tribute to the complexities of H.D.'s writing: 'The three most important meta-languages in *Trilogy* – the discourses of mysticism, politics, and feminism – are intricately interwoven.'[53] Morris deploys these meta-languages in considering the significance of ritual as cultural practice for the community (of readers) in the political context of the Second World War. Morris argues that feminist criticism such as Gubar's and Duplessis's 'tend[s] to mute the mysticism of H.D.'s practice by turning it back to the material realm and using it to reshape social definitions of gender'.[54] She locates her reading of *Trilogy* in the context of Friedman's, Ostriker's and Robert Duncan's work, arguing that the re-telling of the Christmas story in *The Flowering of the Rod* transforms traditional paradigms into a ritual that 'responds to current cultural dilemmas [...] [and] rejoins the secular and the sacred, in-time and out-of-time, politics and mysticism'.[55] However, the difficulty of aligning feminism and mysticism is demonstrated here, as Morris does not explain *how* the two come together except to say that *Trilogy* works to undermine estrangement that pits men against women. While this is no small thing, it does not encompass the liberation agenda that is feminism's hallmark.

Morris's monograph *How to Live / What to Do: H.D.'s Cultural Poetics* (2003) develops her earlier material. In this volume Morris argues for 'a case for poetic language [...] as an agent of thought, perception, and meaning in the ongoing life of a culture'.[56] She argues that a feature of this kind of language, and of H.D.'s poetry in particular, is a 'pressure of ongoingness, a generativity'.[57] It is this open dynamism that forms H.D.'s continued relevance to late twentieth-century poetry and cultural life. In focusing on thinking and action, Morris's project differs from writing on H.D. that emphasizes her cultural context, or the complexities of the subject positions and desires in the texts. *How to Live / What to Do* does not focus on religion but Morris does approach the topic obliquely. In exploring alchemical projection as a significant concept for H.D., Morris highlights the connection between writer and reader; the 'throwing forward' meaning of projection suggests the image 'forcibly cast onto the reader's imagination'.[58] Alchemy is an important process for *Trilogy* as it indicates creation and transformation and informs the imagery and structure of the poem. I will return to Morris's analysis in my exploration of alchemy in *Trilogy* in Chapter Three; my focus is the explicit alchemical ritual within the poem and its relationship to writing and reading, rather than alchemy as a meta-discourse.

Eileen Gregory's monograph *H.D. and Hellenism: Classic Lines* (1997) is largely concerned with charting H.D.'s lifelong engagement with Hellenic art, literature and mythology in the context of the emerging twentieth-century formulations of classicism. Two areas of her work have influenced the understanding of H.D. and religion developed in this book; the exploration of early twentieth-century fascination with myth and ritual and the influence of Walter Pater's Hermeticism on H.D. Gregory considers the impact of archaeology and

Jane Harrison's work on myth, ritual and their relationship to art in H.D.'s work.[59] The ecstasy of Dionysian ritual and sacred marriage and birth as providing the ritual form of the Eleusinian mysteries are elements of Harrison's theories that resonate with H.D.'s writing. The drama of ancient ritual lends an active formulation to the abstract theories of Hermeticism, while reinforcing their creative potential.[60] In his writing on the Renaissance, Pater shaped a literary approach to pagan mysteries, a visionary approach which utilized the 'poetic theology' of Renaissance thinkers who 'borrowed from the Alexandrian *Hermetica* a metaphorical language of the pagan mysteries, suggesting manifestations to initiates of the God hidden within appearances.'[61] The use of sacred metaphors enabled literature itself to be a vehicle for divine encounter. Moreover, it enables the humanist emphasis on this world (rather than an otherworld beyond death) as a place of sacred reality.[62] This Romantic/Hermetic understanding of the sacred imbuing all of life is crucial for H.D. Gregory places H.D.'s early poetry in a Romantic tradition of theophanic poetry in which the revelation of sacred presence manifests itself not in the appearance of the gods but in a transformation of vision.[63]

The foregoing body of criticism tends to read religious vision as an analogue for poetic vision and to consider H.D.'s work as an exploration of feminine creativity or to treat the religious significance of her work as a small element of a larger project. The criticism that does foreground discussion of religion in H.D.'s work is limited to short articles, book chapters or introductions to editions of H.D.'s prose. Timothy Materer and Demetres Tryphonopoulos both argue for the primacy of Hermeticism and the occult in H.D.'s thinking and stylistics: 'Perhaps the most distinctive feature of occult writing is its radical syncretism. I consider H.D. an "occult" writer primarily because in her prose and poetry radical syncretism constitutes the very fabric of her thought.'[64] Tryphonopoulos describes H.D.'s project as 'a matter of collecting fragments of a faith forgotten – reconstituting [...] [the wisdom of] mystery religions.'[65] Materer joins Chisholm and Friedman in arguing that occultism and psychoanalysis are united in H.D.'s work because 'both explore the hidden.'[66] Like Tryphonopolous, he emphasizes H.D.'s syncretism, arguing that her approach to ancient wisdom 'is seen in her conception of a secret, syncretic wisdom best described as Hermeticism.'[67] However, Materer's attention to psychoanalysis forestalls a fuller exploration of Hermeticism in H.D.'s work.

Despite the importance numerous scholars attribute to Friedman's *Psyche Reborn*, few pick up the religious themes explored in the volume's second half. However, the recent critical editions of the 1940s and 1950s novels, which deal largely with spiritual and religious themes, are one expression of a growing scholarly interest in H.D. and religion. In addition to the recent special issue of *The Journal of Cultural and Religious Theory* on 'H.D. and the Archaeology of Religion', a number of scholars include H.D. in their larger projects on modernism and religion, while texts with a different focus, such as Madelyn Detloff's *The Persistence of Modernism*'s (2009) emphasis on modernism and trauma, also engage with H.D.'s spiritual concerns.[68]

The growing interest in religion and spirituality in H.D. studies intersects with a similar interest within the broader field of modernist studies. Early explorations into this domain include Leon Surette's *The Birth of Modernism* (1993) which argues for the presence of the occult in Pound, Eliot and Yeats and refutes readings that gloss over this influence or assert that it is simply a matter of metaphor and aesthetic style. Surette argues that occult texts form an important intellectual context for these modernist poets and occult figures and tropes form an integral part of the poetry's content. One of the intriguing aspects of Surette's study is his defensive tone. He clearly expects his readers to be taken aback by the claims of his book and goes to great lengths to outline and refute scholarship that insist on the secular and sceptical nature of modernism. Two decades later, his interest in the occult roots of modernist literature does not seem so unusual. Work by scholars such as Alex Owen, Helen Sword, Leigh Eric Schmidt, Pamela Thurschwell, and more recently Suzanne Hobson, Pericles Lewis and Lara Vetter, has seen the field of modernism and religion expand in a number of different directions.[69]

In *Ghostwriting Modernism* (2002), Helen Sword argues that many modernists were caught up in the popular fascination with spiritualism in the first half of the twentieth century and that spiritualism itself provided metaphors for writing and suggested ways of engaging with difficult questions of authority, authorship and meaning. Modernist texts are rife with haunting as they encode the losses, traumas and fragmentation of their historical moment.[70] I will return to Sword's comments on spiritualism and writing in Chapter One, but here I want to emphasize her point that the spiritualism that fascinated the modernists was primarily engaged with the interplay between the seen and unseen, and, as such, is inherently material.[71] Modernist studies' recent interest in the material context of modernism may also be seen in studies of modernism and religion such as Sword's. We also see a concern with the material in Lara Vetter's *Modernist Writings and Religio-scientific Discourse: H.D., Loy and Toomer* (2010). Vetter's study demonstrates that in the early twentieth century science was seen by many to have shifted from the mechanistic, positivist nineteenth-century position that eroded belief and advanced secularism, to the more mysterious relativism of Einstein, and thus was often referred to in religious terms.[72] The volume highlights the interplay of material and spiritual in the discourse of electromagnetism, written about in the language of the soul and sharing a vexed relationship to the body. In her concern with issues of sexuality, gender and race and the vulnerability of the body, Vetter shows how these ostensibly spiritual writings concerned with human ideals and otherworldly strivings are grounded in the material and political. She explores the relationships between notions of electromagnetism, sexuality, movement (based on the early twentieth-century dance and exercise discourse) and spiritualism in H.D.'s prose.[73] Like Surette and Sword, among others, she is primarily concerned with heterodox spirituality.

Pericles Lewis's *Religious Experience and the Modernist Novel* (2010) argues that spiritual concerns have generally been overlooked in studies of the modernist novel but these include 'borderline states of consciousness, forms of the divided self, the process of conversion, the function of ritual, the magical potential inherent in words, moments of sublime experience, and the relationship between social life and sacred power.'[74] Lewis's work resonates with mine in his analysis of transcendence meaning 'experiences that originated in the ordinary world, not the supernatural, but that opened some sort of insight beyond the realm of the ordinary.'[75] This revision of transcendence accords with my understanding of material mysticism in H.D. and Cixous.

Lewis is primarily engaged with the boundary between mainstream religions and secularism, while Suzanne Hobson undertakes an ambitious study that draws together mainstream religion, secularity and heterodox beliefs and practices. In *Angels of Modernism: Religion, Culture, Aesthetics 1910–1960* (2011) Hobson explores the trajectory of the figure of the angel through modernist literature from the well-known angels of history (Benjamin) and the house (Woolf) to the uncanny and haunting angels of war in H.D.'s mature poetry. Hobson argues:

> Angels appear regularly in contradistinction both to modernism's much discussed hostility to traditional religious pieties and its campaign against unnecessary and ornamental figuration in literature. These figures continue to perform significant cultural work even as they are identified as incongruous and untimely.[76]

The angel moves from mainstream religion to the heterodox permutations of astrology, from secular philosophy to fictions of gender-bending and occult poetry; 'in their sheer variety, they register the complex and variegated pattern of belief and disbelief which more accurately characterizes modernism's "religion" than the old disenchanted version.'[77] Modernist writers increase the terminology to deal with spiritual phenomena, but they also use 'ready-made religious language' and may utilize these tropes (such as the angel) in new, imaginative and strange ways.[78] Hobson explores how angels appear in H.D.'s early prose as a marker for both homoeroticism and androgyny, thus suggesting an intersection between sexuality, gender identity and spirituality; she then turns to their appearance in H.D.'s mature poetry as a sign of the conflicted yet persistent modernist utopian imagination of the 1940s and beyond.[79]

Critical engagements that focus on the nexus of the religious, the visionary and the creative, such as this book, suggest that there is further work to be done in modernist studies on the role of the religious imagination in particular. This field of criticism has not fully engaged with the expansive, heterodox vision of the sacred of writers like H.D., or considered how the occult, spiritualism and theosophy intersect with mainstream religion. This book sits aslant to the stream of criticism which reads H.D. as visionary by foregrounding the religious concerns of her work. In attending to the role of Moravian Christianity (albeit a Christianity with an occult cast) in her work, it unites mainstream religion with esoteric beliefs and practices. By exploring the affinity between H.D. and the theoretical work of Cixous, in considering the intersection of spirituality and trauma and in examining the inherence of the sacred within language and material places, this study adds further to our understanding of the variety and complexity of modernist religious imagination.

H.D. and Modernist Religious Imagination: Mysticism and Writing

The following five chapters elaborate the ways in which H.D.'s religious sensibility intersects with creativity, writing and materialism: from her relationships with others in the context of physical and psychic trauma to the performativity of text and ritual, from the unfolding of metaphor to the emplacement of writing. In all of these interventions, attention to the alterity within language enabled by my reading of Cixous and simultaneous grounding of writing in materiality is crucial.

Chapter One, 'Voices of the dead: trauma and spiritualism', examines H.D.'s spiritualism through considering the function of the voices of the dead in *The Sword Went Out to Sea*. The intersection of spiritualism with wartime and previous traumas in H.D.'s texts leads to a discussion of testimony and witnessing which draws upon Cixous's writing on trauma and encounter. Cixous refuses to bar poetry from the scene of trauma, positioning writing as witness, while also refusing to relinquish the delight of writing. Her exploration of the possibilities for poetics' engagement with trauma is illustrated by H.D.'s expression of the dynamic of testimony and witness in a mystical language of community in which the voices of the absent are heard. In *The Sword*, hallucinations and madness also indicate the instability and inherent risk of interpretation. The healing of trauma through narrative frameworks is mitigated by the continued ruptures in the narrative, the insistent questions of spectral figures and ambivalent endings.

Chapter Two, 'Cloud of Witnesses: Moravian spirituality and intimate communities', offers a reading of community and the writing cure in the context of H.D.'s interest in visionary Moravians. For H.D., healing, reintegration and restoration are worked out through her writing and drawn from the resources of her interpretation of Moravian history and spirituality. Here I draw upon archival research to analyse the relationship between H.D.'s research into Moravian history and her Moravian novel *The Gift*. H.D. situates the spirituality of previous generations of Moravians within a visionary context which connects Moravianism to both Hermeticism and creativity. In H.D.'s writing from this period, the voices of the dead allow the narrator to situate herself within community and form a cloud of witnesses that enables creative work. The conclusion of this chapter ties its concerns with intimate community and the writing cure to the previous chapter's focus on haunting and Cixous's emphasis on dialogue with others in the face of trauma.

Chapter Three, 'Writing as Ritual', explores H.D.'s religious syncretism through the lens of ritual. It uses performance approaches to ritual to consider the productive dynamics of drama and ceremonial processions in *The Sword*, Moravian litany in *The Gift* and Hermetic alchemical ritual in *Trilogy*. The chapter closes with an analysis of the connection between ritual and writing, drawing upon the deconstructive practice of Jacques Derrida and Cixous. The difference that mobilizes meaning for Derrida and Cixous is also seen in the Hermetic worldview that sees diversity at the centre of divine being.

Chapter Four, 'Image and Divine Difference', draws on the Hermetic understanding of the imagination as the faculty which enables apprehension of the divine life within the universe to advance a view of the creative imagination that brings a religious dimension to Romantic modernism. The chapter develops a theoretical framework for exploring H.D.'s deployment of the images of the bee, the bee hive and honey by using Paul Ricoeur's work on metaphor as mobilized by the internal dynamic of sameness and difference and the connection between writing, imagination and materiality developed in Cixous's work. The proliferation of these images across H.D.'s writing allows creative explorations of how spirituality and creativity inheres in encounters with others, subjectivity and embodiment. They allow an exploration of difference in language and instantiate material mysticism by drawing together materiality and the sacred.

Chapter Five, 'Writing as Sanctuary: sacred places and pilgrimages', returns to the scene of war, recovery and religion considered in the early chapters. It attends to sacred place in H.D.'s writing through an analysis of three spatial metaphors: garden, flight and sanctuary. The chapter outlines the recent turn to space as a crucial theoretical category for both literary and theological studies before considering gardens, flight and sanctuaries in a more extended reading of Cixous's autobiographical and theoretical writing alongside H.D.'s work. The chapter closes with a consideration of how pilgrimage may be situated within writing: a reformulation that draws upon H.D.'s distinctly modernist religious imagination and the theory of writing as a spiritual practice drawn from Cixous's work.

Notes

1 H.D. 1960. H.D. received an Award of Merit Medal for Poetry in 1960.

2 H.D. 1998a, p. 50. Subsequent references to key texts by H.D. will be given in the text.

3 The bee is both a pagan and a Christian symbol for life and resurrection.

4 In the 1940s, the spiritualist Arthur Bhaduri had a vision of a Viking ship decorated with wings. H.D. was convinced that the word 'wings', communicated during the séance, and Bhaduri's ship vision were a reference to a visionary experience she had in 1920. While sailing to Greece in 1920, H.D. met Peter Welbeck (also called Pieter Rodeck and Peter van Eck in H.D.'s writing) on deck one evening and together they watched a pod of dolphins in the water, illuminated by an otherworldly soft blue light. Later Welbeck did not remember the meeting and H.D. concluded that it was a visionary experience 'out-of-time' in which she approached mythic Atlantis with Welbeck/van Eck initiating her into a sacred mystery; H.D. 2009a, pp. 4, 86–96; H.D. 2007, pp. 14–17.

5 Eliot 1951, pp. 388–401. For further discussion of Eliot's views on the relationship between art and religion see Walton 2007b, pp. 15–17.

6 The Moravian Church, or *Unitas Fratrum* (United Brethren), can be situated within

the German Pietist movements of the eighteenth century, although its roots lie in the late fourteenth- and fifteenth-century Hussite movement. Followers of the pre-Reformation reformer John Hus established the *Unitas Fratrum*, which was suppressed in the course of the Thirty Years War (some Moravian historians claim that the tradition was carried on by a small remnant, the 'Hidden Seed', while most recent scholarship finds this unlikely), and blossomed again under the leadership of Count Nicolas von Zinzendorf in the early eighteenth century. The Moravians emphasized personal piety over orthodox doctrine. Like many other religious groups, they were drawn to the greater freedom of religion in Pennsylvania and established a settlement, Bethlehem, near Philadelphia in 1741; Atwood 2004, p. 21; Hutton 1909, pp. iv, 102–9; de Schweinitz 1885, pp. iv, 109.

H.D. linked the idea of a 'Hidden Seed' to other secret societies including the Knights Templar (this is particularly evident in the late novel *The Mystery*). Her vision of the Hidden Church persisting through the generations, guarding the Church's wisdom, is consistent with her interest in Hermeticism.

7 Bryher, the self-chosen name of Annie Winifred Ellerman, was an heiress, a patron of the arts, devotee of psychoanalysis and active in numerous political and artistic pursuits. She provided support and encouragement to many artists, including H.D., Dorothy Richardson and the Sitwells. She and H.D. lived together off and on from the 1920s to the end of the Second World War. Following the war, H.D. lived in sanatoria and hotels in Switzerland and Italy until her death in 1961 but she and Bryher maintained close contact. Bryher and her second husband, Kenneth Macpherson, legally adopted H.D.'s illegitimate daughter Perdita and were intimately involved with her upbringing.

8 The first part of *Tribute to Freud*, 'Writing on the Walls', was serialized in *Life and Letters Today* in 1945 and 1946; Friedman 1990, p. 283.

9 H.D. 1975, pp. 41, 116, 82; H.D. 1982, p. 19.

10 H.D. 1975, pp. 53–5.

11 Ibid. p. 50.

12 Ibid. p. 40.

13 Ibid. p. 51.

14 Ibid. p. 44.

15 Materer 1995, p. 89. Eileen Gregory has pointed out Hermeticism's significance with relation to her early poetry in *Sea Garden*, while the title of the late long poem, *Hermetic Definition*, suggests its continued relevance to H.D.'s late poetry; 1997, pp. 82–4.

16 Faivre 1995, p. 65.

17 Eco 1990, p. 24.

18 Faivre 1995, p. 67.

19 Materer 1995, p. 104. See also Tryphonopoulos 2009, p. xxiv.

20 Buck 1991; Kloepfer 1989. Buck notes the resonance between Cixous's engagements with Freud and Lacan, and her interest in subjectivity and sexuality as resonant and H.D.'s work; pp. 4–7, 84–5.

21 Sal Renshaw's study is the first book-length work to treat Cixous and spirituality. Her focus is how Cixous's work speaks to, challenges and refines Christian philosophical writing on agape; 2009. Berkowitz (2003, pp. 176–88) and Hollywood (2003a, pp. 145–61) both treat Cixous and spirituality; Berkowitz focuses on Cixous's engagement with the Hebrew Bible and Hollywood writes on Cixous and mysticism while also considering the intersection of spirituality and trauma.

22 Suleiman 1991, p. x.

23 Cixous 1998b, p. 200.

24 Cixous 2008, p. 19.

25 Conley 1992, p. 2; Shiach 1991, p. 23.

26 I follow Abigail Bray's definition of alterity: '[T]he other of the other [...] a form of Otherness which is not reducible to the binary self/other. It is a concept of the other which is autonomous [...]. Alterity signals [...] the space of difference': 2004, pp. 73–4.

27 Cixous and Clément 1996, p. 86; Cixous 1998a, p. 6.

28 Yaeger 1988, p. 16.

29 In *Sexual/Textual Politics*, a book which provided an early Anglophone interpretation of Cixous, Toril Moi asserts that Cixous's work avoids the political in a constant regression to a 'mythological' realm in which all gaps and disruption are filled with a joyous plenitude that has no weight in historical terms. However, Moi disregards the extent that Cixous's attention to gaps maintains, rather than dissolves, difference and this critique fails to adequately account for the potential of 'utopian visions' to provide the 'political inspiration' that Moi herself acknowledges; 1985, pp. 116–26.

30 Anon. 1908–26, p. 83; Dupré and Moore 2005, p. 6341.

31 Bernard McGinn employs a deliberately loose definition: 'the preparation for, the consciousness of, and the reaction to what can be described as the immediate or direct presence of God'; 1992, p. xvii. This is a particularly Western definition; it is appropriate here as my writers are primarily rooted in Western culture, although occult beliefs such as theosophy as well as modernist aesthetics owe a debt to Eastern philosophy, literature and spirituality; Thacker 2011, pp. 59–66.

32 This approach tends to take William James's *Varieties of Religious Experience* as a starting point. For discussion of the development of the understanding of mysticism in the late nineteenth and early twentieth centuries, see Jantzen 1995, pp. 305–21; Schmidt 2003.

33 McGinn 1992, p. xvii.

34 Hollywood 1995, pp. 20–1.

35 Hollenberg 1997, p. 138.

36 In 1944 H.D. wrote an additional section of notes containing greater detail about Moravian history in Europe and America.

37 The history of encounters between European Moravians and Native Americans (mainly Lenape, Mahican, Shawnee, Iroquois and other Algonquian groups) is more complex and compromising than *The Gift* suggests, although the text does not entirely elide the history of conflict. H.D. included a detailed description of massacres of Native American and European Moravians at the hands of hostile tribes and European colonists; H.D. 1998a, pp. 272–4. As Susan Stanford Friedman points out, 'this white betrayal of the peace made between Indians and Moravians was emblematic for H.D. of America's heritage, a mix of peace and violence, gift and theft, freedom and oppression'; 1990, p. 347.

The Moravian Church owned land the Lenape (or Delaware) tribes lost through the fraudulent Walking Purchase, and they contributed to the dispossession of the Native Americans in eastern Pennsylvania, as even peaceful missionary efforts contributed to the weakening of tribal governance and culture; Kaiser 1997, p. 139; Kidwell, Noley and Tinker 2001, p. 177; Olmstead 1991, p. 7. A fuller exploration of this complex history is beyond the scope of this book; however, it is worth pointing out that Native Americans and Moravian communities did live peacefully together for some time despite the conflicts between Native American tribes and British and French colonies (the French and Indian War and the American Revolutionary War did much to erode the relationships between communities); Pencak and Richter 2004, pp. ix–xxi. For further discussion of the encounters between Native American tribes and Moravian colonists see Schutt 2007.

38 Here H.D. puts a syncretist spin on Moravian evangelism; she is much less concerned with the Christian nature of the Moravian and Native American alliances than with the invocation of divine presence.

39 In her introduction to 'H.D. by Delia Alton', Adelaide Morris cautions against reading H.D.'s later work as 'conventional romance', but suggests reading texts such as *The Sword* as a key strand of H.D.'s spiritual writing; 1986, p. 177.

40 In 1937 Douglas Bush criticized H.D.'s poetry for being overly spiritual, emotional and escapist (essentially decadent), while Lawrence Rainey makes a similarly dismissive judgement in his 1998 analysis of the cultural economy of modernism. Rainey sees H.D. as a minor writer who was isolated in a small coterie of admirers, ignoring the variety of her engagements in the cultural sphere and the achievements of her mature writing; Bush 1957, pp. 500–5; Rainey 1998, pp. 146–68.

41 Duplessis 1986; Friedman 1975; Friedman 1981; Gubar 1978; Ostriker 1983.

42 Anthologies such as *The Gender of Modernism* and *Gender in Modernism* give H.D. a greater prominence in modernist history; Scott 1990, pp. 85–138; Scott 2007, pp. 563–73, 809–13, 48–51. However, H.D.'s place in the canon is still a matter of

debate; for an analysis of the critical reception of H.D. and the challenge her work presents to notions of canon see Hickman 2012, pp. 9–22.

43 Letter collections include Friedman 2002; Hollenberg 1997; Zilboorg 2003. The short prose collections include H.D. 2012b; H.D. 2012a.

44 Psychoanalytic approaches to H.D. include Buck 1991; Chisholm 1992; Duplessis 1986; Friedman 1990; Kloepfer 1989. Readings focused on H.D.'s literary context include Collecott 1999; Gregory 1997; Laity 1996. Readings focusing on historical materialist context include Graham 2002, pp. 161–210; Randall 2007, pp. 124–54.

45 Boughn and Coleman 2011, pp. 1–2.

46 Ibid. p. 7.

47 Duncan 2011, p. 471.

48 Friedman 1981, pp. 212–13.

49 Ibid. p. 196.

50 Ostriker 1983, p. 7.

51 Ibid. p. 8.

52 In a letter to Viola Jordan, H.D. described the angels of *Trilogy* as 'planetary angels', suggesting the union of Christian mythology and astrology within *Trilogy*; H.D. 1945b. There are extensive references to astrology across H.D.'s letters to Jordan, an indication that this interest extended beyond her writing.

53 Morris 1990, pp. 127–8.

54 Ibid. p. 130.

55 Ibid. p. 133.

56 Morris 2003, p. 1.

57 Ibid.

58 Ibid. p. 97.

59 The extent to which H.D. was familiar with Jane Harrison's work is unknown. Gregory argues that the affinity between H.D. and Harrison cannot be explained as direct influence but rather 'a broad and diffused intertextuality'; 1997, p. 110. H.D. may not have read Harrison's work but she certainly would have been aware of her ideas as they were widely disseminated and directly influenced many of her friends and contemporaries. Myriad sites for indirect influence include: H.D.'s friendship with D. H. Lawrence, who read *Ancient Art and Ritual* shortly before meeting her; Gilbert Murray's writings, which included summaries of Harrison's arguments; and the novels of Mary Butts, which were influenced by Harrison and read enthusiastically by H.D.; Gregory 1997, p. 11; Friedman 2002, pp. 136–7.

60 Gregory 1997, pp. 119, 22–5.

61 Ibid. p. 77.

62 Ibid. p. 79.

63 Ibid. pp. 83–4. However, Gregory also points out that some of the implications of Pater's Hermetic Romantic Hellenism are problematic for H.D. as a woman writer.

Crystal, asceticism and athletic discipline configure a homoerotic, masculine space that leaves little room for the explorations of a female poet. What is missing is the matrix, 'the material ground out of which the crystal is projected [...] rocky ground, occluded and shadowy body, visceral feeling – the matter out of which desire comes, from which it never escapes'; 1997, p. 88.

64 Tryphonopoulos 2009, p. xxiv.

65 Ibid. p. xxxviii.

66 Materer 1995, p. 88.

67 Ibid. p. 89.

68 Reid 2010, pp. 1–5; Detloff 2009.

69 Owen 2004; Schmidt 2000; Schmidt 2003; Sword 2002; Thurschwell 2001; Hobson 2011; Lewis 2010; Vetter 2010.

70 Sword 2002, p. 57.

71 Ibid. pp. xi–xii.

72 Vetter 2010, pp. 3–7. For a related discussion of the intersection of spiritualism, technology and psychology in modernism, see Thurschwell 2001.

73 Vetter 2010, pp. 57, 61–6, 97–109.

74 Lewis 2010, p. 5.

75 Ibid. p. 20.

76 Hobson 2011, p. 1.

77 Ibid. p. 5.

78 Ibid. p. 9.

79 Ibid. pp. 122–3, 30–4, 56–71.

1

Voices of the Dead: Trauma and spiritualism

In considering her oeuvre in the prose reflection 'H.D. by Delia Alton' (written in 1950), H.D. comments on the significance of community to her identity as a writer: 'the feeling of intimate communion or communication [...] renewed my faith at the end of the war-years'.[1] This 'intimate communion' – with previous generations of Moravians through memory and vision, with the spirits of fallen RAF pilots through séance communication and with her companions in the Blitz through more mundane daily encounters – sounds the keynote of her religious belonging. The Moravian Christianity of her childhood and her spiritualist practice in the 1940s merged with her psychoanalytic pursuits, occult interests and creative activity to yield an idiosyncratic set of beliefs and practices embedded in communities that enabled the renewal not only of H.D.'s faith, but also of her writing.[2] In H.D.'s texts from this period, the voices of the dead allow the narrator to situate herself within community: these voices form a cloud of witnesses that call forth her creative work. The significance of community is such that when she becomes isolated, desolation and breakdown follow. The restoration of communication and community through vision, witness and writing leads to healing and a turn from a focus on the past to openness to the future. This chapter explores the intersection of trauma and spiritualism in H.D.'s writing, while the other significant strands of religious thought in H.D.'s work, Moravian Christianity and Hermeticism, will be addressed in subsequent chapters.

This chapter focuses on the prose work *The Sword Went Out to Sea*. Although *The Sword* was written after the end of the war and is more often compared with H.D.'s other post-war writing the novel's reflections on war lend it to analysis in the context of her work from the early 1940s.[3] *The Sword* is a significant text in terms of H.D.'s development as a writer and religious thinker; it represents a complex engagement with the spiritual, creative and psychoanalytic concerns of her other texts written during the Second World War such as *Trilogy*, *The Gift*, *Majic Ring* and *Tribute to Freud*. The protagonist of *The Sword* is Delia Alton, a pseudonym frequently used by H.D. in her later writing. *The Sword* is a fluid, often highly abstract text; dreams, séances, memories and interlocking fictional vignettes from different epochs are layered together in a jumble of dialogue, imagery and reverie with little exposition to guide the reader. Although Hermeticism is not explicitly emphasized in *The Sword*, *Majic Ring* indicates the significant extent to which the search for hidden wisdom and understanding of previous visionary experiences was a motivating factor in H.D.'s interest in spiritualism. H.D.'s Hermetic spiritualist practice provides a mode for exploring the spiritual resonances and implications of her wartime experiences, of engaging with dreams and visions as well as traumatic memories. The first part of the novel, 'Wintersleep', draws upon the letters and notes on H.D.'s spiritualist activities and earlier visionary experiences collected in *Majic Ring*, while the second part, 'Summerdream', contains fictional vignettes from different times and places that meditate on the themes of the first part in a more abstract way.[4]

Many of H.D.'s texts from the Second World War, including *Trilogy, The Gift* and *The Sword* can be read as trauma narratives.[5] Written in the context of the war and for a post-war, survivor audience, they also address earlier traumas from H.D.'s childhood (*The Gift*) and the First World War (*The Sword*). *The Sword* alludes to painful episodes from the First World War, suggesting that the return of these traumas formed part of the stress of the later conflict.[6] In this chapter, I first outline the terminology of testimony and witnessing in trauma theory. Trauma theory indicates an aporia, the paradoxical necessity and impossibility of testifying and witnessing to traumatic events. Hélène Cixous and H.D. address trauma's aporia by expressing the dynamic of testimony and witness in a mystical language of community which attends to the voices of the absent. I then consider the intersection of spiritualism with H.D.'s wartime and previous traumas in the light of the encounter formed through testimony and witness. The following chapter develops the categories of testimony and witness through a reading of community and the writing cure in *The Gift* and *The Sword*.

Trauma: Testimony and witness

Recent decades have seen a proliferation of theoretical engagements with trauma. From the varied resources of trauma theory, what is most relevant to this project is the terminology of testimony, witness and survival. After providing a brief overview of these terms and their significance for my reading of H.D., I will then consider how Hélène Cixous's work provides a compelling approach to the relationship between these issues and writing. In Cixous's work writing becomes a means of expressing trauma, witnessing to it and generating a creative response. The intersection of Cixous's work and trauma theory provides the framework for my reading of H.D.'s creative and religious response to trauma. For both Cixous and H.D., writing is a mystical practice that opens a way through trauma's aporia, the paradoxical necessity and impossibility of speaking the unspeakable.

Trauma has been defined as an extreme event that disorders the subject's normal capacity for understanding and engaging with the world. Trauma intersects with writing in the discourse of testimony, a term that references both legal and religious discourse. Shoshana Felman's and Dori Laub's formulations retain a sense of the weight of response, responsiveness and responsibility from these other areas. Felman describes testimony as 'a performative speech act', yet the majority of her contribution to *Testimony* (1992) considers literary texts; this suggests that oral narratives are texts to be read and that texts function as speech.[7] Testimony as the discourse of trauma has two primary characteristics; it is fragmentary and excessive in its attempt to delineate an event that evades coherent memory: 'testimony seems to be composed of bits and pieces of a memory that has been overwhelmed by occurrences that have not settled into understanding or remembrance [...] events in excess of our frames of reference.'[8]

This sense of fragmentary narratives, 'bits and pieces of a memory', is developed by Dori Laub, who cites writers such as Holocaust survivor Elie Wiesel who claim a paradoxical impossibility and necessity of writing 'through this silence', of remembering and forgetting.[9] Laub theorizes witnessing, or listening, as the necessary action that enables the testimony to achieve its form, however fragmentary it may be. Thus the discourse of trauma is inherently dynamic and relational. The residue of the courtroom and the religious community in the term testimony emphasizes the relationship between the speaker and those spoken to. As Madelyn Detloff points out, much of trauma theory focuses on the traumatic event as unspeakable, but a helpful strategy for cultural criticism is 'to focus on the potential listener's ability to hear, to see and to recognize trauma when its effects are articulated by others'.[10] In her emphasis on testimony as performative speech, Felman suggests that the role of audience is crucial to testimony's existence. One of the defining factors of testimony is its ability to appoint a witness.[11] Conversely, this encounter depends upon the witness, the listener, to enable the testimony to emerge. Laub argues that the encounter between testifier and listener allows knowledge to emerge, knowledge that was unavailable to the traumatized subject before the encounter:

> My attempt as interviewer and as listener was precisely to respect [...] the subtle balance between what the woman knew and what she did not, or could not, know. It was only at the price of this respect, I felt, [...] that what the woman did know in a way that none of us did [...] could come forth and could receive, indeed, a hearing.[12]

This encounter is the site of dynamic knowledge production, as knowledge emerges that the speaker may not have had prior access to.[13] As we will see in my later analysis of *The Gift*, H.D. experiences a similar discovery of knowledge when her inner exploration of war trauma reveals the spiritual insights of her childhood that she had unconsciously buried.

The therapeutic nature of the encounter is integral. The responsibility of the witness for containing the distress and hopelessness of the testifier is immense, but it is precisely this affect which allows the testimony to be heard.[14] This 'libidinal investment', the containment and development of safe space for knowledge to unfold, brings 'witness' closer to the religious community than the courtroom. In considering the response of theology to trauma, Rita Nakashima Brock and Rebecca Parker argue that '[s]alvation begins with the courage of witnesses whose gaze is steady'.[15] However, as Brock and Parker admit in their analysis of the effects of violence, the transforming presence of the witness is all too often threatened and (nearly) annihilated. I would suggest that a theology of provisional presence holds together the gaze of the witness, the hope for transformation and the acknowledgement of fragility.

Rebecca Chopp suggests a reconfiguration of theology and theory in relationship to texts of testimony: 'I prefer to speak of the poetics of testimony for those discourses – poetry, novels, theory, theology – that speak of the unspeakable and tell of the suffering and hope of particular communities who have not been authorized to speak.'[16] In considering testimony's challenge to theory and theology, Chopp remains close to the space of alterity: 'I want to underscore the importance of respecting and protecting this gap between the named and the unnamable.'[17] In this way Chopp reiterates Felman's claim that testimony exceeds our frameworks for understanding. However, like Brock and Parker, Chopp is interested in testimony's power for transformation: 'poetics seeks [...] to refigure, to reimagine and refashion the world. Poetics is discourse that [...] calls into question the ordering of discourse within [...] the "social imaginary".'[18] Here, Chopp is close to H.D.'s and Cixous's engagement with poetic language as transformative, a point I will return to in a variety of ways across this book.

Chopp argues that the purpose of testimony is survival: 'The telling of these stories is for life, for the mending of life, the healing of life, the ability of life to live and survive and thus conquer this extremity. [...] [S]urviving is both resistance and hope.'[19] Chopp's argument leads to a consideration of healing which is latent, if not explicit, in much of trauma studies. In a contrasting understanding of survival, Cathy Caruth argues that survival itself is traumatic and presents a challenge to assimilation: 'Repetition, in other words, is not simply the attempt to grasp that one has almost died but, more fundamentally and enigmatically, the very attempt *to claim one's own survival*.'[20] H.D.'s work demonstrates the tension between these two modes of understanding survival and traumatic return, as she continues to struggle to make meaning out of her own survival.[21] This aligns with Bruno Bettelheim's understanding of survivorship in which the post-traumatic subject is faced with the burden of 'how to live with an existential predicament which does not permit of any solution'.[22] Bettelheim suggests that reintegration after the disintegration caused by profound trauma is a precarious, ongoing process.[23]

As Felman argues, texts of testimony may provoke a witness but this is not a straightforward relation. Testimony is bound up with alterity, with what we cannot know: 'the texts that testify do not simply *report facts* but, in different ways, encounter – and make us encounter – *strangeness*.'[24] I suggest that this is exactly the work Cixous's writing performs. Through the terms 'texts', 'encounter' and 'strangeness' she develops a mystical framework for the aporia of testimony, crafting a space for testimony and witness in which the witnesses not only encounter strangeness, but are transformed by it.

Cixous's work invokes the etymology of trauma as wound. In her preface to the collection of essays, *Stigmata* (1998), she stresses two contrasting results of a wound – scars and stigmata: 'The stigma is a scar that is difficult to efface. [...] The scar adds, the stigma digs, excavates [...] the literature in me wants to maintain and reanimate traces.'[25] The scar denotes both the healing of a wound and the inevitable, ongoing remnant of the wound, while stigmata encode an absence, the indentation of the wound without the addition of scar tissue. This notion of reanimated traces indicates the spectral return, the haunting, that is so prevalent in texts of trauma. The echoes of both the living and the dead animate Cixous's writing as she crafts her work into an act of witnessing. For Cixous, the categories of life and death, witnessing to trauma and constructive renewal, are always blurred as she continues to claim the value of artistic practice: 'My own recipe stays always the same. It consists in urging readers to plant flowers, both metaphorically and concretely.'[26]

The connection between reader and writer is crucial to Cixous; reading and writing are as intertwined as testimony and witness. For Cixous, writing-reading is the place of encounter. She has recently written of Derrida: 'We speak to one another so as to hear ourselves read, to know how to read, to write ourselves speaking, to give ourselves the writing that is in speech, sometimes so as to take words from each other's mouths.'[27] She develops her understanding of writing as a movement towards encounter through the work of Paul Celan:

> As Celan's themes tell us, poetry addresses and moves toward the other. Eventually, it becomes a calling to the other. [...] We have to go to its encounter. Such is poetic process, a move that becomes a political activity in an ethical mode. If we have a sense of the delicacy of the world, this is exactly what we have to do.[28]

This calling to the other can be understood as testimony, while the place of encounter is that of the nexus of witness, testimony and confession. Cixous situates her writing and reading practice in the midst of hope and despair, where the stakes are high and yet the delicacy of the world, the fragility of survival and 'the joy of loving a leaf' also demand expression and a witness.[29]

In Celan's essay 'The Meridian', we see 'encounter' brought together with 'strangeness' in the poem's movement towards the Other: 'But doesn't the poem [...] at this point participate in an encounter – *in the mystery of an encounter*?'[30] The sense of mystery involved in the encounter with the Other suggests the precarious and always only partially known development of mystical community as well as the contribution that poetry makes to political responses to trauma. Celan draws upon the language of the sublime to indicate his understanding of the encounter that is both mysterious and intimate. He makes an ethical claim here, asserting the task of the poem to speak 'in the cause of an Other'.[31] I would suggest that this involves eliding the distinction between witness and testimony, that this poetic speech is testimony to witnessing. With Cixous we can see the dangers of appropriating the voices of others in this configuration. Yet this is also required if silence is not to be the only response to trauma.

The rest of this chapter considers H.D.'s work in this context of testimony and witness. This is a Cixousian reading that explores spiritualism and writing as creative activities located in the ambivalent spaces of trauma and encounter. In *The Sword*, séances allow Delia to forge a precarious community by attending to the voices of the dead. Her own wartime traumas are folded with the ongoing haunting within her texts. The following chapter explores the importance of encounter as evidenced by the intimate communion with others emphasized in *The Gift* and then turns to the role of writing in enabling survival.

Haunting: Spiritualism, trauma and memory

Discussions of trauma, survival and witness inevitably raise spectral questions: what of those who have not survived? Indeed, the traumatic event may be the witness of another's death with its attendant loss. Patricia Yaeger argues that, when writing of trauma, we have a responsibility to the dead to consider 'not only what is our stake in their narratives, but what is their stake in ours'.[32] H.D.'s engagement with the dead – fallen RAF pilots, her own family members, past generations of Moravians and their Algonquian neighbours – suggests that their narratives and hers are mutually implicated.[33] They remain part of her audience and interlocutors. However, it is important to note that H.D. is not a passive listener. As author and narrator, her own voice and vision hold the primary place in her work. Her writing is always as much self-exploration as attention to the other. Yet these others do remain a crucial – at times enabling, at times challenging – haunting presence in her texts.

Marina MacKay argues that many modernist writers 'made the guilty compromise' of supporting the Second World War despite pacifist leaning and distrust of the type of propaganda and nationalism rife during the First World War.[34] In this way late modernist writing was involved with the public sphere more profoundly than earlier manifestations of modernism. The Second World War was a markedly civilian conflict and thus many texts, including H.D.'s, that are more concerned with domestic contexts than battlefields may still be considered war writing.[35] Madelyn Detloff considers modernist writing from the Second World War and the post-war period as 'a constellation of discourses about wide-spread loss and violence'.[36] Detloff analyses writers (her exemplar is Virginia Woolf) who explore 'the terrain between resignation and redemption' in refusing to transcend trauma or idealize sacrifice but also recognizing the possibility of survival and of living into the future.[37] This resilient writing is evident in H.D.'s prose from the 1940s as she refuses to glorify war or to re-write it into a myth of a challenge overcome.

In its attempt to find a mystical meaning or purpose in the midst of war, H.D.'s work, *Trilogy* in particular, has been criticized as escapist, triumphalist and dangerously deterministic, the totalizing narrative of redemption eliding the reality of suffering and loss.[38] Detloff argues that *Trilogy*, like Eliot's *Four*

Quartets, deploys apocalyptic discourse in service of a transcendence that privileges narrative closure over the ongoing historical reality of suffering.[39] However, in linking *Trilogy* with *Four Quartets* Detloff elides important distinctions between the two texts, in particular *Trilogy*'s emphasis on multiple meanings that resist closure, its emphasis on materiality and the contingency of H.D.'s mysticism.[40]

Tony Trigilio gives a reading of apocalypse in *Trilogy* that places H.D. in the radical tradition of Blake, arguing that she, like Blake, reconfigures traditional versions of prophecy and apocalypse that support singular authority and a violent vision of the end of history. Her 'endlessly transmutable [...] alchemical language' enables a creative practice in which language and meaning proliferate and transcendence is reimagined as 'immanent [...] rebirth'.[41] The Hermetic precept 'as above, so below' reminds us that Venus is reflected 'in the field-furrow/the rain water' (H.D. 1998b, *Angels* 10:1–2).[42] In H.D.'s war writing, the starry heavenly hosts are figures of the threshold and share humanity's connection to the earth.[43] The insistence of the material, and therefore the contingent and historical, within her work undermines readings that regard her vision as overly transcendent.

Hobson stresses the contingency of H.D.'s visions of redemption; the occult practices she draws upon (astrology, Tarot, etc.) are presented in her writing as resistant to deterministic, fated revelations; instead they are precarious, open and conditional.[44] The risks of H.D.'s poetic strategies and ambivalence within her vision are a 'constituent part of the [visionary and creative] gift itself'.[45] Hobson points out that H.D.'s response to sensing herself at odds with her contemporaries was to align herself with an imagined group of spiritual seekers stretching into the past while also acknowledging that being part of such a group 'brought about its own dangers including that of being taken for a fraud or a trickster'. Yet Hermes is the patron of tricksters, the consummate trickster, and H.D. was prepared to embrace the risk. She does so out of commitment to utopian imagination, for which angels are a marker in her mature poetry. Here Cixous is again helpful for my reading of H.D. Cixous has also been criticized for a-historicism in her work.[46] However, this critique undervalues the commitment to utopian imagination in her work and how writing within this genre allows for flights of imagination that do not so much ignore politics as insist that political action alone will not transform the world. For H.D. as for Cixous, the more the modernist utopian imagination appears to have failed, the greater the urgency of providing a space for such imaginings within writing.[47] Her myth-making retains a degree of ambivalence and a hope for healing that does not close off the traumatic ruptures in the text. In H.D.'s writing, creative and spiritual practice embedded in intimate communities of both the living and the dead provide a means for consolation and continuing to live.

Both the First and Second World Wars witnessed a dramatic resurgence in spiritualism; the bereaved took up 'the paradoxical practice of mourning the dead by refusing to let them die [...] as millions of new clients flocked to spirit mediums in hopes of making contact with their dead.'[48] In this sense, the devotees of spiritualism have more in common with Derrida's melancholic subjects who strive to keep the dead present through discursive openings than with Freud's mourners who seek to incorporate the object of loss or to re-focus libidinal energies and so resolve grief.[49] Perhaps the most significant difference between spiritualist practice and other forms of haunting is intentionality and desire. A medium may be surprised by the spirits she encounters and the nature of their messages; nevertheless, the presence of the dead is actively sought.[50] In his study of nineteenth-century popular religion and the attendant manifestations of spiritual hearing, Leigh Eric Schmidt defines 'hearkening' as hearing 'a beckoning voice that requires a reply' or an interior listening, and he argues that it is the essential component of spiritualism, among other charismatic religious practices.[51] The practice of spiritualism is a process of listening to what the spirits of the dead have to say to the living. Schmidt frames spiritualist discourse as a communal activity, entered into willingly by mediums and spirits and constituting a certain intimacy. It involves both the inner lives of adherents and an external community in the form of the medium's circle.

Colin Davis argues that the living dead – ghosts – destabilize the categories of presence and absence, past and present, life and death. In many narratives, the dead return in order to present some requirement. Once this demand has been fulfilled by the living the ghosts are banished, thus enacting what is essentially a second death. Conversely, in other narratives the disturbance remains; the function of the narrative (and the ghost) is to prevent closure: 'The tidy restoration of moral and epistemological orders is resisted, as is the clear delineation of the domains of the living and the dead. [...] They provide ways of thinking about how, in trauma, sadness or fond memory, we live with the dead.'[52] H.D.'s writing blurs Davis's distinction between narratives of closure and narratives of disruption. In *The Sword* and *The Gift* the dead return for a particular purpose (to share visionary experiences, to pass on the message of peace, and to urge the prevention of war) and yet even as this purpose is fulfilled – the message given or the gift passed on – they do not fully depart, but instead constitute an ongoing openness in the text. The sense of strangeness, the names and voices of the dead, are clearly present at the close of both texts. Far from a return to the status quo the texts' resolutions point to a new future. In *The Gift* and *The Sword* H.D. makes her peace with the dead yet continues to attend to them.

In her book on spiritualism and modernism Helen Sword claims that '[v]irtually everything that H.D. wrote during and about the Second World War years [...] bears witness to an abiding obsession with otherworldly communication, ghostly return, and the spectral phenomenology of memory.'[53] She goes on to argue that H.D.'s post-war writing, particularly *The Sword*, shows a marked change from the optimistic writing of the war period itself due to her post-war breakdown. *The Gift*, 'Writing on the Wall', *Majic Ring* and *Trilogy* all reveal H.D.'s conviction of 'the reality and importance of otherworldly inspiration'; however, 'never again would she write so optimistically about prophetic and visionary experience as during the war years'.[54] While I concur that H.D.'s writing changes tone after 1945, I find continuity between *The Sword* and the works composed between 1941 and 1945 in terms of H.D.'s preoccupation with religious experience and artistic practice in the context of war. *The Sword* demonstrates H.D.'s ongoing commitment to her vision, tempered with a greater awareness of the risks and personal cost of such commitment. This sense of cost mitigates the optimism of her earlier work, but provides greater urgency to her sense of vocation.

H.D.'s active interest in spiritualism began in 1941 and spirits appear in her writing from this year.[55] In *The Sword* spiritualism forms the connection between Delia Alton and Lord John Howell as well as allowing the development of a circle of companions, both living and dead. Delia begins a circle with the medium Ben Manisi, his mother and Gareth (Bryher), eventually acting as a medium herself and finally working entirely on her own. It is at this point that she receives messages from a group of fallen RAF pilots. The airmen's messages, while ambiguous in terms of exact content, are clearly directed towards political ends: an end to war and prevention of future disasters (p. 47).[56] As a medium, Delia acts as a witness to war traumas, although, her dreams and hallucinations contain more traumatic detail, while the RAF spirits do not share their own traumas. The dead airmen's reiterated calls for peace indicate H.D.'s desire to resolve the question of survival in a meaningful way. Even a spectral return must have some purpose beyond consolation.[57]

Delia reiterates her conviction of the interrelation between psychological experience, politics and spiritual realities: 'Probably, it was the struggle to comprehend the incomprehensible actions that were taking place outside, that forced me by a law of compensation, to try to grapple with the forces inside myself, or outside the material world' (p. 67). There is a refusal of sentimentality here, an insistence on a practical aim and moving towards the future rather than mourning the past. It is not Delia's own dead who return to her but strangers. However, there is a double-haunting in the narrative, as the séances evoke Delia's memories of the First World War, the breakdown of her marriage and eventual deaths of her husband and her brother.[58] Presence and absence mingle; the RAF ghosts themselves are present in the spirit and absent in the flesh. Moreover, the presence of the ghosts indicates the absence of those dead who are not among their company. The descriptions of the séances convey an uncanny intimacy as Delia becomes attached to these anonymous spirits and vows to memorialize them (p. 133).

Although H.D. did not continue to practise as a medium after her post-war breakdown, and her letters to Bryher in 1946 indicate wariness with regard to spiritualism, *The Sword* does not repudiate this practice or the ghosts themselves.[59] The historical vignettes provide an opportunity to restage and resolve the war's conflicts and traumas but she also reiterates the significance of the paradoxical presence and absence of the airmen, as the text concludes with a mention of the names of the fallen written in The Battle of Britain book in the Memorial Chapel in Westminster Abbey (p. 267). Following the series of vignettes that layer the personal and the historical, the text concludes with this formalized, official remembrance. This short final chapter is titled 'Goldwings', which alludes to the RAF pilots, the eagle carried by the Duke of Normandy in the last historical story and 'Golden Wings', a poem by William Morris about a land of peace that must eventually go to war.[60] Additionally, 'wings' is one of the key words for Delia's initial encounters with the medium Ben Manisi, so the word symbolizes her spiritualism and her creative work which are also linked through the William Morris table which was used for their séances (pp. 4–16).[61] Thus the final chapter brings together official remembrance with informal spiritualist practice and a creative vision that insists on the ongoing presence of the absent.

Helen Sword argues that, in H.D.'s Second World War writing, 'memory proves a welcome and redemptive ghost'.[62] However, in *The Gift* and even more so in *The Sword* there is a negative side to this spectre. Many of the memories evoked in both novels are painful or destructive and must be transformed before they can be redemptive. The importance of intimate communities to H.D. is also emphasized through the negative consequences of their loss. In *The Gift* we see the threat to community by the physical and psychological destruction of total war as an echo of the massacre of Native Americans after the peace with the Moravians was broken.[63] In *The Sword*, when communication is interrupted (by Lord Howell), Delia becomes isolated, which leads to confusion, hallucinations and breakdown: 'It was then that I felt myself plague-stricken. It was then that I visualized the streets of gibbets. It was then that I walked with eyes wide open, into Hell' (p. 95). Delia sees the disruption of her attempts at communion with the RAF pilots and Howell as the catalyst for her breakdown. Here we see the connection between social and spiritual bonds and belonging in the world. Without a recognized place and project within a circle of others, Delia feels herself absolutely displaced.

The editors of *The Sword* point out that the description of H.D.'s breakdown is not 'simply a catalogue of Delia's hallucinations, but also a revisionary reading of them'.[64] *The Gift* and *The Sword* are not purely confessional texts (if there are such things) but complex literary constructions in which H.D.'s experience is selectively recounted in such a way as to contribute to her pacifist project. Hogue and Vandivere suggest that *The Sword* is primarily a work of mourning:

> [A] testament to and working through of [...] the grief sustained, repressed, sublimated by the generation of women who saw two world wars and were called 'shrill' or mad or both when they tried to protest that *war* is mad. [...] One might say that it is a mad grief – something that looks like madness but isn't, something that is closer to fury.[65]

By writing out the repressed grief and fury of a generation, H.D. attempts to map out a cure through creative practice, a point I will return to in the following chapter. Paradoxically, she presents madness as a reasonable response to the terrors of war, while simultaneously presenting Lord Howell as lacking in courage to face up to the consequences of the spirits' visits:

> His barbed shaft had not killed me; perhaps, he feared that mine might drive him mad. Madness might do; provided I didn't gibber and hurl things at people, I didn't mind if he thought me a little crazy. But I didn't think I was. Later, I was to reconstruct a world of fantastic terror; I heard sirens and guns, after the war was over. I thought my friends were dead and the city struck down with plague. (p. 90)[66]

Despite her desolation at Lord Howell's rejection, Delia indicates that her spiritualist experiences are not the result of madness, although her later hallucinations may be. She writes on madness in a dual register, presenting it at one moment as a chosen refuge in which to express her grief and anger and the next moment as a terrifying episode of hallucinations and confusion. The text oscillates between Delia's confidence in her visions and despair at the meaninglessness of these experiences when they remain unshared:

> [T]hrough the mediation of the little table, [the RAF pilots] were not dead. They spoke, they laughed, they crowded around the table. But what they said or what they would have said, could now no more concern us. There was the roll of drums. There was the moon-circle that was broken. It was all a dream, a fantasy, a delusion. [...] They were dead and I was a middle-aged, tired woman. (p. 91)

Here H.D. blurs the lines between madness and sanity, 'mad grief' and desolation. The subsequent historical narratives play against and alongside the initial hallucinatory return of the immediate past as she searches for meaning for her losses in the distant past and imagines alternative outcomes. Detloff argues that the critical tendency to code madness as a metaphor for something else can lead to over-determined readings where texts become metaphors for a wounded psyche and thus their creative formal innovations are ignored.[67] Yet H.D. crafts a text that explodes such restricted readings by explicitly foregrounding madness as 'a resource as well as a disability', one that may be crafted into political interventions and aesthetic innovations.[68]

By foregrounding her 'mad grief' H.D. sets the stage for the rest of the narrative to develop various strategies for healing from the practical – removal from the scene of trauma – to the visionary – Delia experiences consolatory as well as frightening hallucinations. The text becomes a 'recovery document' as the psychoanalytic cast to the narrative highlights.[69] The analytic voice emerges early in the narrative, revealing how the changes to the physical cityscape prompt internal upheavals:

> The debris that cluttered the streets of London, sometimes left a half-house open. [...] One looked into rooms in another dimension. So I think this externalization of peoples' private lives, somehow in the end, sliced open one's own house. One looked into one's own interior private life, a life shut off until now, even to oneself. (p. 57)[70]

The reversal of inner and outer lives gives psychic and spiritual experiences greater political and social relevance, as well as establishing the reflection on Delia's inner life that will continue throughout the text. Her recovery is affected by returning to the distressing symptoms of her illness and seeking to make sense of her breakdown by relating it first to her own previous experiences and then to the larger pattern she traces through the historical vignettes. Eventually, she consoles herself by explaining Howell's rejection as paradoxically sustaining her fragile health, arguing that if she had stayed in London her health would have broken down completely, so the mental collapse that led to her removal to Switzerland was a blessing in disguise (p. 121).

Delia and Howell are here portrayed as led by the spirits, who have a greater awareness of their frailties. Delia adjusts her purpose from communicating the RAF pilots' message to Lord Howell to the broader project of writing *The Sword*. Therefore, writing becomes both a mode of self-analysis and the means of channelling personal experience into a creative project with a wider visionary scope addressed to all who have suffered the wounds of war.

Conclusion: Haunted hermeneutics

Critical discussion of haunted modernism repeatedly emphasizes the hermeneutical significance of ghosts: 'Ghosts, after all, are hermeneutic entities, both etymologically – like Hermes, the Greek messenger god, they possess a privileged ability to pass between the worlds of the living and the dead – and practically: all ghosts demand interpretation.'[71] H.D.'s description of the medium as translator emphasizes the hermeneutic framing of spectral activity. Rather than a passive ventriloquist of the spirits' voices, the medium is an active participant, a translator (p. 88). She aligns artistic and spiritualist practice, representing the medium as an artist in her own right. As a translator Delia is implicitly a member of a community of both living and dead, interpreting one to the other. For H.D. haunting is something to be decoded like other visionary or mystical experiences.[72] However, in *The Sword* Delia's hallucinations and madness also indicate the instability and inherent risk of interpretation while the repetition and variation of characters and events through the historical vignettes indicate the proliferation of meaning in which a final outcome or interpretation is never fixed. In H.D.'s writing from the Second World War, ghosts and memories indicate an excess of meaning, desire and wonder; they are compelling, intrusive and demand action.

Writing is aligned with haunting; as the ghosts seek to pass on messages to Delia, so H.D. in turn seeks to pass on these messages to the reader. Daniel Cottom argues that the spiritualist movement was primarily a *way* of speaking and writing. Spiritualism's appropriation of language made it 'appear more theatrical than instrumental, more creative than instructive, more potential than referential'.[73] Cottom's emphasis on the potentiality of language in spiritualist discourse suggests that the openness within texts created by the movement of spirits undermines any totalizing impetus of narrative. This understanding of spiritualism as primarily a creative, uncertain hermeneutical activity brings us back to Cixous's theories of writing as a response to trauma that is ambivalent, mysterious and oriented towards the future. As Bettelheim suggests, reintegration is an ongoing process and the outcome of an encounter with strangeness is never guaranteed. The following chapter explores the significance of intimate communities, focusing on H.D.'s autobiographical Moravian novel *The Gift* and the writing cure as response to the traumas of war.

Notes

1 H.D. 1986, p. 195. At the end of the Second World War H.D. suffered a physical and mental breakdown.

2 H.D. joined the London Society for Psychical Research in 1941, where she met the medium, Arthur Bhaduri, and soon developed a spiritualist circle including herself, Bryher, Bhaduri (called Ben Manisi in *The Sword*) and his mother; Sword 1995, p. 347.

3 Augustine 1996, pp. 121–32; Laity 1996, pp. 116–17.

4 For an introduction to *Majic Ring* and an analysis of its relationship to *Trilogy*, see Sword 1995, pp. 347–62; Tryphonopoulos 2009, pp. xxi–xxxix.

5 See Detloff 2009, pp. 88–101; Friedman 1990, pp. 329–50; Graham 2007, pp. 299–319; Henke 2000, pp. 25–42.

6 The First World War was an exceptionally traumatic time for H.D. with a stillbirth, the breakup of her marriage, the death of her brother in France and her father's subsequent death in February 1919. Following the war, H.D. and her baby daughter nearly died of influenza. H.D. considered her lost child a war casualty, claiming that the stillbirth was brought about by the shock of hearing of the sinking of the *Lusitania*; H.D 1975, p. 40. Trudi Tate discusses H.D.'s understanding of war trauma extending to her unborn child in the context of discourse on civilian war neuroses in the First World War; 1998, pp. 10–20. See also Henke 2000, pp. 42–53.

7 Felman and Laub 1992, p. 5.

8 Ibid.

9 Ibid. p. 65.

10 Detloff 2009, p. 14.

11 Felman and Laub 1992, pp. 2–6.

12 Ibid. p. 61.

13 Ibid. p. 62.

14 Ibid. p. 71.

15 Brock and Parker 2001, p. 250. *Proverbs of Ashes* deconstructs theologies built on models of redemptive suffering and turns to the language of trauma studies to consider alternatives.

16 Chopp 2001, p. 61.

17 Ibid. p. 64.

18 Ibid.

19 Ibid. p. 62.

20 Caruth 1996, p. 64.

21 Friedman describes *The Gift* and *Trilogy* as 'testaments to survival'; I would add *The Sword* to this list; 1990, p. 351. As Bruno Bettelheim points out, although these questions are common among survivors it is important to affirm that survivors have no obligation to prove they were *worth* saving as this would suggest that those who did not survive were *not worth* saving; 1986, p. 39.

22 Bettelheim 1986, p. 36.

23 Ibid. pp. 36–48.

24 Felman and Laub 1992, p. 7.

25 Cixous 1998b, pp. x, xiv.

26 Cixous 1992, p. 122.

27 Cixous 2007, p. 13.

28 Cixous 1992, p. 149. Celan is an important writer for trauma studies and forms another point of contact between Cixous and Felman. For further discussion of his work in the context of testimony and poetics see Cixous 1992, pp. 130–2; Felman and Laub 1992, pp. 25–42; Walton 2007a, pp. 46–7, 57–8.

29 Cixous 1979, p. 78.

30 Celan 1978, p. 37.

31 Ibid. pp. 35–6.

32 Yaeger 1997, p. 230.

33 Many of the tribes who had contact with the Moravians in what is now Eastern Pennsylvania spoke Algonquian languages, including the Lenape, the Shawnee, the Nanticokes and the Mahicans and thus the related languages delineate a way of referring to these interrelated tribes as a group; Pencak and Richter 2004, p. xiv; Schutt 2007, p. 3.

34 MacKay 2007, p. 10.

35 Ibid. p. 6.

36 Detloff 2009, p. 4.

37 Ibid. pp. 14–15.

38 Hobson 2011, pp. 156, 64; Rainey 1998, p. 163.

39 Detloff 2009, pp. 83–7.

40 For a fuller commentary on the relationship between transcendence and materialism in *Trilogy* and *Four Quartets* see Anderson 2012, in press.

41 Trigilio 2000, pp. 84–7, 111.
42 References to *Trilogy* and H.D.'s other long poems include volume, section and line numbers.
43 Cacciari quoted in Hobson 2011, p. 161.
44 Ibid. p. 154.
45 Ibid. p. 170. See also Trigilio on ambivalence within H.D.'s vision; 2000, p. 113.
46 Moi 1985, pp. 120–1.
47 Hobson 2011, p. 171.
48 Sword 2002, p. 3. Spiritualism emerged in the United States in 1850 and spread to England, where it was popular from the 1860s to the 1880s: Armstrong 2005, p. 123; Owen 1989, p. 1. For more on the popularity of spiritualism and the occult in the First and Second World Wars see Armstrong 2005, p. 18; Augustine 1996, p. 1.
49 Derrida 2001; Freud 2005, pp. 201–18.
50 For a discussion of the role of the medium in relation to gender and authority (literary, social and political), see Sword 2002; Braude 1989; Owen 1989.
51 Schmidt 2000, p. 35.
52 Davis 2007, p. 157.
53 Sword 2002, p. 123.
54 Ibid. p. 254.
55 A poem from 1941, titled 'R.A.F.', describes an encounter with the ghost of a pilot who is compared to Hermes as a winged divine messenger; H.D. 1983, pp. 485–92.
56 *Majic Ring* gives far more detail of individual séances; it indicates H.D.'s ongoing occult interests: her notes on spiritualist sessions are replete with occult references and refer at length to H.D.'s earlier visionary experiences. In the fictionalized version, *The Sword*, H.D. embeds her Hermetic understanding, occult interests and visionary experiences in the narrative arc of Delia's wartime experience and the historical vignettes that form the later part of the text.
57 This is not to disregard the importance of consolation and the relief that contact with the spirits of dead loved ones provided for many people.
58 This is a clear example of the fictionalization of H.D.'s life in *The Sword*. H.D.'s husband, Richard Aldington, did not die in the First World War, although they did separate at that time. Their relationship became more amiable in the late 1930s. They finally divorced in 1938 but in 1937 they renewed a correspondence that continued until H.D.'s death in 1961; Zilboorg 2003, pp. 1, 241. Although Aldington read the text in draft, we have no indication of his reaction to being fictionally killed off.
59 On 6 October, 1946 H.D. wrote to Bryher, 'Do not worry about *Voices*, Fido dear. That is all over now. But there is still the common-or-garden Voice of inspiration and of Love – may I keep that? I did go too far. You were quite right'; H.D. 1946.

60 Hogue and Vandivere 2007, p. xliii.

61 See also H.D. 2009a, pp. 4, 15–16.

62 Sword 2002, p. 124.

63 In her notes to *The Gift* H.D. describes how peace was established and then broken by European settlers; H.D. 1998a, p. 273. Jane Augustine notes that '[i]n order to break down the stereotype of the Native American "savage" and to connect with the Second World War context, H.D. refers to the "white savages" as "'Aryan,' the Nazis of their time"; H.D. 1998a, p. 287 n. 20.

64 Hogue and Vandivere 2007, p. xxxiv.

65 Ibid. p. xv.

66 I use the word 'madness' here deliberately, partly because H.D. uses it herself in the course of *The Sword*, but also in order to avoid an anachronistic use of clinical language. To modern readers, it seems fairly likely that Delia suffers from some kind of post-traumatic stress disorder. However, this is problematic partially because this diagnosis did not come into use until the 1970s and also because the symptoms are unclear (the text does not specify if Delia's experiences are hallucinations, flashbacks or memories). *The Sword* is autobiographical fiction, not a case study, and there is no diagnosis presented in the text (there is very little about Delia's treatment in the novel). Therefore I find it more appropriate to use a generic word like 'madness' to indicate the strange, hallucinatory experience Delia undergoes, rather than a term like 'mental illness' that carries clinical connotations. Moreover, 'madness' also denotes the rage Delia feels at the ongoing destruction of war.

67 Detloff 2009, p. 26. Detloff refers to readings of Virginia Woolf as a trauma survivor.

68 Ibid.

69 Augustine 1996, p. 130.

70 The psychological reading of architectural destruction resonates with H.D.'s other Second World War writing. For further discussion of the significance of the London cityscape in *The Walls Do Not Fall* see Graham 2002, pp. 164–7, 79–80.

71 Sword 2002, p. 165.

72 For an analysis of coding, decoding and hieroglyphics in H.D.'s poetry, see Ibid. pp. 118–21.

73 Cottom 1991, pp. 109–10.

2

Cloud of Witnesses: Moravian spirituality and intimate communities

Chapter One considered H.D.'s spiritualist practice during the Second World War as a way of building community and nurturing creativity as a response to the individual and corporate traumas of war. This chapter continues this engagement with the violent context of H.D.'s 1940s writing but turns its focus to Moravian spirituality. In this chapter I explore H.D.'s interest in eighteenth-century Moravians as well as her own Moravian upbringing. Moravian spirituality forms another significant strand of H.D.'s religious belonging and provides a context for her to explore the connections between spiritual and creative gifts. Thus Moravian spirituality, like spiritualism, fuels her own creative practice and provides resources for H.D.'s creative response to war trauma. Before moving from the previous chapter's focus on trauma and spiritualism to a reading of visionary communities and the writing cure in *The Gift* and *The Sword*, I outline the significant elements of Moravian history for H.D.; its affective, erotic spirituality and emphasis on ritualizing communities.[1] For H.D., healing, reintegration and restoration are worked out through her writing and drawn from the resources of her interpretation of Moravian history and spirituality and her spiritualist practice.

The Gift may be read as a self-analysis in which H.D. uses the tools from her encounter with Freud to grapple with both newly remembered traumas from her childhood and current wartime traumas. In conducting a self-analysis, H.D. acts as witness to her own testimony – her writing providing the space for containment and libidinal investment needed to enable testimony and its associated knowledge to emerge. However, *The Gift* is not entirely framed by psychoanalysis; it is a spiritual narrative in which a mystical communion with current companions, family members and long dead Moravians provides a way through the impossibility of testimony. Here the voices of the dead (or absent) are not those of young men killed in war but H.D.'s own family (particularly her grandmother) and previous generations of Moravians. Through construction of female genealogies H.D. connects her personal and familial memories to Moravian history.

Moravian genealogy and history

Although much of *The Gift* focuses on H.D.'s childhood memories, it is not an escapist novel of nostalgic desire but a deliberate return to the past in order to recover the wisdom hidden in childhood for the benefit of the war-torn present.[2] *The Gift*'s population of spectral figures is not limited to living memory. H.D. knits her immediate family to the wider Moravian church by constructing spiritual as well as familial genealogies. Her engagement with early Moravians in *The Gift* is expanded in the book's concluding series of notes, which include lengthy meditations on Moravian history.[3] Before considering H.D.'s appropriation and deployment of Moravian history and spirituality, I will briefly outline aspects of Moravian history, theology and practice relevant to the concerns of this book, including Zinzendorf's affective theology, the emphasis on ritual in community life and the intersection of gender, sexuality and spirituality (as we will see, this gender–sexuality–spirituality complex is particularly evident in blood and wounds devotion). In particular, the significance of community and affective spirituality and their expression in liturgy and hymnody reveal the importance of voice to Moravian spirituality. The voices of dead Moravians form a powerful presence within *The Gift* as their spiritual legacy is expressed in both H.D.'s audition of humming voices and the encoding of secret messages in musical scores. The elements of Moravian spirituality outlined below are crucial to understanding the visions in *The Gift* and contribute to the spiritual and creative resources that enable H.D.'s recovery from war trauma and inspire her subsequent writing.

Following Pietist trends (although going much further than many of his contemporaries found acceptable), Count Nicholas von Zinzendorf developed an affective theology, a 'religion of the heart', while leading the Moravian Church in the mid-eighteenth century.[4] He did not reject rationalism so much as an over-reliance on rationalism as key to the mysteries of the universe. He insisted that it was not possible to understand the mystery at the heart of God, and therefore Christians should focus their efforts on devotion to Jesus. Zinzendorf's view of incarnation, that Jesus Christ's identity held all the fullness of God, led to a side-lining of the first person of the Trinity in Moravian worship, with a devotional focus on Christ as both creator and saviour and the Holy Spirit who nurtured the Church and facilitated salvation. Zinzendorf believed that salvation for all was accomplished by Jesus' life and death, therefore Jesus' suffering was a cause for believers' rejoicing, not sorrow.[5] Because Zinzendorf was more concerned with joyful devotion and ethical practice than doctrine, 'all life became a liturgy' for eighteenth-century Moravians. Ritual and communal life erased traditional distinctions between secular and sacred.[6] Community life was an essential part of Moravian religion. During the eighteenth century, Moravian communities were centred not around nuclear families, but rather on 'choirs', groups based on gender, age and marital status.[7] The choir system was enabled by a communal system (known as the General Economy) in which labour and its fruits were shared.[8]

The more controversial elements of Zinzendorf's theology included his understanding of the Trinity, his view of a divine marriage between Christ and each soul (and the implications for human sexuality) and zealous devotion to Jesus' blood and wounds. Zinzendorf radically revised the language used to discuss the Trinity and the relationships between the three persons. His theology delineated a remarkable gender-bending. He advanced a view of the Trinity as a family; the creator as father and the Holy Spirit as mother to the son. The Spirit 'prepared [Jesus] in the womb, hovered over him, and finally brought him into the light. She gave him certainly into the arms of his mother, but with invisible hands carried him more than his mother did.'[9] Zinzendorf repeatedly refers to the Holy Spirit as mother in sermons and hymns; she is mother to all living things (because she participates in creation) and mother to individual believers because she is 'the active agent in conversion'.[10] Finally, and most importantly for Moravian life and worship, she is mother to the community, acting within to draw the community together and to uphold its common purpose. In arguing for the Holy Spirit's 'maternal office' Zinzendorf and other Moravian leaders advanced a metaphorical view of gender, side-stepping biology and refuting claims that they were making metaphysical statements about God's being.[11] However, language is crucial to our understanding of gender (and of the divine) and thus Zinzendorf's creative metaphors can be seen as a feminization of the Trinity.[12] When it comes to the identity of Jesus, this re-gendering process becomes more complicated.

For Zinzendorf the primary expression of the relationship between human and divine was erotic. The mystical marriage between Christ and the Church was a common trope in medieval Europe. However, Zinzendorf went further than most in his endorsement of a physical expression of this marriage in terms of human sexuality and explicitly erotic devotion.[13] Zinzendorf insisted that male believers had to become feminine in order to approach Christ as bridegroom, while also standing in for Christ in their sexual relations with their wives (no such slippage was necessary or available for women, nor were women encouraged to take on the role of Christ in relation to their husbands). Although the configuration of male believer and male husband/saviour does indicate homoeroticism, Atwood argues that the emphasis on heterosexual marriage within the community and a heterosexual alignment of believer and saviour effectively suppress any homosexual tendencies.[14] However, Aaron Fogleman argues that one way of resolving the problem of an erotic relationship between a male Jesus and male believers was to embrace it, and he points out that the single-sex choir system may have allowed for a certain amount of homosexual activity.[15]

Fogleman also finds evidence of a feminine Jesus in Moravian iconography and hymnody.[16] The side-wound of the crucified Jesus was depicted as both a womb and a vagina and was the object of great devotion; thus Jesus becomes both mother and lover. The 'blood and wounds' theology of Zinzendorf formed the devotional locus for affective Moravian piety: a sign of Jesus' humanity, suffering and salvation, blood and wounds dominated the imagery of much Moravian liturgy, a point I will return to in Chapter Three.[17] Although Moravian devotion emphasized Jesus' suffering, this is in the context of its life-giving properties:

> In Zinzendorfian piety, blood is thus a concrete symbol of health and well-being. It is symbolic of the healing of the soul and the release from sin and death. [...] Christ's blood becomes the lasting connection between the heart of the Christian and the heart of the Savior. It is a symbol of immersion in the divine life.[18]

The maternity of Jesus and the Holy Spirit are here united as the believers are reborn through the side-wound and delivered into salvation by the Holy Spirit.[19] Wound iconography takes an erotic turn in the devotional cards carried by many Moravians that depict the wound – often entirely separate from the rest of Jesus' body – with vaginal or womb-like imagery.[20] The distinction between human sexuality and religious devotion was elided by the use of these cards during conjugal visits (with married couples living separately, sexual encounters were regulated by the community).[21] Moravians were encouraged to view their own sexual experiences as a physical manifestation of a spiritual relationship. Taken together, the views found in Zinzendorf's writing and wider Moravian devotion suggest an androgynous Christ as depicted in hymn verses such as

'My King [. . .] Thy royal desire [. . .] leads me on the militant path/with motherly love'.[22] What this theological and liturgical discourse meant for real women is of course an open question. Fogleman argues that an additional controversy surrounding the Moravians stemmed from the practice of gender equity.[23] Zinzendorf rejected a view of sin which blamed women and found sexuality a source of wickedness, but his emphasis on Jesus' masculinity upheld traditional gender hierarchy and gender roles. The feminization of men in a mystical sense did not lead to complete gender equality. On the other hand, Zinzendorf did emphasize a need for mutual devotion and honour between men and women. The dispersal of the patriarchal family allowed women to take on many leadership roles within the community. Women such as Anna Nitschmann, who became an elder at 15, were highly regarded as spiritual leaders. Another controversy surrounding the Moravians was provoked by women's practice of teaching and preaching. However, Zinzendorf oscillated between advocating for women preachers and retreating from this position by arguing that their role was circumscribed. Despite the egalitarian rhetoric, Moravian women seemed afflicted with a glass ceiling of their own. Most of their pastoral work involved the women choirs, they seldom achieved the prominence of male leaders and their preaching was often presented as exceptional rather than normative. After Zinzendorf's death the prominence of women in the church and their speaking and teaching roles declined, along with many other controversial elements of his theology and devotional practice.[24]

The reconfiguration of the nuclear family for the sake of an alternative vision; the imaginative linguistic virtuosity that challenges rigid understandings of body and gender (while at the same time affirming the importance of the physical); the conception of sexuality as sacred; and the unity of secular and sacred brought about by a community focused on liturgy – all resonate with H.D.'s writing.[25] In eighteenth-century Moravian theology, gender is produced by shifting layers of bodily and spiritual experience. Jesus is and is not female, is husband, mother and sibling (the Holy Spirit being mother of both Jesus and the Church).[26] These ideas are consistent with the fluid sexuality evident in H.D.'s writing, the connection she draws between sexuality and the sacred and the situation of rituals and visions in the midst of the everyday. I will return to rituals and visions in H.D.'s writing in the following chapter, and sacred sexuality in Chapter Four. For now I will focus on the significance of community and its voices in *The Gift* and *The Sword* as sites of trauma's intersection with religion. In these texts, writing is the force that expresses attention to the voices of the dead and mobilizes post-traumatic reintegration.

'Intimate Communion': Circles of belonging

The Moravian emphasis on the communal nature of religion, evidenced by the significance of ritual and the elision of any distinction between sacred and secular, resonates with H.D.'s work in many ways. As Adelaide Morris has aptly noted, her poetry has a communal cast from the early Imagist poems: 'The sustaining pronoun of H.D.'s poetry, however, is not "I" but "we." Most of her poems are social, creating an "I" that is one of a choros, rewriting shared mythologies, or enacting rituals designed to draw others into alliance.'[27] Likewise, Rachel Connor emphasizes the enabling presence of others to H.D.'s creative and spiritual visions.[28] Just as Bryher's presence is necessary to enable and support the visions described in *Tribute to Freud* and *Majic Ring*, so the support of the spiritualist medium Ben Manisi provides the impetus for Delia's spiritualist experiences in *The Sword*. The communal experience of vision extends to other characters; Hilda's presence (and perhaps the distant but audible presence of other family members) draws forth Mamalie's recitation of her earlier visionary experience, and the RAF pilots appear as a group. Hilda's grandmother, Mamalie, is both a catalyst for Hilda's apprehension of the gift of vision and an important figure in H.D.'s constructed genealogy. Mamalie connects Hilda/H.D. to the early Moravians and their Algonquian neighbours, thus drawing together overlapping circles of community that encompass many generations, extending beyond living memory.

The use of the first person plural and the narrator's commentary draw the reader into the circles of the texts. Thus, in addition to self-analysis, H.D. sets up a structure for the reader to act as witness to her writing as testimony. Throughout H.D.'s writing, even the most personal visions are embedded in her commitment to community (and they are idiosyncratic; she is not particularly interested in any kind of orthodoxy). *The Gift* focuses on family and Moravian history while *The Sword* has a broader historical sweep, but each text emphasizes the significance of a small, intimate group of fellow believers or practitioners.

In both texts H.D. focuses on her place in a small group of initiates nested within a larger community.[29] In *The Gift* this is the Hidden Church of the early Moravians, Zinzendorf and his companions, re-discovered by Mamalie and her first husband and revealed to the child, Hilda.[30] In *The Sword* the spiritualist circle of Ben Manisi, Gareth and Delia first provides the necessary group of initiates within the larger group of spiritualists. As Rachel Connor argues, the emphasis on connections (between members of the circle as well as between the medium and the spirits) of popular spiritualism and its use of the discourse of mass communication technology (H.D. echoes this discourse in describing the circle as a wireless) enables a reading of H.D.'s spiritualist writing as committed to the wider community. Connor acknowledges that this aspect of H.D.'s writing runs counter to her efforts to situate herself among the literary and cultural elite (such as joining the Society for Psychical Research).[31] Some of the secrecy that surrounds the involvement of H.D. and Bryher in spiritualism can be located in their anxiety about cultural status, yet it is clear from H.D.'s writing that a greater concern was protecting something she saw as precious from ridicule.[32] Moreover, H.D.'s emphasis on privacy created a safe space for intimacy to flourish. Alex Owen describes the unfixed gender and sexual identities enabled by the spiritualist circle where the medium was often possessed by spirits of the opposite, or indeterminate, gender and typical gender hierarchies were undermined as 'witness to [...] the polymorphous nature of desire'.[33] Connor considers unorthodox spirituality as a location for transgressive desire, suggesting that the spiritual experiences shared by H.D. and Bryher periodically over many decades undermines the heterosexual discourse by the construction of an elaborate performance of cross-gender and sexual identities.[34] H.D.'s spiritual experiences were characterized by eroticism and intimacy; they were inherently relational as well as encouraging self-exploration.

Following the breakup of Manisi's circle, the spirits of the RAF pilots form the community around Delia, although she continues to seek living communion in the form of an alliance with Lord John Howell. Howell is figured as part of the group of RAF pilots, partly as a father figure but more specifically through H.D.'s physical descriptions: 'I was looking straight into a white face and staring, grey eyes [...] he looked haunted. He looked like a ghost' (H.D. 2007, p. 36). Describing Howell as a ghost marks the ongoing haunting in the text by constructing a (tenuous) community of the living and the dead. Clearly Howell is a significant figure in *The Sword* but, while I don't wish to underplay his role, I want to emphasize the significance of female partners and mentors in H.D.'s texts. In *The Gift* and *The Sword* Bryher (Gareth) is a background figure but one whose presence is steady and assuring. In the historical vignettes in *The Sword* there are older female figures such as Mother Beata and Rose Beauvais who provide wisdom and guidance to the young Blanchfleur, who is just beginning to discover the importance of a spiritual element in working for peace, while in *The Gift* Mamalie, Anna von Pahlen and Morning Star provide Hilda with spiritual guidance.

The Gift and the writing cure

As we have seen in the presence of the RAF pilots, loss is a part of H.D.'s experience of intimate communities, and this is also evident in *The Gift*. An active incorporation of the lost into intimate communities is one way of containing grief. At the beginning of the text Hilda begins elaborating her own interpretation of her genealogy by describing old family portraits and graves in the nearby cemetery (H.D. 1998a, p. 35). On the first page of the novel the death of a liminal character (she is one of the students at the Seminary and so not an outsider, but she is neither named nor a member of the family) is twinned with the death of children that Hilda (and Hilda's mother before her) cannot remember. Each generation has its lost children: Hilda's Aunt Fanny (who died when her mother was a baby), Hilda's sisters Alice and Edith, and H.D.'s own stillborn child of 1915 (although this child is not mentioned here). Hilda first defines herself in the family figuration by her fascination with these domestic ghosts. She marks herself as the repository of family history and inheritor of memories; through the novel this role will expand until her inheritance includes the family's spiritual and creative gifts as well.

The Gift and *The Sword* can be read as dual deployments of community belonging, as Hilda explores her identity as part of a Moravian family in Bethlehem, Pennsylvania, and the adult H.D. grapples with the threat to her community in London. There is a significant emphasis on choice as H.D. reiterates her decision to remain in London during the Blitz as a sign of solidarity with her adopted country.[35] In her openness to her own visions and the stories told her by Mamalie, and her more active participation both spiritually (as a medium) and materially (by her location in London), she suggests that community belonging is a matter of individual action, not simply historical chance.

In attempting to make sense of Mamalie's revelations, Hilda incorporates the memory of Moravians past to her own unusual family, drawing upon the Moravian emphasis on community: 'Only if we were *United Brethren* and I was one of them, then it was really in the family' (H.D. 1998a, p. 157).[36] Hilda reconfigures her family tree to include the Shawnee chief Paxnous, who was connected to her through his wife's Moravian baptism and the former spouses of her father and grandmother. She sees her own identity as mutable and defined, in part, by how her relatives refer to her, just as she shapes their identity by her own terms of reference.

Hilda's ability to redraw kinship lines is continued in a variety of ways by H.D. as an adult. Towards the end of *The Gift*, H.D. describes the community forged by the air raids to Bryher: 'I propped the front-door open and Mrs Williamson across the hall, sent her maid over to see if I were all right [...] People from upstairs came down and people below, dragged out their bedding and slept in the hall' (p. 214). H.D.'s correspondence is peppered with references to gifts exchanged within her circle of friends and acquaintances. Certainly rationing and scarcity led to the increased value of material goods, but more significant is the excess value of affection mobilized and displayed by such gift-giving.[37] The exchange of domestic goods – tea, honey, flowers – marks and maintains these circles of friendship. H.D.'s correspondence with Bryher reveals similar exchanges but far greater intimacy. H.D. returns to key moments in their relationship many times in the course of her prose oeuvre, attaching great meaning to particular shared experiences. Bryher helped H.D. in 1919 when she had just given birth and was ill with influenza. In 1938 H.D. returned to this moment when she wrote in response to a gift of flowers from Bryher: 'Now Fido [...] a most lovely thing, one of those great wood boxes has just come and masses and masses of daffodils that come before the swallow dares. [...] The room is filled with you and 1919, and all you did and ever do for me. [...] They are especially lovely and have that fragrance, like [...] forgetfulness and healing.'[38] In her writing of the Second World War H.D. often returned to the scenes of the First World War and the intense experiences which followed. In 1945, when the strain of the war was beginning to fray her nerves, she wrote to Bryher: 'maybe, I will get a new lease of life and if so, I will owe this next re-birth after this war to you, as I did the re-birth after the last.'[39] Letters such as these indicate the longevity and vitality of H.D. and Bryher's relationship and H.D.'s awareness of the interconnectedness of the two world wars at a deeply personal level.

Pennsylvania and London are brought together by psychological and spiritual resonances, as the secret of the Hidden Church becomes the means for H.D.'s psychic survival of the Blitz and the continuity of her community. The 'secret' of the Hidden Church is revealed as the promise of intimacy given by Jesus in the Gospel of Matthew, as Mamalie tells Hilda: 'The Secret that my Christian explained to me seemed very simple. It was simply belief in what was said – *and lo, I am with you alway, even unto the end of the world*' (H.D. 1998a, p. 157). The ongoing presence of Anna von Pahlen, Paxnous and other members of the Hidden Church indicates not only the significance of maternal genealogy but of the endurance of this unorthodox communion of saints. In receiving their secret, H.D. sees herself as linked to this group of initiates that spans many generations. She sees Mamalie's sharing of her memories as an initiation in which her spiritual gifts are awakened. This gift she in turn must pass on through her creative work.

Through Hilda's memories of the intimate world of the Moravian community in Pennsylvania, H.D. constructs a female genealogy in which artistic and spiritual giftedness are entwined. Mamalie understands the secret of the Hidden Church through her knowledge of music; the message was encoded in musical notations in old documents. When Mamalie shares her memories of the visionary experience she had as a young woman, Hilda stores the tale for later interpretation. By using two narrative voices, H.D. weaves together the terrors and discoveries of childhood with her adult fears and hopes; this palimpsest provides the key to understanding the gift itself. The gift is initially defined as artistic – 'Artists are people who are gifted' – but even this straightforward definition is immediately complicated: 'an artist is someone who – well – he can draw or paint or write a book or even do other things' (p. 43). The hesitation and vague reference to 'other things' suggests that the gift is not readily defined and it will take Hilda/H.D. the rest of the book to reach a mystical understanding of the gift: 'The Gift was a Gift of Vision, it was the Gift of Wisdom, the Gift of the Holy Spirit, the *Sanctus Spiritus*' (p. 214).

The presence of the Hidden Church is marked by moments of visionary consciousness where the mystic becomes one with the spirits of the earlier initiates and is sustained by the telling of this vision. Because she is a musician, it is unsurprising that Mamalie's hearkening to the voices of her spiritual ancestors takes the form of sound and music:

> [I]n trying over and putting together the indicated rhythms, she herself became one with the *Wunden Eiland* initiates and herself spoke with tongues. [...] [W]e all laughed like scales running up and down. [...] The laughter ran over us and the deep tones of the men's voices and the high pure silver of Anna's voice, mingled in a sort of breathing hymn. (p. 169)

The rapture Mamalie experiences culminates in a hymn, the musical expression of her religious community, a point I will return to in the following chapter on ritual. What I want to emphasize here is the integration of music, voice and community. Here H.D. draws upon the traditional emphasis on hymn singing in Moravian devotion. Such singing is important as an act of devotion that gives voice to and strengthens community bonds. It is the relationships between the initiates, Mamalie, her husband and his uncle, that give the vision its value.

Through identifying herself with these spiritual forebears, Hilda claims the gift of her inheritance. When she hears Mamalie's story, she engages in a complex weaving of names and relationships, situating herself as part of the visionary Hidden Church:

> [N]ow I understood that I had another name; now I was Agnes, now I would really be Agnes and Aunt Aggie's name was Agnes Angelica, so perhaps they had named her Angelica because of Anna von Pahlen, then I would be part of Anna von Pahlen, too, and I would be part of the ceremony at *Wunden Eiland* and I would be Morning Star along with Anna. (pp. 163–4)[40]

Here Hilda's understanding of her own identity shifts again. Not only does her identity emerge from her family, but through those links she is united with the eighteenth-century Moravian Anna von Pahlen, who in turn was linked with Morning Star when they exchanged names. Thus H.D. is able to call upon a rich and diverse spiritual inheritance.

Only as an adult in war-torn London does H.D. come into a full understanding of Mamalie's gift. The development of Hilda/H.D.'s spiritual understanding is revealed in the narrative form of the central chapter of *The Gift*, 'The Secret', which contains the episode of Mamalie sharing her memories with Hilda. The narrative is primarily told by the child, but the adult's voice occasionally breaks in, adding a reflective layer to the text in the form of analysis of both Hilda and Mamalie. This dual register suggests that, in dwelling on her childhood memories, H.D. is bringing the Hidden Church into the present moment of 1940s London.

She goes on to explain that a traumatic event caused the child Hilda to repress Mamalie's secret. Hilda was the first of her family to see her father returning home with blood on his face after falling from a trolley. She was unaware of the cause of his injury and was terrified. Furthermore, he does not respond to Hilda, and the children are brushed aside by the adults and left alone. This silencing is deeply distressing to Hilda as she wishes to tell the story and be recognized for her discovery.[41] The narrator reiterates the numerous questions that Hilda wishes her mother would ask; these questions would have allowed her to tell her story (p. 106). The silencing of Hilda's narrative and lack of explanation by the adults cause her to become even more frightened and bewildered and may have contributed to the memory's suppression. The subsequent trauma of the Blitz leads to an 'earthquake' in H.D.'s mind; memories are brought to consciousness and she finally tells her story (p. 50).[42] The scene of writing provides a witness which allows H.D.'s testimony and its hidden knowledge to emerge, as described by Dori Laub. Thus H.D.'s initiation into the mysteries of the gift is twofold; the child receives Mamalie's vision and the adult endures the traumas of war terror which return this vision to consciousness. Giving expression to this vision in writing brings healing for both old and new psychic wounds.

The presence of the Hidden Church in London is made explicit in the concluding chapter when H.D recognizes first England and then the world as *Wunden Eiland*, a place of sacred belonging (pp. 221, 223). In linking the shattered world of the 1940s with a Moravian holy place, H.D. implies that sacred communion can flourish even in the midst of destruction, while she also acknowledges the fragility of these places. The secret of communion and peace becomes H.D.'s gift to her companions in London and the wider community of her readership as she brings the spiritual resources of an intimate moment between grandmother and granddaughter to the predicament of a world at war. However, in *The Sword* the vision of peace sustained by H.D.'s memories of Moravian community is obscured by further trauma. In this text she utilizes a broader historical scope and a greater emphasis on writing to respond to her own post-war breakdown.

As in *The Gift,* H.D.'s conviction in *The Sword* is the urgency of passing on the message of peace, which is located in a complex interplay between past, present and future. She reiterates the interconnection between individual and social health, suggesting that healing must come from within, radiating outward towards others:

> I have said if you have consolation, do not try to share it, but eventually, if you are consoled or integrated, you help console and integrate the scattered remnant. I don't think society can be reconstructed from outside. [...] In saving oneself, one creates a shell, not the isolated, highly individual spiral-shell I spoke of, but a minute coral-shell, one of a million, or a single wax-cell of the honey-comb. (p. 67)

This passage suggests the intersubjectivity mobilized by the reciprocity of testimony and witness following the traumatic event. In stressing the balance of individual and communal identity, H.D. resists privileging one over the other. There is repeated textual confusion over who is healed in *The Sword* – H.D., Delia, Delia's community, or, indeed, H.D.'s community. The blurring of the lines between character, author and intra- and extra-textual communities suggests that these distinctions are less important than the cure itself. Although community belonging is essential for psychic and spiritual health, H.D. emphasizes the responsibility of individuals to build and rebuild their communities by attending to inner life as well as external concerns. Therefore, her interest in psychoanalysis and psychic health is not a turning away from society but a way of understanding the social world from the inside out, and her devotion to her communities is matched by commitment to her particular vision.

Delia's recovery involves a renewal of her writing; psychic, spiritual and creative health is presented as unified and mutually enabling. In both *The Gift* and *The Sword* H.D. responds to personal and social crisis with a deeper commitment to writing. *The Gift* describes the development of her understanding of her vocation, which climaxes in the midst of an air raid:

> [H]ow could I see and be and live and endure these passionate and terrible hours of hovering between life and death, and at the same time, write about them? Yet now [...] I passionately regretted only this. That the message that had been conveyed to me, that the message that my grandmother had received, would again be lost. (p. 213)

She comes to understand the dual nature of the gift as creative *and* spiritual and believes that her inheritance is the task of reviving it. I suggest that this is H.D.'s way of making sense of her survival of the Blitz and her later breakdown and thus attaining reintegration.[43] Her fear and anxiety is subsumed by the urgency of passing on the secret of the Moravian and Algonquian peaceful alliances. Likewise, in *The Sword* the requirement of passing on the RAF message dominates the text. The prophetic nature of these messages unites H.D.'s religious thinking and experience with writing. In *The Gift* and *The Sword* the urgency of witnessing to consolation as well as trauma becomes the driving force of the narrative. This leads to an emphasis on survival and the importance of a witnessing presence as explored by Chopp, Brock and Parker. In attending to the voices of the dead, and inviting them to resonate with her own experiences and to resound within her texts, H.D. explores a model of attention and renewal that allows her to move beyond trauma without disregarding the ongoing presence of its wounds.

Conclusion

The end of *The Sword* employs a performance metaphor: 'We went on with the play' (p. 267). This is an ambivalent ending; it can be read as an affirmation of ongoing life or as an indication of the hopeless repetitions of violent histories and the marginalization of non-violent interventions. I suggest that it indicates the repetition of the writing cure itself. The writing cure is a practice that must be engaged with again and again as trauma returns either through haunting memories or new catastrophes. This repeated return is evident in Cixous's numerous engagements with the poetics of memory, wound and writing.

However, not all returns are traumatic; haunted gaps also make space for creative interventions, new growth and the mysterious proliferation of meaning. For H.D., as for Cixous, reading and writing themselves are seldom traumatic, but rather involve a process of witnessing which affirms, and moves towards, reintegration. It is those who return – the RAF pilots, her grandmother, the Moravians Anna von Pahlen and Christian Renatus – who call H.D. to the writing cure. The scene of encounter, whether one encounters the spectral return of the dead or the precarious testimony of the survivor, demands a witness. The openness in the text creates the space for this encounter which, according to Cixous, also partakes of an intimate communion. Alterity haunts Cixous's writing as she seeks to write a path towards the mysterious encounter. The unknown becomes present *through* poetic writing. Survival itself bears the mark of strangeness. The community of witnesses carries traces of alterity as the process of testimony itself is a mystical one that escapes containment and explanation.

The unknown haunts domestic ruins. Cixous makes no claims for the clue to survival, but she insists that the encounter with the miraculous, the unknown from elsewhere, is one that takes place *within*. It returns us to ourselves, but to a self that contains an untamed alterity. Both *The Gift* and *The Sword* are texts that commit to the writing cure and the exploration of the resources of visions for healing, consolation and inspiration, resolving trauma through its incorporation in meaningful patterns of spiritual gift and creative practice. However, the healing of trauma through narrative frameworks is mitigated by the continued ruptures in the narrative, the insistent questions of spectral figures, named and unnamed, and ambivalent endings. H.D.'s writing is a practice of hope rather than certainty.

Notes

1 Susan Stanford Friedman associates the writing cure with *The Gift* in her psychoanalytic reading of the text, while Colbey Emmerson Reid argues that H.D. refashions the Freudian talking cure into 'a religious discourse of oracular interpretation' which allowed her to re-enter writing; Friedman 1990, p. 329; Reid

2010, p. 2. Diane Chisholm also reads *The Gift* in the context of a writing cure that engages with female sexuality and spirituality; 1992, pp. 121–64.

2 Augustine 1998, p. 3.

3 The notes section of *The Gift* not only reveals H.D.'s deep interest in Moravian history but also suggests an attempt to legitimize her work as historically based; ibid. pp. 14–15.

4 Atwood 2004, p. 77. Zinzendorf was an aristocrat who offered sanctuary to Bohemian Protestants on his lands in Saxony and re-established the *Unitas Fratrum* or the Moravian Church in 1727. He was a charismatic leader who travelled across Europe and North America visiting Moravian communities. His writings, including sermons and hymns, were also highly influential for eighteenth-century Moravians. For an analysis of Zinzendorf and Moravian historiography see Atwood 2004, pp. 9–19. H.D.'s interest in Zinzendorf is evident from the notes to *The Gift*, which contain lengthy meditations on his work with the Moravian communities; her later novel *The Mystery*, in which fictionalized members of his family appear as main characters; and her unpublished notes on Moravian history and spirituality which include numerous references to him; H.D. 1951.

5 At this time Moravians downplayed Christ's resurrection; theological and liturgical emphasis was on the passion and death; Miles 2005, p. 362.

6 Fogleman 2007, pp. 89–90.

7 Zinzendorf believed that all stages of life were sacred because Jesus was born as an infant, grew to maturity and then died, thus blessing every stage of life. Childcare was communal from a young age, leaving parents free to work as missionaries or in other roles within the larger community; there were also separate choirs for young women, young men, married women, married men, widows and widowers. Atwood points out that a weakness of this theology is that those aspects of human life not experienced by Jesus would be downplayed in Moravian spirituality, particularly old age; Zinzendorf wrote extensively on death but not on old age; 2004, pp. 87–90.

8 During the period of the General Economy the church owned the land, buildings and businesses. The breadth of economic communalism was unique to Bethlehem; most other Moravian communities had a more limited social communalism; ibid. p. 118.

9 Ibid. p. 68. Those who have experienced the physical cost of bearing children might be less than thrilled with this diminution of Mary's role.

10 Ibid. p. 69. See also Fogleman 2007, p. 75.

11 Ibid. p. 76.

12 This is the view of both Atwood (2004, p. 68) and Fogleman (2007, pp. 75–6); Kinkle argues otherwise, claiming that Zinzendorf's maternal metaphor is functional and thus not a new doctrine: 'The motherly office of the Holy Spirit referred to the Spirit's function, the Spirit's activity. It was a name for God in

relation to humanity – a name for God in God's graciousness. [...] It was not an attempt to speculate about the divine life'; Kinkle 1990, p. 9. However, Kinkle overlooks the significance of God's actions for our understanding of divine life. Zinzendorf's formulations may be metaphorical rather than ontological but that does not make them any less formative for Moravian understanding and practice.

13 Atwood 2004, p. 91; Fogleman 2007, pp. 78–82.

14 Atwood 2004, p. 93.

15 Fogelman also draws on evidence from Herrnhaag (a German Moravian community) during The Sifting Time when a group of young men around Zinzendorf's son, Christian Renatus (who figures in *The Gift*), turned to explicitly homoerotic rituals involving penetration of Christ's side-wound. This activity drew much criticism from surrounding Protestant groups and led to the persecution of Moravians, and was repudiated by Moravian leaders and subsequent Moravian historians; 2007, p. 79.

16 A feminine Jesus is not, of course, Zinzendorf's invention. Many medieval images and texts emphasize Jesus' nurturing qualities and compare blood to milk as Christians feed from the wound in the crucified Jesus' side, while Julian of Norwich described Jesus as 'our Mother for we are for ever [sic] being born of him'; Lochrie 1991, p. 118; Wolters 1966, p. 164.

17 Devotion to Jesus' body and blood was also a feature of medieval piety. Bynum outlines the complexity of conflict over Jesus' body and its fragmentation that was represented by controversies around blood piety. She argues that devotion to Jesus' body (represented by the host in the Eucharist) emphasized resurrection, containment and community, while blood was contradictory, symbolizing life and death, salvation and destruction. Bynum also points out the violent legacy of devotion to Jesus' blood: its emphasis on destruction, sacrifice and accusation led to anti-Semitic violence in pogroms and crusades as the Jews (along with heretics, non-believers, or other marginal figures) were blamed for Jesus' suffering and death; 2002, pp. 699, 702–7. Here, we can locate the contrast with the later Moravian piety: the focus on Jesus' wounds brings body and blood together, but the Moravian emphasis is on the life-giving properties of blood, incorporation into Jesus' body and thus a matter for rejoicing, not condemnation or horror. Asceticism or other practices of imitative suffering were not a part of Moravian practice. Zinzendorf disagreed with many other Pietists on the necessity of suffering (i.e. Christ's suffering may be a consolation to Christians when they suffer but it is not a requirement of conversion); Atwood 2005, pp. 21–4.

18 Ibid. p. 22.

19 Ibid.; Fogleman 2007, p. 77.

20 Some of these small cards, of watercolour on card stock, had devotional verses and a simple red oval painted on them; others had larger red or pink ovals with verses

printed inside them or on the rim and detailed domestic images – such as a bed, chair and window, or the exterior of a house – within the oval; Fogleman 2007, plates 4–5.

21 Ibid. p. 82.

22 Quoted in Ibid. p. 78.

23 Ibid. p. 90.

24 Atwood 2004, p. 90; Miles 2005, p. 363. In North America, much of the contact between European Moravians and their Algonquian neighbours was between women; as women began to play a less prominent role in Moravian society, the relationships between the groups also eroded; Schutt 2004, pp. 87–103. For further discussion of the role of women in the Moravian church in the eighteenth century, see Fogleman 2007, pp. 95–104; Vogt 1998, pp. 227–47.

25 Adalaide Morris argues that H.D.'s unusual family life, especially her arrangements for her daughter's care (Perdita was adopted by Bryher and her then husband, Kenneth MacPherson, and often cared for by H.D.'s mother and aunt while H.D. and Bryher travelled) are best understood in the context of a gift economy; 2003, pp. 124–6.

26 Katherine Faull argues for an interpretation of Moravian spirituality that emphasizes a 'polyvalent signification of male and female sexualities' in the figure of Christ; however, her analysis underplays the feminine attributes of Jesus; 2004, p. 39.

27 Morris 2003, p. 135. See also Ostriker 1990, pp. 346–7.

28 Connor 2004, p. 45.

29 H.D.'s communities are intimate but not exclusive. Her goal is to pass on her knowledge and experience; as she writes in *Trilogy*: 'that way of inspiration / is always open, / and open to everyone'; H.D. 1998b, *Walls* 20:5–7.

30 It is also worth noting that H.D. frequently uses the other name for the Moravians, the *Unitas Fratrum* or United Brethren, which directly invokes the relational aspects of the denomination.

31 Connor 2004, pp. 117–18.

32 This protectiveness is also evident in H.D.'s attitude towards her tarot readings, astrology charts and other occult activities.

33 Owen 1989, p. 222.

34 Connor 2004, pp. 125–7.

35 As she wrote to Viola Jordan, 'if one has taken joy and comfort from a country, one does not like to leave it, when there is trouble about'; H.D. 1941.

36 Hilda refers to Paxnous, or Paxinosa, the Shawnee chief whose wife H.D. called Morning Star; he is a historical figure and is mentioned in Moravian records of meetings with Shawnee and Nanticoke tribes; Anon. 2000–9.

37 Sitwell 194-.

38 H.D. 1938.

39 H.D. 1945a.

40 *Wunden Eiland* was an island in the middle of a river near the Moravian settlement where the Hidden Church met. H.D. draws upon historical records to describe the place in her notes to *The Gift*: 'Its name, "the Island of the Wounds," meant that it was dedicated to the remembrance of the wounds of Jesus, as then dwelt upon in certain special liturgies and hymns'; Bishop Joseph Levering, quoted in H.D. 1998a, p. 262.

41 Madelyn Detloff notes *The Gift*'s repeated representation of burning or dead girls and argues persuasively for the evidence of sexual endangerment and survival that is alluded to cryptically in the text. The silencing that Hilda experiences after rescuing her father may well also refer to other periods of silence. Detloff is at pains to connect private, sexual trauma with the public traumas of war, an example of H.D.'s continual recasting of history, both personal and public, and her refusal to posit ultimate distinctions between them: 2009, pp. 95–101.

42 See also Friedman 1990, p. 333. The recovery of this memory during the Blitz is fictionalized in *The Gift*. H.D. had in fact discussed this incident with her first analyst, Mary Chadwick, and also with Freud in the 1930s; Henke 2000, p. 26.

43 This correlates with Bruno Bettelheim's analysis of survival: 'all attempts to extract meaning from life are to a very large measure actually a projecting of meaning into life. This can occur only when and to the degree that a person is able to find meaning within himself [sic], which he [sic] can then project outward. One must invest life with meaning, so that one may be able to extract insight from it'; 1986, p. 48.

3

Writing as Ritual

In her article 'Signaling: Feminism, Politics, and Mysticism in H.D.'s War Trilogy', Adalaide Morris argues that *Trilogy* is oriented towards the community of Londoners in which H.D. was situated during the Second World War. In addressing itself to the community in a mystical mode the epic poem is like a ritual: 'it labours to create a formal break with everyday life, a ritual space that invites the reader to return to, re-examine, and rearrange the *ethos* of a community in crisis. The work *Trilogy* initiates is the work of cultural reconstruction.'[1] Having examined the significance of intimate communities and religious belonging as the context and catalyst for the writing cure in H.D.'s Second World War texts *The Gift* and *The Sword Went Out to Sea*, I now come to a consideration of ritual as a primary activity of religious communities, an activity which both expresses and shapes the cultural reconstruction called for by *Trilogy*, *The Gift* and *The Sword*.

Demetres P. Tryphonopoulos argues that *Trilogy* is a palingenic, or soul-making, text in its 'incantations and liturgical or ritualistic rhythms'.[2] This soul-making activity takes place throughout the poem, from the smallest movement – the worm spinning its own shroud – to expansive flights of vision. These movements, which indicate the regenerative transformations at the heart of *Trilogy*, are supported by the 'ritualistic rhythms' of the poem. *The Gift* is bracketed by a procession and play in the first chapter and a litany in the final chapter. The mystical experience at the end of the text unites liturgy, performance, visionary consciousness and community, while ritual processions and plays throughout *The Sword* demonstrate the significance of these forms for the vitality of the community.[3] The interplay between art and ritual emphasizes the performative element of each.

Recent scholarship on ritual has emphasized the power of rituals to create and shape culture rather than simply reflecting social values.[4] The performance approach to ritual studies establishes a link between aesthetic and sacred activity by developing a dynamic model of ritual. Morris uses Victor Turner's analysis of social drama as a way into the ritual dynamic of *Trilogy*, and while this is productive I would argue that the emphasis on transformation in Richard Schechner's theory of performance is more relevant to the entirety of H.D.'s 1940s oeuvre. Turner argues that social drama is about conflict and resolution and consists of four stages: breach, crisis, restorative action and reintegration or schism (harmony is restored either by a group's reintegration or by complete separation).[5] Morris locates *Trilogy* in the third stage of social drama in which society reflects and acts – often in a ritual, liminal space – in order to move to the final stage, the resolution of conflict.[6] However, my reading of *Trilogy*, as well as prose texts such as *The Gift* and *The Sword*, finds transformation as the texts' focus, while conflict forms their context.

Schechner argues that the essential drama is located in transformation and that theatre is used as 'a way to experiment with, act out, and ratify change'.[7] Changes may be temporary or permanent or a more complex iteration in which transformation for the individual is permanent while the performance works to maintain a system-wide status quo. Schechner distinguishes between aesthetic drama – theatre – and social drama only to elaborate a way of comparing the two: '[t]he function of aesthetic drama is *to do for the consciousness of the audience what social drama does for its participants*: providing a place for, and means of, transformation. Rituals carry participants across limens, transforming them into different persons'.[8] Thus ritual can be seen as related to both theatre and social drama in its ability to affect transformation.

This chapter explores the relationships between ritual, performance and vision through three examples: the sacred dramas in *The Sword*; the Moravian litany in the final vision of *The Gift*; and the Hermetic, alchemical ritual in *Trilogy*. While I use this rubric to separate the three texts for clarity of structure and ease of analysis, it should be noted that there is significant overlap and resonance between them. H.D.'s syncretism is such that the devotion to Moravian Christianity explored in *The Gift* does not conflict with the veneration of pagan deities such as Hermes and Venus evident in *Trilogy*. As I discussed in the Introduction, this syncretism is held together by an overarching search for ancient wisdom, her Hermeticism, and its expression and development through a materially grounded creative practice. Hermeticism as a mode of interpretation enables a discussion of writing and ritual with which the chapter closes.

In *Trilogy*, writing is a spiritual activity that both expresses and instantiates the dynamic interplay between ritual-as-performance and signification. An analysis of *Trilogy* alongside Jacques Derrida and Hélène Cixous shows the dynamism of writing, or signification, as a ritual performance in time and space that depends on the proliferation of difference. My use of ritual as a framework for this chapter functions in two ways. First, it allows for close readings of various ritual elements within H.D.'s writing; second, it is a heuristic choice that allows me to develop my understanding of material mysticism in H.D. In this way the chapter itself is a reading performance that is primarily concerned with the activities of texts.

Drama and ritual in *The Sword Went Out to Sea*

In both *The Gift* and *The Sword*, domestic and folk traditions are juxtaposed with more formal art forms such as Greek drama. These variations on dramatic performance form important elements of H.D.'s understanding of the gift and constitute a connecting thread through the different stories told in *The Sword*. The presence of drama in this text highlights a crucial aspect of writing for H.D. – the performativity that is essential to understanding the text as cure. Delia comes to understand her 'mad grief' as connected to the creativity she sees as the vibrant heart of culture: 'I have [...] traced my own madness to its source, the source of all western poetry, the source of philosophy and mythology, the Greek drama' (H.D. 2007, p. 101). By identifying her madness with Greek drama/poetry, she realigns it with creativity, rather than destruction, and, therefore, embraces the possibilities for renewal nascent in even this painful episode. Although somewhat grandiose, this is an effective strategy for reconciling painful experiences, but there is more going on here than self-analysis and rehabilitation. H.D. also emphasizes the connection between drama and poetry; she configures writing as performative, as an event as well as a material object.

If *The Sword* can be understood as the product of a writing cure, suggesting that art is a source of healing for a society as well as individuals ravaged by war, then one of the primary modes in which this cure is effected is drama. As Cynthia Hogue and Julie Vandivere argue, drama forms the central nexus of artistic practice and psychic health in *The Sword*:

> [T]he approach H.D. adopts to work through her experience, representing it as a healing dream for a broken land, is to turn the 'theatre of war' into the culturally originary ritual of the drama festival (that is, to *poetry*), as potential, curative performance: quite literally, acting/writing (out) *as* cure.[9]

H.D. plays on the expression 'theatre of war' when she describes the bombed houses as a 'stage-set' (p. 57). The nexus of writing/drama and religion is evident through the relationship of drama and ritual, which *The Sword* presents as a site for healing, a performed cure. Hogue and Vandivere argue that the proliferation of performances in the text provides numerous sites for acting out psychic and spiritual cure.[10] While this is a crucial insight for understanding *The Sword*, Hogue and Vandivere collapse religious rites into artistic pageantry, thus eliding H.D.'s emphasis on the sacred. The placement of sacred processions at Delphi and in Athens alongside Greek tragedies and court plays implies not only that religious ceremonies are 'culturally originary', but also that plays are sacred rituals themselves.

Performance functions as both a structuring device for *The Sword* and a flexible metaphor which allows H.D. imaginative scope to engage with themes such as memory, history, creativity and vision. In this text H.D. refines the metaphors deployed in earlier texts such as *The Gift* and *Trilogy*. In bringing together drama, vision and ritual H.D constructs a meta-discourse that allows her to comment on her own process of reading and writing history. Early in the novel she indicates that performances will be used throughout the text to indicate the significance of vision to a view of history as palimpsestuous: 'The veil [...] was very thin. One saw right through it. Or, like a curtain before a play, the veil was drawn aside from time to time, and one looked on scenes of the near or far past or even of the future' (p. 64).[11] This metaphor indicates a potential reading strategy as the figure of the seer and the theatre-goer merge into one and plays assume a prophetic function. H.D. hints that the reader may also draw aside the veil in looking upon *The Sword*'s scenes. Scenes of past and future are layered in the text through the recurring themes and performances of both plays and rituals that are embedded in the historical vignettes.

As is typical in H.D.'s work, the connection between ritual and drama is figured and refigured in *The Sword*: from ceremonial processions both ancient and modern, to the Elizabethan and Venetian plays, to the classical dramas presented in both ancient Athens and twentieth-century Philadelphia. The theatre of ritual is tied to the theatre of war through the procession and ritual remembrance of the fallen of the Battle of Britain. Delia attends a memorial service in London's Westminster Abbey; in the context of the other rituals in the text this becomes a radical alignment of modern, state-sanctioned Christian rites with ancient, pagan, gynocentric rituals. H.D. believes that this ancient source will nurture healing for herself and her own society. Through the historical vignettes and reincarnated characters H.D. links Athenian military culture (aligned with the modern world at war) with the older, goddess culture of Minoan Crete when the Painted Lady claims that the two cannot be fully separated: 'We can not [sic] dismiss the serpent-goddess from the citadel. She has been there too long. It was not only the Delphian [...] Apollo who came from the cradle of Zeus, his sister came with him' (pp. 172–3).[12] In this narrative of besieged Athens, the Painted Lady asserts her confidence in the longevity of the serpent-goddess while simultaneously confessing her fear that this tradition will be lost. The presence of the older goddess is suggested in another scene which points again to an earlier Greece. The Cretan spring festival – a procession with the goddess – is disrupted by war, but an Ariadne figure, later called Daystar, continues the rituals: 'I sang songs with the old words. I wove garlands of wood-violets, and placed them on a flat stone for an altar' (pp. 176, 180).[13] H.D. draws together this simple ritual with more elaborate theatricals when she writes of the Sacred College of Delphi staging plays for the Athenian Dionysian festival (pp. 195–6).

Like many other modernists, H.D.'s interest in ancient Greek religion was influenced by the myth and ritual theories current in the early twentieth century. The work of Jane Harrison, one of the Cambridge ritualists, resonates with H.D.'s writing, particularly her theories about art's basis in ritual and the common purpose of art and religion.[14] Harrison argued that ritual preceded mythology; therefore, studying what the Greeks *did* in relation to the sacred would yield greater knowledge of their religion as a whole.[15] Unlike many of her colleagues, Harrison critiqued the imposition of patriarchal Olympian theology over ancient matriarchal cults.[16] She argued that the Olympian religion replaced an older worship of earth spirits. However, she looked to the Olympians and their rituals for traces of the older gods: 'Apollo held the oracle, but Apollo [...] was preceded by a succession of women goddesses [...] Gaia the Earth was first.'[17] The movement of religion towards mythology and theology evacuated the intensity from ritual, leaving it available for the development of art:

> So long as people believed that by excited dancing [...] you could induce the coming of Spring, so long would the dromena [...] be enacted with intense enthusiasm. [...] [T]hese rites repeated year by year ended [...] in the mental creation of some sort of daemon or god. [...] In place of *dromena*, things done, we get gods worshipped. [...] So the *dromenon* [...] wanes, the prayer, the praise, the sacrifice waxes. Religion moves away from drama towards theology, but the ritual mould [...] is left ready for a new content.[18]

The new content that she alludes to is Greek drama and subsequent art forms. Harrison emphasized the chorus as the remnant of ritual within drama, which resonates with H.D.'s use of the chorus in her poetry to emphasize community belonging.[19] Harrison understood ritual as a collective activity.[20]

The significance of the community for the performance of ritual further underscores the centrality of community to H.D.'s writing. Eileen Gregory connects H.D.'s early poetry's concern with ritual with the responsibility of the artist to common life:

> She conceives of the lyric as *dramatic* not in the traditional sense of emphasizing individuality and character [...] but precisely in the sense suggested by Harrison: drama as associated with *dromenon*, with liminal passage, with 'common life'. [...] She certainly saw her engagement with the lyric as a socially responsible gesture, a form of spiritual mediation.[21]

This engagement with community which Gregory sees as part of H.D.'s early lyric poetry becomes more explicit in her writing of the Second World War, where artistic practice and ritual is embedded in intimate religious communities.

H.D. configures history as both a drama and a ritual. In *The Sword*, as in most of her writing, the significance of religion is not lodged in particular beliefs but in sacred practices, places and objects (I will return to the significance of objects in H.D.'s writing in Chapter Four). Periodic moments of vision serve to weave together various strands of history and ritual:

> I saw the Parthenon frieze [...]. I could see Orestes pursued by the Furies. He found the sanctuary by the altar of the goddess. I would stand by the altar. We were pursued by the Furies. Rat-ta-ta-tat – the years were revolving on their pedestal. They went slowly at first, then faster, faster as the drum beat louder. (p. 83)

The insistent beat calls to mind the drums of war and the pursuit of the Furies suggests the all-too-present threat of destruction and the madness suffered. However, the drumbeat also may indicate the beat of an ancient ritual performance. Throughout *The Sword*, these two are held in tension: sacred ritual over and against the threat of destruction. The writer positions herself as the participant in ritual. She chooses to stand by the altar, but this choice will need to be made again and again through the numerous folds of time, as the Furies of madness and war continue to disrupt ritual's rhythm.

In H.D.'s prose, classical plays are joined by the medieval mystery play. The English mystery play provides a metaphorical vehicle to shift the scene from Athens to England. H.D. uses the mystery play to indicate the convergence of history, mythology and religion. The mystery plays were groups of pageants whose scope extended from early narratives in the Hebrew Bible to the end of time or doomsday and centring on the life, death and resurrection of Christ.[22]

The cycles were performed in medieval English towns from the fourteenth to sixteenth centuries as part of the celebrations of the feast of Corpus Christi. Authorized by the pope in 1264, Corpus Christi is a liturgy in celebration of liturgy with devotion to the sacrament at its centre (the mass concludes with the priest processing with the host held aloft).[23] This reflexive ritual creates a space conducive to the development of pageants concerned with layers of history and cosmology. Mervyn James argues that the location of the plays as part of this feast day indicates the significance of the body to urban society; it provided an organizing concept allowing the affirmation of 'social wholeness and social differentiation' while simultaneously marking the creative tension between them.[24] Wholeness and differentiation can be seen in H.D.'s use of the mystery play as a metaphor for the complexities of belonging and the relationship of past, present and future. H.D. mobilizes the themes addressed by such plays and their position between ritual procession and formal theatre to suggest the role of the artist as ritual participant: 'At last, I had a place in the vast pageant and a place that was near the altar' (H.D. 2007, p. 106). Delia is a participant, but through the act of writing the text (itself a performance) H.D. claims an authority for the artist as interpreter and creator of ritual.

Moravian litany in *The Gift*

As she does in *The Sword,* H.D. uses performance to explore artistic vocation, the connections between different historical moments and the gift that is simultaneously creative, spiritual and visionary, in *The Gift*. However, there are important distinctions between the texts. In *The Gift* the historical focus is tighter as H.D. considers her family's heritage. Four different times are drawn together: the London Blitz; H.D.'s childhood in Bethlehem, Pennsylvania; her grandmother's discovery of the Moravian Hidden Church as a young woman; and the early years of the Moravian colony and their Algonquian neighbours (primarily Lenape, Nanticoke and Shawnee) in the eighteenth century.[25] Contrasting with this precise historical framework, the use of performance throughout the text is much looser, ranging from a ritualized encounter with a fortune teller to processions, musical performances, religious rituals and a single play.

The correlation between drama and ritual is highlighted in the frame of the narrative. In the opening chapter a production of *Uncle Tom's Cabin* is one of Hilda's first experiences of the gift, and the novel closes with a litany that brings together vision, liturgy, community and music.[26] H.D. describes the play as a

'Medieval miracle-play procession', a metaphor she uses in *The Sword* as previously discussed (pp. 47–8). For Hilda the miracle of the play is how it transforms the world around her: 'the street would never be the same again, it would always be different, really everything would be different' (p. 47). Moreover, she explicitly links the play with religious ritual: 'The theatre was dark and the lights [...] were like ours in Church, when we sit in rows, grown people and children like this, and the Sisters walk down the aisles to hand the candles to the children' (p. 46). Before she becomes a writer herself, Hilda experiences artistic practice as something that changes the way she *sees*, something that partakes of vision and imbues the world with the sacred.

Hilda also attends to the musical aspects of the play and imagines that her family's musical endeavours will bring the dramatic into her everyday domestic life. Music forms a significant element of her family's identity; her mother experiences the suppression of her musical gift after her father's mockery as a significant loss, while Hilda's uncle is a renowned musician, frequently singing and playing. Most importantly for *The Gift*, her grandmother's music is a thread through the text and is crucial to the rediscovery of the Moravian Hidden Church. One of the original members, John Pyrlaeus, wrote down the secrets of the Hidden Church in a code formed by musical notation. Mamalie discovers this code through her knowledge of musical theory. Thus H.D. correlates music and text. She emphasizes that music is not just a sound to be heard but also has a written language of its own. With John Pyrlaeus's hidden message with the musical score H.D. introduces the possibility of a text within a text, a hidden meaning that is only available to the initiated, an example of her Hermetic view of Moravian Christianity. However, as we will see, H.D. draws together musical performance and musical text. Before turning to the audition which the musical text inspires – where Mamalie hears past generations of Moravians singing – I will briefly outline the significance of hymn singing to Moravian devotion and H.D.'s spirituality.

Hymns play a central role in H.D.'s consideration of the nexus of musical performance, community and religious experience. From the days of Zinzendorf the Moravian Church has been characterized by a strong tradition of hymn-singing.[27] In 1755 the Bethlehem bookstore had 15 different hymnals and the community owned thousands of published and unpublished hymns and litanies.[28] Hymns knit together the community, providing communication as well as common worship. H.D. describes how her mother knew whether there had been a death or a birth in the community, and the gender of the deceased, based on what hymn she could hear from the church (H.D. 1998a, p. 57).

The enthusiasm for blood and wounds piety found expression in hymns that scandalized many other Protestants. Although these hymns were eventually dropped from Moravian hymnals, H.D. was aware of them through her research on Moravian history. Henry Rimius based much of his criticism of the Moravians on such hymns.[29] In her notes on Rimius H.D. copied out the following, amongst others: 'My heart dwells in Jesus Side,/I kiss with the greatest Tenderness/the Scars on his Hands and Feet,' and:

> Doth, not a little Child stick
> wittingly to his little Mother: For this
> Reason am I so much wrapped up in the Mark of his Side,
> there is my Place, my House, my Hall,
> my little bed and my little Table.
> there make I – Ye Wounds![30]

Here everyday domesticity is conflated with religious devotion. The wounds of Jesus become a domestic scene where the relationship between Jesus and the devotees is configured as that between a mother and a child. This scene is comprised of ordinary objects – a bed, a table – which indicate the pleasure, comfort and sanctuary offered by devotions to the wounds. While the emphasis on blood and wounds piety may be mitigated in modern Moravian devotion, the central role of hymns remains. H.D.'s modern liturgical guides are primarily hymnals.[31] The liturgies for communion are mostly hymns, with only brief words of institution.[32] Several of the hymns reference blood and wounds before and after the words of institution for the wine, such as: 'E'er since by faith I saw the stream,/Thy flowing wounds supply,/Redeeming love has been my theme,/ And shall be till I die'.[33]

The hymns' attention to the physicality of Christ's body, while inscribing a celebration of divine presence rather than an emphasis on suffering, correlates with H.D.'s continued search for the sacred within the material. Moreover, the radical interpretation of gender and the focus on the domestic suggest H.D.'s view of Moravian devotion as centred in the family and female genealogy. During a more intimate scene in *The Gift* hymns mark the nexus of religious devotion, creativity and domestic life that reaches its peak at Christmas. Hilda sees the story of the Nativity played out around her as candles, moss and evergreens, ginger-bread and the Moravian *putz* (crèche) suggest the presence of the sacred in both church and domestic life. Creativity meets divinity as suggested by the hymn: '*Fir tree and pine and the laurel bough, We are twining in wreaths to greet thee now*' (p. 88).

Throughout *The Gift* music forms the connection between the different generations of the Hidden Church as well as between the different stages of H.D.'s own life. She turns to the hymns of her childhood to express her fears during the Blitz:

> I will be afraid too, there will be the *Storm of Death* that *roars sweeping by* that I sang to you in a hymn, and it was just a word in a hymn but it will be the *Storm of Death* and it will roar over my head. (pp. 181–2)

Initially H.D. is sceptical of the significance of hymns but her attitude changes when she begins to see their relevance to her current situation: 'the trite, old words of the familiar, long forgotten hymn-tunes had come true. What had I known of the *darkness deepens* when I sang to my grandmother?' (p. 217). The hymns express the hope that she sometimes wearies of maintaining and this hope comes to fruition when she finally understands Mamalie's gift. The gift, the legacy of the Hidden Church, is re-discovered by Hilda's grandmother and her first husband. Rituals are at the heart of this legacy: 'The later Christian [...] pieced out the story of the meeting, deciphered actually the words of strange pledges passed, strange words spoken, strange rhythms sung.' H.D. emphasizes the interplay between custom and inspiration; the words and rhythms 'were prompted [...] by the Power of the Holy Spirit' (p. 168). This suggests that the rituals of the *Wunden Eiland* may have been loosely structured with room for improvisation and a tenuous relationship with the practice of the wider Moravian community. This would allow H.D. to describe, or invent, a tradition within a tradition.

Mamalie's discovery in the musical manuscripts gives rise to a mystical audition. She hears voices of the older Moravians and the Shawnee leaders:

> [T]he actual Power that had fallen on Anna and Zeisberger and Paxnous and Morning Star, fell, a hundred years afterwards, on the younger Christian Seidel and his wife, Elizabeth Caroline, who was our grandmother. It seemed, [...] that in trying over and putting together the indicated rhythms, she herself became one with the *Wunden Eiland* initiates and herself spoke with tongues, hymns of the spirits in the air, of spirits at sun-rise and sun-setting, of the deer and the wild squirrel, the beaver, the otter, the king-fisher and the hawk and eagle. [...] 'O,' said Mamalie, 'I could not tell you of that laughter, it was the laughter of leaves, of wind, of snow swirling, it was the laughter of the water; indeed, it was the outpouring of the Mystic Chalice [...] it poured from the sky or from the inner realm of the Spirit, this laughter that ran over us.
>
> The laughter ran over us and the deep tones of the men's voices and the

high pure silver of Anna's voice, mingled in a sort of breathing hymn; it was breathing, it was breath'. (p. 169)

'The Power' is earlier referred to as 'the Gift', indicating that spiritual inspiration is aligned with artistic vocation. Thus the hymn, which partakes of both art and religion, is an appropriate vehicle to express this power.[34] H.D. describes a mystical experience that goes beyond Christianity as the spirits of the natural world join the Holy Spirit and the sacred chalice. The spirits of the sun and the animals, the laughter of wind and snow suggest the paganism that is never far from H.D.'s conception of Christianity. How much this passage is influenced by H.D.'s knowledge of Algonquian religions is unclear, but certainly the sentience of the natural world plays a significant part in the cosmology and rituals of many Native American tribes.[35]

The Gift's dramatic opening – the play *Uncle Tom's Cabin* and the actors' procession through the town – is paired with a liturgical closing. The final scene includes the adult H.D.'s audition of the Moravian 'Litany of the Wounds'. The Blitz brings the adult H.D. to a moment that reconfigures Mamalie's discovery of the secret of the Hidden Church and her ecstatic mystical audition. Here her childhood memories coincide with the psychic shifts H.D. has experienced through war trauma. This leads to a visionary experience, which, like Mamalie's, is primarily auditory and liturgical.

Not only was hymn-singing a primary feature of Moravian liturgy, but rituals themselves were at the centre of Moravian life. Before considering the significance of H.D.'s audition for understanding the role of ritual in *The Gift*, it is important to place it in the context of the original 'Litany of the Wounds'.[36] *The Gift*'s litany is markedly different from the eighteenth-century Moravian litany. In the original the litany is set for two choirs, the second making responses to the statements of the first.[37] Over its course, the litany praises Christ, invokes the blessing of the Trinity, requests mercy and culminates in a long set of responses requesting blessings for the Moravian community and the wider world which encourages adoration of the wounds themselves. Salvation and sanctification are clearly invoked – 'Wondrous wounds of Jesus,/*Holy fissures, you make sinners holy, and thieves from saints*' – but more of the petitions celebrate an ongoing intimacy with Jesus in which the believers are nourished by the wounds: 'Soft wounds of Jesus,/*I like lying calm, gently, and quiet and warm. What should I do? I crawl to you*', and 'Eternal wounds of Jesus,/*[You are] my house to dwell in. In a million eons you will still be new*'.[38] Although the litany clearly refers to Jesus' crucified body, what is invoked here is his living presence. Not all the responses are so abstract; blood is part of this devotion: 'Powerful wounds of Jesus,/*So moist, so gory, bleed on my heart so that I may remain brave and like the wounds*' and 'Purple wounds of Jesus,/*You are so succulent, whatever comes near becomes like wounds and flowing with blood*'.[39] However, even here the Moravians wish to share the qualities of the wounds, not in Jesus' physical suffering. The wounds do not begin with crucifixion but with birth and circumcision:

> May your painful first birth — Make us love our humanness!
> May your holy first wound — Help us circumcise our hearts!
> May your childlikeness — Help us to have childlike joy!
> May your first exile — Teach us to be at home everywhere![40]

The entirety of Jesus' life is part of the litany; it emphasizes the common humanity of Jesus and his worshippers and thus the relevance of his life as a model.

Returning to *The Gift*, in an instance of hearkening, or spiritual hearing, the communal nature of ritual is emphasized as H.D. connects the members of the Hidden Church (represented by Christian Renatus, Zinzendorf's son) with the wider Moravian community (the choir) and her own family (her great-grandfather).[41] Moreover, this hearkening occurs in the midst of the Blitz, thus drawing together H.D.'s Moravian past with her present community in London and suggesting that the spiritual resources of the former may be a gift for the latter. Consonant with her previous configurations of religion and domesticity, H.D.'s audition occurs in a mundane environment; after an air-raid, she walks into the kitchen and into a mystical experience:

> I heard Christian Renatus saying:
> Wound of Christ,
> Wound of God,
> Wound of Beauty,
> Wound of Blessing,
> Wound of Poverty,
> Wound of Peace,
>
> and it went on and on, while underneath it, there was the deep bee-like humming of the choir of Single Brothers and then the deeper sustained bass-note that must have been Christian David who had a voice like my great-grandfather who made clocks and kept bees and was called *princeps facile* of musicians. (p. 222)

H.D.'s litany is an abbreviation, almost a citation, rather than a full responsorial prayer. The response here is the humming of the choir and the overlaid memory of Hilda's great-grandfather. Christian Renatus's address to the wounds reflects H.D.'s belief in the Hidden Church as the caretaker of an ongoing mystical tradition. The description of the wounds is much more abstract than in Zinzendorf's version, indicating the general values of the Moravian community. The wounds are removed from their close identification with Jesus' crucified body, while still continuing to signal the living presence of the divine. Another point of connection may be found in H.D.'s subsequent recognition of the whole earth as 'a wounded island' (p. 223). The wound as a *place* is emphasized in both the earlier litany and H.D.'s visionary counterpart, while the domesticity of the wounds as a place of rest accords with the domestic setting of H.D.'s audition.

The 'bee-like', hymn-like humming of the choir recapitulates the voices of Anna von Pahlen and Paxnous, as well as the commingling of human voices with the voices of the natural world heard by Mamalie.[42] In this way H.D.'s audition re-stages the visionary experience of her grandmother that was given to her second-hand as a child. This repetition allows the adult H.D. to fully inhabit her own childhood experience and bring this shared wisdom to fruition. The words suggest a sacred plenitude, drawing together divine presence, aesthetics and an end to war. She goes on to emphasize the liturgical nature of her audition, thus drawing together the ritual and the visionary consciousness that is the gift Hilda received from Mamalie. H.D. reconfigures blood and wounds piety. She aligns this liturgical tradition with the Secret of the Hidden Church, which is both the peace exemplified in the pacts between Algonquian tribes and Moravians, and the divine presence indicated by the words discovered by Mamalie's husband: '*lo, I am with you alway* [sic], *even unto the end of the world*' (p. 157). In *The Gift*, sacred presence leads to visionary transformation; the way one sees is changed. Such transformations are enacted through the performative rituals of litany and music.

Alchemical ritual and Hermeticism in *Trilogy*

In *Trilogy* ritual is allied with writing rather than with the performances that are so prominent in *The Sword* and *The Gift*. Reading the three texts together allows performance and writing to be drawn together. The poem's ritual aspects can be read in terms of performance approaches to ritual.[43] Before I turn to a consideration of the complex interactions of textuality, ritual and performance, I wish to consider alchemical ritual and its underlying philosophy, Hermeticism, in *Trilogy*. Among the many strands of H.D.'s religious syncretism, Hermeticism provides a worldview that allows diverse elements to be brought together in the search for ancient wisdom and hidden knowledge. I have demonstrated how this shapes her approach to her Moravian Christian heritage; I now turn to the more obvious occultism of *Trilogy*. Amidst the numerous invocations, initiates, offerings and altars of *Trilogy*, the poem's central ritual – the ritual that prepares the way for the subsequent visions of the burnt yet blossoming tree, the Lady and the presence of the angels – is alchemical. H.D. uses this ritual and the multivalent interpretations mobilized by Hermeticism to explore the relationship between writing, materiality and the sacred.

As Morris and others have argued, *Trilogy* is concerned with a quest for healing a community damaged by the traumas of war.[44] Read alongside H.D.'s other Second World War writing, this common theme emerges even more clearly. The poet exhorts herself and the reader to undertake an inner journey in search of mystical knowledge that draws on Hermetic traditions in order to effect healing:

> living within,
> you beget, self-out-of-self,
> [...]
> we are the keepers of the secret,
> the carriers, the spinners
>
> of the rare intangible thread
> that binds all humanity
>
> to ancient wisdom. (H.D. *Walls* 4:43–15:9)

Critics have read the references to initiates and initiation in *Trilogy* in numerous ways: as coded references to poetry, spiritualism, feminist spirituality or Hermeticism. I suggest that, while all of these readings may be valid and there is certainly evidence for them, whether intra- or intertextual, the invocation of ancient wisdom suggests the centrality of Hermeticism in the text. Indeed, Hermeticism can be seen to subsume the others, not by exclusion but by inclusion; it is a framework for thinking that does not exclude other practices or beliefs. Erik Hornung argues that, because 'Hermes Trismegistus is a god of harmony, of reconciliation and transformation', Hermeticism is by nature tolerant, with no rigid dogma.[45]

Hermeticism is a philosophical tradition with its roots in the cultural milieu of Alexandrian Egypt, the contact zone of Greek and Egyptian culture.[46] It was transmitted to European culture via Greek texts known to early Christian apologists; Arabic writings (particularly on alchemy) disseminated during the

Middle Ages; and more widely circulated translations of the older texts during the Renaissance. Hermeticism is more of a worldview than a set of doctrines. It is marked by devotion to Hermes (both god and sage), mediator between the divine and humanity, and the search for ancient wisdom, which will bring the seeker to God's presence.

The role of Hermes in Western culture is complex and varied. The messenger of the gods, he is the founder of cities, the creator of writing, the arts and alchemy, the bearer of souls to the afterworld, a trickster and a thief. He is the patron of 'poets, orators, thieves' (H.D. 1998b, *Angels* 1:6). His thievery involves returning hidden treasures to circulation and thus is related to relays of knowledge.[47] Hermeticists conflate the Greek Hermes with the Egyptian Thoth, also credited with inventing writing (and, by extension, all of culture) and judging the souls of the dead as well as regulating the fate of the living.[48] Hermeticism takes its name from texts ascribed to the Egyptian sage Hermes Trismegistus, reputed to be of ancient origin. Hermes Trismegistus shares many of the attributes of Hermes/Thoth and is sometimes considered the grandson of the god, or his avatar.[49]

The conversion of Hermes from god to sage allowed the resurgence of interest in Hermeticism in the Renaissance, as Christians could revere the sage and consider his writings to be a means of connecting pagan and Christian wisdom.[50] Many texts of diverse provenance have been ascribed to Hermes Trismegistus. A collection of these writings, the *Corpus Hermeticum* (or *Hermetica*), was translated into Latin in the fifteenth century by Marsilio Ficino, enabling the circulation of Hermeticism through Europe during the Renaissance.[51] In 1614 Isaac Casaubon from Geneva discredited the ancient origin of most Hermetica, proving that most of the texts dated from the early centuries of the Common Era, although some still argued for ancient Egyptian theology in the *Asclepius* (another Hermetic text from the first centuries of the Common Era).[52] However, Faivre suggests that this may well have reinforced 'belief in a hidden Tradition, all the more secret or primordial because one could no longer date it', while Umberto Eco explains Hermeticists' dismissal of Casaubon's findings by their refusal of linear causality, which extends even to history.[53]

Like Gnosticism and related systems, Hermeticism indicates that salvation comes through knowledge. However, this knowledge is not primarily rational or intellectual but experiential, attained through spiritual discipline, study and practice, passed on from teacher to disciple.[54] The Hermeticist seeks '*gnosis*, or direct awareness of the Divine'.[55] Hermeticism suggests that the divine is the soul of the world and is hidden and revealed in creation.[56] Thus all of nature is sentient, full of the spirit of God; Paracelsus, a Renaissance alchemist, taught that 'there is no corporeal thing, which hath not a spirit lying hid in it, as also a life'.[57] The Hermetic understanding of the nature of God and creation thus differs from orthodox Christian doctrine: 'The Nous, the divine Self, is indeed uncreated and invisible, as in Christian theology, but it manifests itself in the physical world, which it has *generated*, not made.'[58] In the *Hermetica*, God reveals this wisdom to Hermes Trismegistus:

> And do you say 'God is invisible'? Speak not so. Who is more manifest than God? For this very purpose has he made all things, that through all things you may see him. [...] Nothing is invisible, not even an incorporeal thing; mind is seen in its thinking, and God in his working. [...] Everywhere God will come to meet you, everywhere he will appear to you, at places and times at which you look not for it, in your waking hours, and in your sleep, when you are journeying by water and by land, in the night-time and in the day-time.[59]

Here, then, is Hermeticism's distinction from Gnosticism, which considers the material world to be irrevocably flawed or even evil, and Neoplatonism, which also stresses a desired transcendence of the material world through a series of hierarchical levels culminating in a perfect ideal.[60]

This understanding of the world as the living revelation of divine being leads to an attention to the particular, as all of creation is understood as incarnation.[61] Both divinity and the created world are seen to be as mutually unfolding and dynamic rather than static: 'even the divine image is not complete'.[62] Divine dynamism undergirds a way of reasoning by analogy; everything in the universe is related to every other part of the 'living whole'.[63] This holistic view includes incorporeal, spiritual and psychic realities as well materiality. In *The Emerald Tablet* Hermes Trismegistus sums up this web of interrelated material and spiritual realms: 'That which is above is like to that which is below and that which is below is like to that which is above.'[64] The law of correspondences suggests that each thing is also an analogy for something else; thus the world is a web of signification. The world as signifying web allows knowledge to be hidden as well as revealed. The analogical relationship between things allows the Hermeticist to see the universe as a text to be decoded and read.[65] Part of the *gnosis* attained by the Hermeticist is the ability to see this web of connection and understand the ways in which the material expresses the spiritual: 'they find sense everywhere in things'.[66] As I discussed in the Introduction, this way of reasoning by analogy is crucial to understanding H.D.'s stylistics. In both her poetry and her prose, she repeatedly brings together differing concepts, images and experiences in order to establish 'a web of correspondences' that both reveals and conceals the complexities of her vision. I will return to this point in my discussion of ritual, language and writing later in this chapter.

In addition to his numerous other attributes, Hermes Trismegistus is the founder and patron of alchemy, with Hermeticism forming its philosophical basis.[67] Like Hermeticism, alchemy has a complex, diverse history. Some strands of the tradition focus on the pragmatic arts of metallurgy, goldsmithing and glass-making, while others are more concerned with the theological and philosophical implications of the transformation of all nature. In this formulation alchemy becomes another mode of ancient wisdom as the alchemist attempts to understand God and creation.[68] At the heart of alchemy is the Hermeticist understanding of all matter as alive and in dynamic relation. Alchemy seeks to harness the principle of transformation at the centre of life towards the perfecting of all things. The two strands are not mutually exclusive; turning lead into gold, or creating the philosopher's stone (which bestows eternal life), may also be seen as metaphors for spiritual, as well as physical, transformation. Many alchemists believed that personal transformation and spiritual purity were required before the physical processes would be successful.[69]

The prototypical alchemical ritual describes a sacred marriage between sulphur (male) and mercury (female), which results in a holy birth – the elixir of life that will 'redeem all life to its highest form'.[70] This ritual can be mapped onto the Eleusinian mysteries and the Moravian formulation of the Trinity as Father, Mother and androgynous Son, where the holy child is the redeemer, the elixir of life.[71] With its resonance across diverse traditions this ritual is a powerful metaphor for H.D. As Adalaide Morris notes, the process of distillation, transformation and birth of new forms is referenced repeatedly throughout *Trilogy*. From the metamorphosis of seed, shell and chrysalis, to the larger narratives of the poem which suggest alchemical change effected in the crucible of war, these transformations culminate in 't]he ultimate, audacious hope [...] that [*Trilogy*] might itself carry and transmit a formula for regeneration'.[72] Here Morris returns to her earlier formulation of *Trilogy* as a ritual and refines this reading by focusing on the poem's alchemical references.

The quest for hidden knowledge, if not ancient then certainly of earlier epochs, is implicit in *The Gift* and *The Sword* but is most evident in *Trilogy* where questions of inspiration, discovery of ancient wisdom and transformation are introduced in the opening sections and continue through all three volumes. H.D.'s interest in Hermes is evident from her earliest poetry. In 'Hermes of the Ways', from her first volume of poetry, *Sea Garden*, the god is the changeable figure who watches over boundaries, pathways and meeting points.[73] The Hermetic understanding of the universe as participating in divine life is evident in the way H.D. describes materiality as suffused with the sacred, the individual as indissolubly material and spiritual and the juxtaposition of the quotidian and the extraordinary. Throughout *Trilogy* H.D. emphasizes the interplay of the human individual, the natural world and divinity in her material mysticism: the star Venus is reflected 'In the field-furrow/the rain-water' (*Angels* 10:1–2). Timothy Materer argues that H.D. gives Hermeticism a twentieth-century cast by blending psychoanalysis and the subversion of traditional sexual and gender identities with Hermeticism and channelling all three into visionary poetics.[74]

For the remainder of this section I will focus on the alchemical ritual that is described in greatest detail in *Trilogy*, and trace its reverberations across *Tribute to the Angels* (where it first appears) and *The Flowering of the Rod*. As we have already seen in *The Sword* and *The Gift*, ritual and vision are closely connected for H.D.; ritual mobilizes visionary consciousness. The visions that proliferate in these texts instantiate a material mysticism as the rituals work to set the dynamism at the heart of Hermeticism's analogical system in motion. H.D. puts an idiosyncratic spin on Hermeticism by constructing an alchemical process that distils not metals or other matter but words. Materer reads H.D.'s use of alchemy in the context of her interest in psychoanalysis, arguing that H.D.'s wordplay can be described by Lacan's 'play of the signifier'.[75] However, I would suggest that, while H.D. certainly does emphasize a verbal alchemy, material transformation is not discarded. She draws a correspondence between the poet and the alchemist when the distillation of words converts into matter (a jewel) and back into language. This oscillating word/jewel allows H.D. to align the philosophy of Hermeticism and dynamic practice of alchemy with artistic practice.

In *Angels*' alchemical ritual particular words (cognates of myrrh) become a jewel which in turn becomes the word 'Venus/Aphrodite', redeemed from negative connotations. Through linguistic alchemy the connotations of Venus are shifted from 'venery [...] venereous, lascivious' to 'venerate,/venerator' (*Angels* 11:6–8, 12:–10). The possibilities of change mobilized by language are explored more fully in the alchemy of *marah*:

Now polish the crucible
and set the jet of flame

under, til *marah-mar*
are melted, fuse and join

and change and alter,
mer, mere, mère, mater, Maia, Mary,

Star of the Sea,
Mother. (*Angels* 8:7–14)

This transformation of words culminates in a bitter jewel. The emphasis on the interplay between words and things is a point I will return to in the following chapter. The poet wishes to participate in the alchemical process herself, contemplating the jewel and wishing to be drawn into it. The alchemical ritual presents a twist on the earlier metaphors of transformation; this time H.D. refers not to a natural process but to human intervention in the natural world, or art.[76] The words are subject to change, but it is the process of distillation that brings about this transformation. As many critics have noted, this ritual reclaims a hidden tradition of the feminine divine.[77] The words 'marah' and 'mar' (meaning bitterness) go through repetitive transformations; they become brine, sea, the mother goddess, the Roman goddess of the spring (Maia), the Star of the Sea (Astarte or Aphrodite/Venus), and finally Mary (both the Virgin Mary and Mary Magdalene). In this process of transmutation, the bitterness of marah and brine are retained, suggesting that this is an essential part of the word–goddess–jewel transformation. All is transformed: word, material, divinity, the poet herself.

As a reflection of the Hermeticist worldview, not only is the jewel transformed, it lives, with a 'faint/heart-beat, pulse-beat' thus suggesting the divine life hidden in the heart of things (*Angels* 14:8–9). H.D. stresses the provisional and fluid by refusing to categorize the properties of the living, mutable jewel:

I do not know what it gives,
a vibration that we can not name
[…]
I said, I can not name it,
there is no name;
[…]
I said, it lived, it gave –
fragrance – was near enough

to explain that quality
for which there is no name. (*Angels* 13:9–14:16)

Like the entirety of creation, the jewel is incomplete and its significance continues to unfold. The dashes before and after 'fragrance' bracket the word off, suggesting that it is special in some way. This invites the reader to ponder the strange quality of this 'jewel-in-formation'.[78] The syntax is awkward, as if the word 'fragrance' needs to be read twice. It can be read as either 'it gave fragrance', or 'fragrance was near enough to explain that quality'. The dash could also indicate a hesitation while the poet searches for the appropriate word. The reader is left wondering if 'fragrance' is indeed what the jewel gives, or if some other word would better convey the unnameable quality. Used ambiguously and in association with the 'unnamable', this hyphen might be better named an apophatic dash.[79] H.D. draws attention to the undecidability of the jewel itself, as well as fragrance, grammatically as well as metaphorically.

Fragrance is uncontained by the ritual and drifts inexorably through *Trilogy*, drawing together the alchemical ritual and the first scene of the poem, the war-torn city. Morris reminds us that the crucible that contains the entirety of *Trilogy* is the crucible of war.[80] The regeneration represented by the alchemical jewel corresponds to the renewal of bombed London; H.D. likens a may-tree found in the city to the jewel (*Angels* 17:17–20). By analogy, the blossoming may-tree takes the elixir of life into the streets, the fragrance of jewel and tree consecrating the cityscape: 'no temple/but everywhere,/the outer precincts and squares/are fragrant' (*Angels* 18:1–4).

However provisionally the poet marks the word 'fragrance', it is the quality that unites the word/jewel, the blossoming tree and myrrh. Myrrh is an image that recurs throughout *Trilogy*. It brings together the blossoming tree, alchemical rituals and Mary Magdalene, who plays an alchemical role in *The Flowering of the Rod*. In the figure of Mary H.D. draws a connection between the alchemical ritual that transmutes words and substances and the personal transformation also sought by alchemists. She plays on the linguistic connections between Mary, marah/bitterness and myrrh. Morris argues that Kaspar (one of the three wise men who followed the star to Bethlehem in the Gospel of Matthew) and Mary represent the distilled (masculine) sulphur and (feminine) mercury needed for the 'chemical marriage', and the product of the sacred marriage is the jar of myrrh, or the elixir of life. Thus, in anointing Christ before the crucifixion with myrrh, Mary becomes the alchemist who prepares the way for transformation and resurrection.[81] However, Mary herself is also represented as myrrh:

> I am Mary, the incense-flower of the incense-tree,
> myself worshipping, weeping, shall be changed to myrrh (*Rod* 19:1–2).

Mary indicates that her identity mirrors the alchemical ritual in which the word 'marah' becomes 'Mary'. She participates in the alchemical process as the poet longs to do.[82]

Through word play and analogy, H.D. suggests that the resonances of alchemical rituals in *Trilogy* move in a number of directions simultaneously. The mutability of myrrh and its drifting fragrance reveal Hermetic dynamism. Myrrh is an image for the divine life that permeates the universe, revealed by the alchemical practices of distillation and projection.[83] Like Mary Magdalene and the word/jewel, the Christ child at *Trilogy*'s close is also represented as 'the bundle of myrrh' which gives off 'a most beautiful fragrance/as of all flowering things together' (*Rod* 43:3–7). Sensory but unseen, fragrance indicates the mingling of spiritual and material, vision and object. Fragrance reveals the close connection between incarnation, epiphany and resurrection, which suggests the importance of materiality and vision for redemption. H.D. aligns fragrance with the wide variety of visions, rituals and experiences throughout the poem; it indicates bitterness and sweetness, death and resurrection, sensory experience and imagination, healing and transformation.

Ritual and language

Since antiquity Hermes has been associated with speech and language. Plato suggests that those aspects of language that have to do with circulation, trickery and transformation are the particular mode of Hermes; he is the interpreter, the messenger, the thief, the liar.[84] Lewis Hyde points out that Hermes, along with other trickster figures, is no ordinary liar: 'When he lies and steals, it isn't so much to get away with something or get rich as to disturb the established categories of truth and property and, by so doing, open the road to possible new worlds.'[85] Another thief, a thief on the wing (Hermes' wings?), is Hélène Cixous's figure of the woman writer, who performs the trick of re-negotiating her cultural status in order to access writing, thus disrupting established categories: 'Flying is a woman's gesture – flying in language and making it fly. [...] [F]or centuries we've been able to possess anything only by flying: we've lived in flight, stealing away, finding, when desired, narrow passageways, hidden crossovers.'[86] Language must be stolen, but, for Cixous, wings themselves are writing: '*I* can only count on my own wings. I unsheathed them. Crumpled, two leaves of paper.'[87] Hermes, like the woman writer, disrupts, as well as creates, culture.[88] Hermes' association with language and the creation and disruption of culture involves not only writing but the related art of reading, or interpretation. Not only is Hermeticism a philosophy but it is also a mode of interpretation.[89] As I have previously indicated, for the Hermeticist all things are related to each other as participants in divine life. The dynamic of revelation and concealment leads to a way of interpreting the world which functions analogically; each thing is related to each other thing through a web of association. The universe is a text to be read, a code to be cracked.

Umberto Eco points out that this interconnectedness suggests layers and multiple analogies in which each expression points to another. None are fully revelatory; all contain some measure of hidden wisdom: 'The original One is self-contradictory [...]. The One can be expressed only by negation and approximation, so that every possible representation of it cannot but refer to another representation, equally obscure and contradictory.'[90] This understanding of the multiplicity at the heart of reality, an irreducible difference, replicated in the world emanating from the divine, is related to the Hermetic mode of analogical analysis. Hermetic readings are always diverse and multiple.[91] Eco suggests that Hermeticism may be linked to a style of hermeneutics:

> I shall call Hermetic drift the interpretive habit [...] which is based on the principles of universal analogy and sympathy, according to which every item of the furniture of the world is linked to every other element (or to many) of this sublunar world and to every element (or to many) of the superior world by means of similitudes or resemblances.[92]

Here Eco unpacks, in a somewhat convoluted way, the Hermetic axiom 'as above, so below'; the traces of connection between material and spiritual, heavenly and earthly, nature and culture, are there to be read. He goes on to argue that what makes interpretation possible is that textual 'symbols are anchored to their context'. The play of meaning is indefinite but not infinite: 'any act of interpretation is a dialectic between openness and form'.[93] Eco implies a relationship between context and form, indicating that it is literary context as well as wider social, historical and material contexts that give structure to the hermeneutic project. The specificity of each text will suggest pathways of interpretation, some more compelling than others, and each hermeneutic decision closes off numerous alternatives. A text may mean many things in an ongoing unfolding, but it cannot mean everything. Although the relationship between sign and referent may be arbitrary, those relationships often find general agreement within interpretative communities. Without these structured agreements, communication would be impossible, but without the play of (many) possible (mis)interpretations there would be no meaning. Both the hidden and the revealed are required for the dynamic of interpretation to be set in motion.

The slippage of meaning in a web of symbols is evident in *Trilogy*. Eco's Hermetic drift is evident in H.D.'s stylistics in which 'one mythical figure or image merges into another in a manner that defies "fixed meanings", and in a process that her ply-over-ply stanza forms re-enforces'.[94] The associative chain of couplets that comprises *Trilogy* allows for digressions and wandering, inscribing a quest that is more unsymmetrical spiral than clear trajectory. Alicia Ostriker argues that *Trilogy*'s prosody is balanced 'between a sensation of crisp clarity and one of fluidity; between the closed and the open'; the regularity of the couplets is balanced by nonmetrical lines of varying length which are unrhymed but full of off-rhymes within the lines creating a unified web of sounds.[95] Ostriker finds a poetics (and a politics) of openness emphasized in *Trilogy* through its 'forward momentum' (crafted through enjambed stanza breaks, long discursive sentences broken by pauses, repetitions and qualifications), open imagery and inclusion of the reader.[96]

Ritual provides a useful lens for viewing the relationship between form and content in *Trilogy*. As I pointed out at the beginning of this chapter, the poem in its entirety has been read as a ritual, while, within the poem, the connection between writing and ritual is emphasized by the invocation of Hermes/Thoth as sacred inventor of writing and the alchemical transformations of the word *marah-mar* into Mary (myrrh)/Mother. The process of this transformation, in the form of the accretion of numerous words, constructs a web of association. The connection between form and content is revealed within the poem itself. In her justification of the value of poetry the poet draws attention to her own writing; she attends to 'what words conceal', thus assigning her writing to the realm of Hermeticism (*Walls* 8:18). Her frequent return to images of signification such as writing, hieroglyphics and maps emphasizes the signifying object of *Trilogy* itself. The connection between form and content is usefully explicated by the metaphor of the hinge, which both separates and connects, allowing movement between the inside and the outside of the text. For Derrida the hinge is a crucial image of the writing of difference. This writing 'permits the difference between space and time to be articulated' and articulation (the hinge) is the connection that turns, the connection that preserves difference.[97] As a metaphor for writing, the hinge marks the movement within the separations and connections of language that implies a displacement which generates meaning.[98] Derrida himself is somewhat of a trickster; Hermes, after all, is 'god of the hinge'.[99]

The rituals discussed in this chapter are textual; they are literarily, rather than literally, performed. However, the rituals of reading and writing are the hinge which connects extra- and intratextual spaces; they are both literal and literary. Moreover, they highlight the text's performativity; in *Trilogy* writing is a ritual: 'scrape a palette,/point pen or brush,/prepare papyrus or parchment,/ offer incense to Thoth' (*Walls* 35:5–8). Stones speak for H.D. as hieroglyphics 'continue to prophesy' (*Walls* 1:8). The distillation of words in an alchemical ritual, the Lady's 'blank pages/of the unwritten volume of the new' and the stylus of Thoth all indicate that writing and interpretation are sacred activities (*Angels* 38:11–12). The distillation of *marah-mar* in the crucible in *Tribute to the Angels* reveals the dynamism that words have for H.D.; language is slippage, movement, transformation, and the poet is the sacred scribe who presides over this process and is transformed by it.

Turning aside from the linguistic associations and sacred rituals of Hermetic alchemy, we can also trace a connection between ritual and language through the signifying properties of performance. Amy Hollywood argues that rituals (as bodily practices) can be seen as signifying practices in which performance constructs meaning. She argues that, for both Catherine Bell and Derrida, 'ritual is like language' in that 'rituals are actions that generate meaning'.[100] She makes this claim against scholars who would either discount ritual by privileging belief or dismiss the meaningful content of rituals by focusing exclusively on their form. In this sense, rituals are not static texts that encode a prior reality, but dynamic processes that produce meaning: 'just as language can be a form of action, so too can actions be forms of signification'.[101] Hollywood draws upon Derrida to extend this understanding of ritual as signification to an understanding of all language as ritualized performance:

> For Derrida, all language takes on the character of the performative and of ritual. [...] Key for Derrida is the iterability or repeatability of the sign; it is this reiterative structure, the fact that the sign is the same and yet also differs and defers (both from possible referents and from other signs) that marks its force (and its power of signification).[102]

The repeatability of the sign brings us to a consideration of writing as the scene of these iterations, of differing and deferral.

Differing, the 'difference between this and that',[103] enables deferral, the displacement of meaning from one sign to another in an associative chain that enables signification (here the affinity between deconstruction and Hermeticism becomes evident):

> *The trace is the differance* which opens appearance [...] and signification. [...] [O]rigin of all repetition, origin of ideality, the trace is not more ideal than real, not more intelligible than sensible, not more a transparent signification than an opaque energy and *no concept of metaphysics can describe it*.[104]

An 'opaque energy' that is outside metaphysical and physical systems and yet enabling both, the trace is what makes language like a ritual. Paradoxically, it is the origin of repetition yet repetition is undermined by the proliferation of differences. The paradox of same-but-different marks the tension (the energy) that generates meaning. Derrida coins 'differance' – a word whose only difference from 'difference' is the substitution of an 'a' for an 'e' (a shift that can only be read; it cannot be heard and therefore is entirely textual) – to indicate the 'systematic play of differences, of traces of differences, of the *spacing* by means of which elements are related to each other'.[105] The play of differences implies spatiality; relation requires space for connectivity and distinction. Differences, then, are produced by differance. The focus on the dynamism of differences, their production and proliferation, their *action*, brings us back to reiteration (ritual) and writing.

For Derrida, writing ('arche-writing') is more than writing-as-script, as letters on a page (or hieroglyphics on stone).[106] It is the signifying dynamic that contains language-as-script/glyph/graphie, language-as-speech, language-as-gesture, etc. To what extent this is also true of Cixous is difficult to ascertain. Certainly her writing on writing suggests a wider field of signification than marks on the page – she employs such a wide range of metaphors and modes of engaging with writing that it appears to exceed the merely graphic: writing is wings, a lover in the night, an unexpected wild cat, breath and blood, the quenching of thirst. However, she tethers these expansive descriptions to an emphasis on the physical, psychological and practical process of writing-as-scripting:

> I had written without turning on the light so as not to risk scaring the Comer [the book] off, quick, without a sound, I grab the pad of paper that never leaves my bedside and the thick-tipped pen for scribbling big across the page.[107]

For Cixous, writing precedes authorship: 'writing engenders the author'.[108] She reverses the usual metaphor; here the author is the child of the work. The process of writing draws the author into being; through the performance of writing the author is transformed.

H.D. and Cixous both traverse the divide between text and context, written word and material world, while their style draws attention to the writerly, to wordiness. Like *Trilogy*, Cixous's texts frequently refer to their own production:

> For us writers, on the contrary, what's important is the process. The tempest, the rough draft. [...] That's love – that is, what passes away. It's the difference that passes away, it's what escapes us.
>
> This is why I've always had a passion for a particular kind of book: *books that get away*. [...] That can't be closed, that leave us behind, that can't be finished.[109]

In describing the process of writing, Cixous also makes broader claims for a more theoretical approach to texts. She complicates the distinction between reader and writer. In the passage above it is unclear whether she is referring merely to her own texts and finishing as the finale in the performance of writing, or to books by other authors, whose final pages are never reached, or, once reached, continue to produce alternative meanings and to haunt the reader. The text goes on ahead while the writer-reader scrambles behind.

The address to the reader forms another hinge between inside and outside in H.D.'s and Cixous's ritualizing style. They continually invite the reader into their texts. This is evident most clearly in their use of pronouns: the shift between 'I', 'we' and 'you'. Of course, 'we' can also be read antagonistically, as an attempt by the writer to co-opt the reader. The slippage between 'I' and 'we' can be a violent disruption of a necessary boundary. However, I suggest an invitational reading; the reader is invited to participate in the dynamics inscribed within writing. These texts demonstrate a keen awareness of the reader's role in the construction of meaning. The narrators portray themselves as readers as well as writers and writing as a gift: 'The books for which I am the scribe belong to everyone.'[110]

H.D. and Cixous consistently represent writing as emerging from, returning to, and involved with, the material. This is not an attempt to identify signifier with signified, sign with referent, but a gesture towards the mutual implication of the corporeal and non-corporeal context of writing; there is no outside to the field of signification. Their texts posit a reciprocal intimacy between writing and the material world (including the bodily); hence their wordplay which foregrounds undecidability. For example, in addition to the delight she takes in *voler* – to fly/steal, Cixous plays on the metaphor of an organic leaf and a leaf as a page:

> In God's place I have [...] both sides of a leaf of paper. [...] When I write I never know what side I'm on [...] if I'm writing on you or if you're writing on me; constantly I twist and turn. [...] Slight, infinite creature, tricky marvel of nature.[111]

Likewise, for H.D., divine wisdom is hidden in the commonplace: 'their [the gods'] secret is stored/in man's very speech' (*Walls* 8:25–6). What is hidden may be found, decoded. Throughout *Trilogy* H.D. emphasizes the physicality of writing as a practice, the scraping of parchment, the scratch of the stylus, the more casual scribbles and jottings in the margins. The emphasis on the actions of the craft suggests that performance is an element of writing. The ritualized language surrounding this emphasis on the material indicates that this is an activity that sacralizes the mundane.

The emphasis on the physicality of writing turns in two directions: writing as verb and writing as noun. Writing is both a physical activity and a material object. The materiality of the written object is suggested in the text by references to the permanence of writing scratched on parchment and etched in stone – the palimpsest that cannot be erased – and, conversely, the vulnerability of books and manuscripts to destruction by fire. By using words as the elements to be distilled and transmuted in the alchemical process, H.D. suggests that words are material substances that can be physically manipulated. Associating that same process with Venus, Maia and Mary indicates not only that both divinity and humanity are subject to transformation, but also that we participate, with the divine, in the web of signification. We are not separate from language.

To return to the spacing indicated by the dynamic of differing and deferral, Derrida calls differance 'a structure and a movement'; it is both a space, and the process of making space.[112] Spacing troubles the distinction between inside and outside.[113] Likewise, the trace is neither fully present nor fully absent, and so it troubles the distinction between them. Cixous likens the writer to the trace: 'Presence and absence are my wings.'[114] Spacing, or spatial and temporal distinctions, the slippage between presence and absence, enables the framework of ritualized repetition. It is the formed space in between gestures, speech and written words that gives their repetitions structure and allows meaning to inhere within them. However, the formality of spacing does not negate play and spontaneity. The performance of writing correlates to movement. Just as vision provides an idiosyncratic experience of ritual, so the movements of writing cannot be contained. For Cixous and H.D., writing is also a journey, a wild flight or 'a departure, an embarkation, an expedition'.[115] Departure, not arrival, is emphasized here, a point I will return to in Chapter Five.

The movements of ritualized writing – the sacred dramas and visionary songs and literary alchemy – are associated with the sacred in H.D. and Cixous: 'One must play language quick and true like an honest musician, not leap over a single word-beat. Find the slowness inside the speed. [...] This speed is not superficial. It strikes deep. It is grace.'[116] This is a different suggestion of the divine than that found in *Of Grammatology*.[117] The differance at the heart of God, emanating throughout the world and setting multiplicity in motion, unfolds in divinity not as a transcendent being whose presence guarantees meaning, but as one whose drifting, hidden presence generates meaning through difference.

Notes

1 Morris 1990, pp. 121–2.
2 Tryphonopoulos 2009, p. xxv.
3 Vision may seem an unusual element to add to a consideration of ritual and performance, yet H.D.'s texts continually associate visionary consciousness with any artistic endeavour or ritual practice.
4 Kapferer 2005, pp. 129–30. For an overview of the performance approach to ritual see Bell 1998, pp. 205–24.
5 Turner 1975, pp. 38–41.
6 Victor Turner defines liminality as 'any condition outside or on the peripheries of everyday life. It is often a sacred condition or can readily become one'; Ibid. p. 47.
7 Schechner 1988, p. 170.
8 Ibid. p. 171.
9 Hogue and Vandivere 2007, p. xxxvi.
10 Ibid. p. xxxix.
11 Sarah Dillon defines 'palimpsestuousness' as 'a simultaneous relation of intimacy and separation [...] preserving the distinctness of texts, while at the same time allowing for their essential contamination and interdependence'; 2007, pp. 3–4.
12 For further discussion of the feminine divine in *The Sword* and her significance as a resource for waging peace, see Hogue and Vandivere 2007, pp. xxxviii–xli.
13 Although this character is unnamed in this vignette, she is like Ariadne in her knowledge of the secrets of the labyrinth.
14 Harrison 1913, pp. 9–10.
15 Harrison 1903, p. a5.
16 Carpentier 1998, p. 46.
17 Harrison 1903, p. 261.
18 Harrison 1913, pp. 137–40. Contemporary ritual theory has been critical of the Cambridge ritualists' search for origins and their developmental models of the relationship between art and ritual. However, I would argue that the turn to performance in ritual studies suggests that the connection itself is vital although I share the opinion that the quest for origins is unnecessary; Bell 1997, pp. 7–8; Schechner 1988, p. 6.
19 Harrison 1912, pp. x–xi.
20 Ibid. p. 48.

21 Gregory 1997, pp. 123–5.

22 Normington 2007, p. 5; Prosser 1961, p. 3.

23 The development of the observance of Corpus Christi is one indication of the growing medieval fascination with the humanity, and thus the body, of Christ. I would suggest that the blood and wounds piety of the eighteenth-century Moravian had its roots in the popular devotions to Christ's body and blood of preceding centuries. For more on blood piety in the Middle Ages see Bynum 2002, pp. 685–714.

24 James 2007, pp. 70–1.

25 In discussing *The Gift* I follow the text in referring to H.D. as a child as Hilda while continuing to refer to the author and adult narrator as H.D.

26 As Madelyn Detloff points out, H.D.'s use of *Uncle Tom's Cabin* is problematic as she is 'blind to the racist implications of her symbolic understanding of slavery as a human condition rather than a historical fact': 2009, p. 94. In focusing on the play as a vehicle for a white child's self-discovery, H.D. overwrites the traumatic history of black slaves.

27 The significance of liturgy and hymnody to the Moravians is acknowledged by numerous scholars, see Gollin 1967, pp. 20–1; Tripp 1978, p. 250. In Bethlehem hymns were often written for special occasions such as birthdays, weddings and funerals; Atwood 2004, p. 142. Zinzendorf himself wrote many hymns. While the more controversial hymns relating to the Holy Spirit as Mother, Jesus as female or explicit devotion to Jesus' blood and wounds have been dropped from nineteenth-and twentieth-century hymnals, many of his hymns remain.

28 Fogleman 2007, p. 89.

29 H.D. took extensive notes on the writing of Henry Rimius on the Moravians; H.D. 1951.

30 Other hymns suggest even greater devotion if less eloquence:
The wounds Cross-God's Covenant's Blood, the Wound's, Wound's, Wound's.
Flood, ye Wounds!
Yea, ye Wounds! Your Wound's, Wound's, Wound's, Good's make Wound's, Wound's, Wound's.
Courage and Wounds, Heart, Wounds.
Wounds! Wounds! Wounds!
Wounds! Wounds! Wounds!
Wounds! O! Ye Wounds! (Ibid.)

31 Moravian Church 1891; Moravian Church 1908. H.D.'s copies of these books (held at the Beinecke Rare Book and Manuscript Library) have handwritten lists of hymns on the back flyleaves.

32 Moravian Church 1908, p. 85.

33 Ibid. Other hymns which denote a milder form of blood and wounds piety include

'Rock of ages, cleft for me/Let me hide myself in Thee' and 'O Sacred Head Sore Wounded'; Fogleman 2007, p. 13.

34 H.D. also indicates here that this power is that of 'the Holy Ghost of the Christian ritualists and the Great Spirit of the Indians' (pp. 168–9). H.D.'s syncretism is evident in her emphasis on a singular divine spirit manifest throughout the material world. Unsurprisingly, she looked for traces of a mystery religion among the Algonquians, which is consistent with her Hermetic slant. Her interest in the history, culture, and language of the Algonquian tribes (particularly Lenape, Mahican and Shawnee) is evident in her notes on *The Gift*, although this research appears largely confined to a romanticized view of eighteenth- and nineteenth-century Native Americans. For further information on contemporary Native American religious beliefs and practices, see Kidwell, Noley and Tinker 2001; Tooker 1979.

35 Kidwell, Noley and Tinker 2001, p. 35.

36 In the middle of the eighteenth century the 'Litany of the Wounds' was the most popular and frequently used litany for Moravians, who declared it to the be the centre of their theology, as well as their devotional practice; Atwood 2004, p. 203.

37 I use Craig Atwood's translation of Zinzendorf's German text; ibid., pp. 'Appendix 3', 233–7.

38 Ibid. pp. 235–7.

39 Ibid. pp. 235–6.

40 Ibid. p. 234.

41 Schmidt 2000, p. 35. Christian Renatus was a central figure at Herrnhaag (a Moravian community in Germany) at the height of blood and wounds piety during the Sifting Time (a time when the wounds devotions became excessive, leading to charges of 'scandalous mysticism' and contributing to the persecution of Moravians); Augustine 1998, p. 21; Fogleman 2007, p. 89.

42 Although this scene lacks the traditional trappings of spiritualism – the table and the tapped-out messages – H.D. signals her role as medium when she describes hearing the voices of the dead; Augustine 1998, pp. 17–18.

43 Morris 1990, p. 126; Gregory 1997, pp. 122–5.

44 Morris 1990, pp. 126–7. See also Graham 2002, pp. 161–6; Pondrom 1987, pp. 156–64.

45 Hornung 2001, p. 201.

46 For more on the relationship between Alexandrian Hellenism and decadence, modernism and H.D., see Gregory 1997, pp. 38–107.

47 Faivre 1995, pp. 15, 21.

48 Fowden 1986, pp. 223; Hornung 2001, p. 52; Seligman 1971, pp. 2723.

49 Fowden 1986, pp. 25–9; Tuveson 1982, p. 8.

50 Ebeling 2007, p. 59; Tuveson 1982, p. 9. This is not to say that Hermeticism

was not present in European culture before the Renaissance. Many theologians, including Peter Abelard and Albertus Magnus, considered Hermes Trismegistus to be a celebrated ancient philosopher. Hermetic alchemy was practised widely enough for Pope John XXII to forbid it in 1317. Early Christian apologists were divided on how to recuperate Hermes Trismegistus for Christianity; some rejected Hermeticism entirely while others championed Hermes Trismegistus as a precursor of Christ and still others chose a middle way; Fowden 1986, pp. 180, 210; Hornung 2001, pp. 78–9.

51 For a history and an overview of the *Corpus Hermeticum* see Copenhaver 1992.

52 Fowden 1986, p. xiv; Hornung 2001, p. 98. The Latin translation of the *Asclepius* is cited by Augustine and became widespread in the twelfth century; Ebeling 2007, p. 10. Although the Hermetic texts are not of ancient origin it is important to bear in mind that the roots of this tradition may go back much further.

53 Faivre 1995, p. 61; Eco 1990, p. 19. This 'spiral-like logic' recalls H.D.'s belief in reincarnation and sense of interconnecting spirals of time, most evident in *The Sword*.

54 Fowden 1986, p. 149.

55 Tryphonopoulos 1992, p. xii.

56 Tuveson 1982, p. xiv.

57 Linden 2003a, p. 15. Paracelsus, quoted in Tuveson 1982, p. 51.

58 Ibid., p. 11.

59 *Hermetica*, trans. Walter Scott, quoted in ibid. pp. 13–14.

60 McKnight 1989, pp. 23–4. Of course, in two traditions as varied as Gnosticism and Hermeticism there will be diverse strands that are more similar and others that are radically opposed. Some scholars suggest there are two strands of Hermeticism; one that affirms the value of the created world, and one (more Gnostic) that is dualistic and rejects the material; Ebeling 2007, p. 32; Faivre 1995, p. 56. For further discussion of the similarities and differences between Gnosticism and Hermeticism, see van den Broek 1998, pp. 1–20.

61 Faivre 1995, p. 58.

62 Tuveson 1982, p. 57.

63 Faivre 1998, p. 119; Tuveson 1982, p. 17.

64 Linden 2003b, p. 28.

65 Faivre 1995, p. 57.

66 Ibid. p. 70.

67 Linden 2003a, p. 9.

68 Ibid. pp. 4–5.

69 Ebeling 2007, p. 26; Linden 2003a, p. 5.

70 Morris 2003, p. 113.

71 Jane Harrison theorized that the Eleusinian Mysteries enacted a sacred marriage

and birth; Gregory 1997, pp. 119–22. Through an analogical system in which chemical processes were aligned with spiritual processes, Christian alchemists considered Christ to be the philosopher's stone or elixir of life; Linden 2003a, p. 22.

72 Morris 2003, p. 115.

73 H.D. 1983, p. 39. Adalaide Morris argues that H.D.'s early work describes a 'world [that] glows with sacred energy'; however, the poet is supplicant, absence haunts the poems and 'the gods function not as the poem's ornament but as its absent center'; 2003, p. 98.

74 Materer 1995, pp. 88–9. Alchemical principles stressed the fusion of 'male' and 'female' elements in the 'alchemical marriage'; alternatively they combined to form the androgyne, the male/female figure of Hermes; Morris 2003, pp. 112–13; Schwarz 2000, p. 65. This philosophy affirmed the importance of the female principal as equal to the male, but it does not necessarily provide any real challenge to gender roles and it clearly privileges heterosexual mythologies. However, I agree with Materer that H.D.'s use of alchemy leans towards subverting sexual and gender roles. The polymorphous nature of sexual and gender identity across her work is evident in the shift of metaphors and images. Even her straight romances are not straightforward and indicate spaces for homoerotic and gender-bending desires to surface.

75 Materer 1995, pp. 100–1. For a nuanced discussion of H.D.'s wordplay in *Trilogy*, see Morris 2003, pp. 40–9.

76 Hermes is the god of art and of cultural construction, as well as of words and communication; Hyde 1998, pp. 261–2.

77 For further discussion of alchemy in *Angels* as the redemption of the feminine divine, see Friedman 1981, pp. 245–53; Gubar 1978, p. 209; Morris 2003, pp. 113–15. Gubar expresses discomfort with the 'mystifications' of the alchemical ritual and the litany of goddesses and considers them secondary to the more abstract 'female spirit'.

78 Morris 2003, p. 214.

79 I am indebted to The Very Reverend Kelvin Holdsworth for formulating this phrase; Holdsworth 2007. Apophatic theology argues that God is completely other to anything that could be said or known about God. Apophasis is the process of 'unsaying' everything that has been said about God. It is the negative way or way of ignorance, of un-knowing; McIntosh 1998, pp. 122–3.

80 Morris 1990, pp. 110–13.

81 Morris 2003, p. 115.

82 The 'incense-flower' which is Mary may have been inspired by references to the Tree of Life from the apocalyptic, ancient Jewish text the *Book of Enoch*: 'And among the trees [...] there was one of unheard-of fragrance; there is no tree

like it upon the earth; its fragrance is the sweetest of all fragrances. [...] And its fragrance shall give sap to their bones'; quoted in Merezhkovsky 1936, p. 107. This passage is marked in H.D.'s copy (held in the Beinecke Rare Book and Manuscript Library), and the dates on the flyleaf suggest that she read the book in the early 1940s.

83 Distillation (or sublimation) is the purification of each substance into its essence, while projection is the final stage in an alchemical process, 'the precipitation of a new, more perfect form', i.e. the philosopher's stone; Linden 2003a, p. 18; Morris 2003, p. 112.

84 Faivre 1995, p. 15.

85 Hyde 1998, p. 13. I will return to the notion of 'possible worlds' in Chapter Four, when I consider Paul Ricoeur's work on metaphor and imagination.

86 Cixous 1997, pp. 356–7.

87 Cixous 1998a, p. 81.

88 For more on the duality of Hermes's relationship to culture, see Hyde 1998, pp. 203–25.

89 Faivre 1995, pp. 66–7; Tuveson 1982, p. 31.

90 Eco 1990, p. 18.

91 Faivre 1995, p. 67.

92 Eco 1990, p. 24.

93 Ibid. p. 21.

94 Materer 1995, p. 104.

95 Ostriker 1990, pp. 339–40.

96 Ibid. pp. 347–48.

97 Derrida 1997, pp. 65–6.

98 Ibid. p. 69.

99 Hyde 1998, p. 209.

100 Hollywood 2003b, p. 76.

101 Ibid. p. 74.

102 Ibid. p. 76.

103 Lucy 2004, p. 27.

104 Derrida 1997, p. 65.

105 Derrida 1981, p. 27.

106 Derrida 1997, pp. 56–7, 70.

107 Cixous 2006, p. 3.

108 Cixous 1998b, p. 189.

109 Ibid. pp. 55–6.

110 Ibid. p. 188. This positioning of writer as scribe is not unlike the role of spiritualist medium translating the messages of the dead.

111 Cixous 1998a, p. 155.

112 Derrida 1981, p. 27.

113 Derrida 1997, p. 70.

114 Cixous 1998a, p. 79.

115 Cixous 1998b, pp. 184–5.

116 Ibid. p. 191.

117 Derrida argues with the God of metaphysics: 'Only infinite being can reduce the difference in presence. In that sense, the name of God, at least as it is pronounced within classical rationalism, is the name of indifference itself'; Derrida 1997, p. 71.

4

Image and Difference

The previous chapter analysed the connection between writing and material mysticism through an exploration of writing as an activity, a ritual, and the production of the written artefact. It drew upon the ritualizing dimension in *The Sword Went Out to Sea*, *The Gift* and *Trilogy* to establish writing as performative, and connected this activity to the Hermetic process of reading the cosmos as a dynamic, unfolding web signifying divine life. The chapter closed with a consideration of ritual, language and the dynamic undecidability of writing that is mobilized by difference. This chapter takes a narrower focus, turning from the broad sweep of writing to concentrate specifically on image and metaphor. In H.D.'s and Cixous's writing images are dynamic as they traverse texts, accruing and dispersing the resonances of multiple meanings. They allow an exploration of difference in language and instantiate material mysticism by drawing together materiality and alterity. Drawing on the Hermetic understanding of the imagination as the faculty which enables apprehension of the divine life within the universe, I advance a view of the creative imagination that partakes of sensory experience and is open to the world, but is not merely the reproduction of sensory input. This chapter investigates the dynamic of imagination and metaphor as they engender the new and how this productivity is fuelled by difference.

The Hermetic tradition emphasizes the transmission of hidden wisdom. However, the acquisition of wisdom is not merely a task for intellect and will but requires the sympathetic involvement of the entire person in a process of understanding and regeneration. Awareness of the universe as participant in divine life is apprehended by the Hermeticist through the imagination.[1] Ernest Lee Tuveson argues that the Hermetic emphasis on transformation (here is where the connection between Hermeticism and alchemy is most evident) is located in the dynamic interaction between world and imagination. For the Hermeticist, rebirth is brought about by the imagination and consists 'not in escaping from the material creation, but in accepting it, celebrating it, identifying with its whole being.'[2] Paracelsus described the imagination as 'the intermediary between thinking and being' which brings about the 'incarnation of thought in the image'.[3]

Tuveson argues that the Romantic preoccupation with the imagination as the faculty that unites the self and the world extends the Hermetic tradition.[4] Although this understanding of the Hermetic imagination can be seen in Cixous and H.D., these twentieth-century thinkers pay more attention to the *construction* of images within language. In their work the relation between self and world is not transparent; subjectivity is shifting and multiple in a way that differs from the confident unity of the Romantic 'I'. David Meakin argues that the self-conscious literary experimentation of modernist writing finds a partner in the playful, deceptive side of Hermes: 'Hermes himself, that tutelary god of alchemists, has frequently been associated with mediation, deviousness and irony, and the element of playfulness that can be read into him proves highly attractive to the spirit of Modernism.'[5] Thus alchemical transformations form an apt metaphor for modernist stylistics, provided the alchemist does not take herself too seriously. Through a reading of Cixous's and H.D.'s ludic engagements with unusual images such as the orange and the bee, I position their creative work on the boundaries that form the domain of the trickster Hermes.

Paul Ricoeur's contention that metaphor functions because of difference and that the unfolding of metaphor's meanings is constitutive of new worlds correlates with the creative, excessive and dynamically open metaphorical writing of Hélène Cixous and H.D. According to Ricoeur's poetics, '[i]magination can be recognized accordingly as the act of responding to a demand for new meaning, the demand of emerging realities to *be* by *being said* in new ways.'[6] Feminists and womanists have been arguing for decades for the need for new realities to be spoken (or written) into being, stressing the complicity of language in both oppressive structures and vehicles of liberation.[7] This implicates language in both creativity and communication. Metaphorical language is the vehicle for expressing the inexpressible to others: 'Language itself is an immoderate testimony to our necessary flair for making present the ineffable, the maybe, the no-longer-here, the not-yet, the big-one-that-got-away.'[8] Images and metaphors are both a net for the ineffable and a way of mobilizing this alterity to create community; they locate the strangeness of the unspeakable *in between*. The paradox of language understood both as communication and as alterity – in other words, as structured around an absence (the 'no-longer-here' and the 'not-yet') yet as positive (a means of conveying the shape of this absence) – provides metaphor with its dynamism. I follow Abigail Bray's definition of alterity as 'the other of the other [...] a form of Otherness which is not reducible to the binary self/other. It is a concept of the other [...] which exceeds the colonizing logic of the self/other binary. [...] Alterity signals [...] the space of difference.'[9]

In considering the relationship between image and metaphor we are already in the realm of ambiguity. The word 'image' comes into English from the Anglo-Norman and Old French and meant 'artificial imitation or representation (in solid or flat form) of a person or object'. The Latin, 'imago', is a 'representation in art of a person or thing, [...] reflection in a mirror, reflection of sound, echo, [...] illusory apparition, phantom, hallucination [...] mental picture'.[10] In a literary context 'image' becomes more complex. Formed with words, it produces a mental picture, although it is important to note that literary images are not exclusively visual, as I will show in my discussion of H.D. and Cixous, and frequently refer to senses other than sight. In literary texts imagery refers to 'those uses of language [...] that evoke sense-impressions by literal or figurative reference to perceptible or "concrete" objects, scenes, actions, or states [...] [including] metaphors.'[11]

An image, then, is essentially a copy, imitation or representation of a material person or object; this copy may be a visual, verbal or mental representation. Although in literary terms metaphor is included in imagery, it is a particular kind of image, and complicates the above definition. In metaphor, two dissimilar things are compared 'in order to suggest some resemblance or make a connection between the two things'.[12] Many definitions of metaphor emphasize similarities, beginning with Aristotle who claimed that 'a good metaphor implies an intuitive perception of the similarity in dissimilars.'[13] However, as we will see, Paul Ricoeur shifts the emphasis onto the dissimilarity between the two halves of a metaphor. He foregrounds the paradoxical nature of metaphor: 'the privileged procedure of metaphor is self-contradiction. The function of metaphor is to make sense with nonsense, to transform a self-contradictory statement into a significant self-contradiction.'[14] What we have here is a kind of image that emphasizes the dissimilarities and imperfections of the copy or echo. Rather than praising the accuracy of representation – a good image as one that is transparent, appearing to occur naturally and perfectly – Ricoeur's emphasis on difference within the metaphoric image highlights the construction involved in both making and interpreting the metaphor. This emphasis on writing as crafted language is consonant with the approach to Cixous and H.D. elaborated in the previous chapter.

In this chapter I will explore Ricoeur's view of alterity within metaphor and then turn to the mobilization of difference in Cixous's writing, demonstrated through an analysis of the image of the orange. The remainder of the chapter consists of a reading of H.D.'s material language, drawing upon Ricoeur and Cixous. I will consider the ways in which the image cluster of the bee/bee hive/honey in H.D.'s work partakes of sacred materiality. Situated in the productive tension between immanence and transcendence, these images accrue a multiplicity of meanings whose excess opens the text to an alterity wherein image is shadowed by mystery.

Ricoeur: Imagination, metaphor and alterity

Paul Ricoeur's work on linguistics leads him to develop an understanding of the imagination as inherently concerned with language. His thinking on the imagination is rooted in his concern with poetic language. For Ricoeur the productivity of metaphor is found in difference rather than sameness:

> [M]etaphor displays the work of resemblance because the literal contradiction preserves difference within the metaphorical statement; 'same' and 'different' are not just mixed together, they also remain opposed. Through this specific trait, enigma lives on in the heart of metaphor. In metaphor, 'the same' operates *in spite of* 'the different'.[15]

The tension between sameness and difference yields a dynamic view of metaphor; both are required for metaphor to function. Metaphors compel their readers to *construct* meaning by recognizing and navigating the tension between sameness and difference. Meaning is not simply inherent in the words of metaphor but created by the recognition, indeed, creation, of similarity between two things thought to be different:

> How do we make sense with self-contradictory statements? [...] [I]n novel metaphors, the similarity is itself the fruit of metaphor. We now see a similarity that nobody had ever noticed before. The difficulty therefore is to understand that we see similarity by constructing it, that the visionary grasping of resemblance is, at the same time, a verbal invention. [...] In other words, a novel metaphor does not merely actualize a potential connotation, it creates it.[16]

The similarity-in-difference that Ricoeur assigns to metaphor is not a case of difference being subsumed into sameness. For metaphors to remain dynamic the tension between sameness and difference must not collapse, otherwise the metaphor dies.[17] Difference is not dissolved within sameness but remains an irreducible presence within metaphor. The persistence of difference is productive, allowing readers to continue to generate new meanings. The production of metaphor is a complex process begun in the text and completed by the reader's act of 'grasping of resemblance'. In this formulation reading is a highly creative activity, as Cixous claims: 'Reading: writing the ten thousand pages of every page'.[18] The understanding of metaphoric language developed by Ricoeur and Cixous suggests a dialogical relationship between text and reader. The construction of meaning that requires the reader to complete the metaphor and grasp similarity-in-difference widens the invitation to the reader that we saw in Chapter Three's exploration of ritual and language. The reader is invited to participate not only through direct address, but through a more subtle involvement with meaning-making.

The new meanings generated by metaphor bring us to the realm of the imagination and the apprehension of possible new worlds. Ricoeur's argument that the attention to language and interpretation as creative activity leading to the new, involves radically revised notions of the imagination:

> We are prepared to inquire into the power of imagination, no longer as the faculty of deriving 'images' from sensory experiences, but as the capacity to let new worlds build our self-understanding. This power would not be conveyed by emerging images but by emerging meanings in our language. Imagination, then, should be treated as a dimension of language.[19]

For Ricoeur, the imagination is generative, and the new worlds it produces are initially formed within the self, thus enlarging self-understanding. However, with the relational dynamic of metaphor, internal possible worlds proliferate through linguistic encounters. The power of the imagination to generate new worlds via metaphor 'point[s] towards a liminal space in language and textuality in which extraordinary things can happen'.[20]

Ricoeur understands imagination not as the reproduction of images of sensory experience, or even creative re-assemblages of the same, but the faculty concerned with the meaning-making activity of language. Richard Kearney suggests that Ricoeur moves image entirely into the verbal dimension: 'Replacing the visual model of the image with the verbal, Ricoeur affirms the more *poetical* role of imagining: its ability to say one thing in terms of another, or to say several things at the same time, thereby creating something *new*'.[21] I would suggest, however, that Ricoeur does in fact forge a connection between sensory experience, the material world and language. The creativity of metaphor is expressed in '*poesis*, that is, fabrication, construction, creation'.[22] I think it is no accident that he uses words that indicate material making; the sensual remains in his argument as an irreducible residue. It may be argued that this is merely metaphoric – that it is impossible to speak of metaphor in any way but by means of metaphors (for example, by describing the process of thinking as 'grasping'). However, the recurrence of these active, bodily metaphors suggests that the world of language and cognition cannot be fully divorced from the material.

Visionary may indeed be the most useful term as it suggests the palimpsest of sensation (sight) and the imaginative emergence of something new, but this visionary language is multi-sensory and tactile, as we have seen in H.D.'s exploration of visionary consciousness. The world, or possible worlds, is/are always present in Ricoeur's understanding of meaning-making and this allows for the interconnection between the material world and the imagination. New worlds not only are the result of metaphor but also partake of sensation. Ricoeur's writing springs from the Protestant tradition, evidenced by his emphasis on the word. His work on metaphor may be read as an implicit Christology in the drawing together of word and flesh. My reading of Ricoeur, which gives greater emphasis to the corporeal residue within language, indicates a stronger incarnational reading. In turn, this reading leads back to the Hermetic view of the physical world as suffused with divine life.

Ricoeur presents a view of textuality that is open to the world rather than closed in on itself or focused on a transcendent beyond:

> [P]oetic language has a mimetic function inasmuch as it is a heuristic fiction preparing a redescription of reality. [...] What is changed by poetic language is our way of dwelling in the world. From poetry we receive a new way of being in the world, of orienting ourselves in this world.[23]

What is crucial here is the configuration of mimesis not as description but as *re*description. By assigning to poetic language, or the smaller unit of metaphor, the ability to transform ways of seeing and ways of being, Ricoeur advances a view of language as profoundly creative. Metaphors do not merely represent or describe the world but, in *re*describing, changing and making new, poetic language transforms the world. The previous chapter considered transformation and language through the lens of ritual and performativity. This chapter takes up transformation again, here through a focus on the image and its movement across texts. The openness in metaphor and text explored by Ricoeur as modes of possibility with attention to worlds and being-in-the-world provide a helpful way of reading Cixous and H.D. Their work is concerned with possible worlds and modes of becoming. This indicates a view of subjectivity as co-constituted between self and other; whether the other is another subject, a material object or a text, alterity is found both without and within.

Cixous and difference

In my reading Cixous's writing provides an exemplar of the play of difference within metaphor delineated by Ricoeur. Her work is highly metaphorical and its style draws heavily on materiality. She can be read in the tradition of surrealist writing; her avant-garde stylistics create a generative space for word play, defamiliarization and experimentation.[24] Her writing constitutes a search for an encounter with alterity and an effort to develop a welcoming stance towards the other that does not appropriate or annihilate, but recognizes, difference. Cixous foregrounds writing as a mode of encounter and transformation. For Cixous, writing gestures toward alterity: 'Writing: touching the mystery, delicately, with the tips of the words'.[25] Here Cixous, like Ricoeur, uses bodily language to refer to poetic language. The images of touch, ingestion and interiority in relation to writing appear frequently in her work. For Cixous, writing is a bodily action and a location of embodied encounter.

Cixous's attention to the material is caught up in alterity; she sees the mysterious presence of the other within the most mundane of objects. She uses these objects as a locus for deconstructing cultural conventions and constructing new meanings. I wish to linger here on her engagement with the orange. This image is a useful case study as it does not appear in many texts, but the issues and ideas which form its textual partners appear frequently. With the orange Cixous spins her own mythology of creativity, knowledge, innocence and experience. It enables her to engage with both her own past and the wider sweep of history while also attending to questions of intimacy with (and as) the other.

In *Vivre l'orange / To Live the Orange* (1979) we see Cixous at her most linguistically virtuosic. She alternates sentences that are overloaded with imagery and carry on for a page or more, with short spare sentences that abruptly pull up the sensual, headlong plunge of the writing. The central image of this text is the orange, which moves between numerous linguistic positions. It marks the space of encounter, responsibility and desire: 'all of the sense relations that every orange keeps alive and circulates [...] the invisible links between fruits and bodies'.[26] It indicates subjects, namely, the women to whom Cixous feels compelled to respond.[27] It is also the gift of another's writing that enables her to begin writing again.[28] So this orange is space(s), person(s) and writing(s). It is a capacious metaphor that allows for word play.

Cixous plays on the phonetic permutations of the word; 'orange' becomes 'oran-je'. Oran is the city in Algeria of Cixous's birth so 'Oran-I' suggests the author's own history and subjectivity.[29] Located in an arid climate, Oran gives Cixous the space to explore the absence of writing as a desert – '*I've wandered ten years in the desert of books*' – and the sweetness of the orange as the oasis, the fluidity of creative practice, the being-able-to-write-again moment:

> [A] writing found me when I was unfindable to myself. [...] From far away, from outside of my history, a voice came to collect the last tear. To save the orange. She put the word in my ear. And it was nearly the nymph of the orange that awakened in my breast and surged forth streaming from the heart's basin.[30]

'She' refers to the writing of Clarice Lispector that Cixous encounters as a call to return to her own writing. The sweet juice of the fruit connotes living creativity that is rooted in the body and the heart. Writing here is a matter of affect and the orange marks the space of literary exchange that is emotional as well as linguistic.

'Oran' is also phonetically close to 'Iran'. During her meditation on writing, delighting in the gift of the sweetness of orange that she finds in Clarice Lispector's work, the author is interrupted by a call to join activists in Paris demonstrating in solidarity with women in Iran. This then prompts a discourse on the relationship between politics and poetry, between writing and activism. The orange is the writing the author yearns for, yet also the women that she yearns to respond to: 'oranges that we have never seen are going out in the streets of Oran [...] oranges of a modern courage daring to give themselves as food for thought'.[31] This brings her to contemplate the scene of history, the destruction of the twentieth century and its many losses.

Asserting the significance of writing as a form of activism itself, Cixous nevertheless turns to a spare style to indicate the harsh responsibility of this position: 'I am not innocent', 'I confess the orange', 'I am unforgiveable'.[32] These short, sharp sentences contrast with longer, fluid sentences that call to others and describe a sensuous garden in the desert, that becomes another way of writing the orange as its sweetness is evoked as an entire landscape, a point I will return to in the following chapter. In the end the only answer Cixous has for the questions she poses is her ongoing fidelity to these questions and to the desire for a witness and an answer, and her commitment to tracing these in writing.

The qualities of the orange – sweet, sticky, compromising – indicate the texture of desire and of Cixous's call for openness to the other. Her choice of metaphor indicates an understanding that alterity inheres in domesticity and wilderness, in the gift of another's writing and the witness of another's activism. Moreover, the orange allows Cixous to explore the bodily nature of these ideas. The juice of the orange gets under her fingernails; it makes her lips sticky. It suggests an intimacy that is frequently a feature of her writing – returning even the most abstract of texts to the immediate moment, suggesting that alterity is not situated in an unknown elsewhere. She suggests that the possibility of an extraordinary encounter is always inherent in even the most mundane of life's encounters.

The multiplicity of subject positions, the ability of an image to constellate numerous references and meanings, the significance of embodiment – all speak to the importance of difference in Cixous's work. Cixous creates a space for 'the singularity of the other's materiality', while acknowledging that '[k]nowledge of the other can only ever be provisional, it is never complete'.[33] Cixous's work inaugurates an exploration of the mysterious without dissipating that mystery by claiming complete knowledge of or mastery over it. Difference is not only located within and between subjects or within and between texts, but also gestures towards a radical alterity that will always disrupt certainties and foreclose on a purely material reading of corporeality. Cixous has increasingly described her writerly engagement with alterity in the language of the sacred:

> When I have finished writing, when I am a hundred and ten, all I will have done will have been to attempt a portrait of God. [...] Of what escapes us and makes us wonder. Of what we do not know but feel. Of what makes us live. I mean our own divinity, awkward, twisted, throbbing, our own mystery. [...] We who are bits of sun, drops of ocean, atoms of the god, and who so often forget this.[34]

Cixous appeals to the Biblical prohibition against crafting images of God.[35] However, this is not quite as straightforward as the passage initially suggests. First, although Cixous uses the language of visual image, she is not a painter and her craft is done with words.[36] Second, this passage can be read as eschatology; the portrait is placed in the future as something Cixous writes towards. This 'finished' writing suggests a time beyond time. However, Cixous is clearly moving beyond orthodoxy in attempting such a portrait of God, as well as in her understanding of divinity. Bits of sun and drops of ocean suggest the Hermetic worldview of the living universe; God is not synonymous with the material world (including human beings) but emerges from and exceeds it.

The escapability of God and the wonderment of author and reader imply a divinity that may be immanent but can never be possessed, fully known or written. Yet the divine is also implicated in writing, in flesh; Cixous refuses to privilege transcendence. Her contemplation of God's portrait is not far from her mystical contemplation of the orange. Both reveal an irreducible mystery within the material and the literary. Cixous's engagement with difference – the divine as well as the human other – within the permutations of language indicates that encounter with alterity is a crucial part of creativity.

H.D.'s bees and honey

My reading of Ricoeur and Cixous foregrounds metaphor as the product of the creative imagination and the space of the dynamic interaction between language, sensory experience and the material world, thus mobilizing possibilities for creating new ways of being in the world. Turning to H.D.'s poetics, we can see how her spiritual and literary commitments intersect in her use of language. In her article on *The Sword* Jane Augustine emphasizes the significance of theosophy for H.D.'s understanding of language; just as theosophists assert that 'thoughts are things', so, 'for H.D., words are things'.[37] Augustine suggests that this materiality of language is a result of H.D.'s spiritualist practice. However, this insight resonates across H.D.'s work of the 1940s, if not further. Indeed, H.D.'s practice has a Romantic precursor in Coleridge, who argued for a material language in a letter to Godwin in 1800: 'I would endeavour to destroy the old antithesis of *Words* and *Things*, elevating, as it were, Words into Things and living Things too.'[38] As we have seen, H.D. does just this in *Trilogy* in the alchemical ritual which produces the word/jewel from the transmutation of words. The suggestion that words could be living things places them within a dynamic world and foregrounds their embeddedness in culture and human exchange (while also suggesting the reverse; things, too, can signify).

The materiality of language works in a number of ways in H.D.'s texts. The previous chapter explored the example of the ritual in which words literally become a thing, and used the performance approach to ritual as a lens to view the materiality of writing as a practice. I will now consider the more subtle expression of material mysticism through the metaphorical density of H.D.'s language and deployment of the image in *Trilogy*, *The Gift* and *The Sword*. The alchemical transmutation of *marah-mar* into Mary can be read not only as a ritual practice but as word play.[39] As I argued when considering Cixous's word play, these practices highlight the indeterminacy of words as meanings slip, slide and mutate.

In her recent book on the process of H.D.'s thought, Adalaide Morris borrows a term from Roland Barthes: 'mana-words'. For Barthes, these words 'function in a writer's vocabulary as nodes and relays of thought'.[40] For Morris, 'mana-words are alive and elastic. [...] [They] are words that lead thought forward across time, sustain its openness and generativity, and maintain its relevance to events at work within a culture.'[41] In borrowing from Barthes and Morris I want to emphasize the first half of this compound term: *mana* – the supernatural power and prestige that can accrue to people or objects.[42] Thus, rather than considering a word purely as a node for thought, I am interested in the sacred charge of the word and its ability to sustain the generativity of the mystical. Barthes's description of mana-words is reminiscent of the flexibility of Cixous's orange and the openness of Ricoeur's metaphors:

> In an author's lexicon, will there not always be a word-as-mana, a word whose ardent, complex, ineffable, and somehow sacred signification gives the illusion that by this word one might answer for everything? Such a word is neither eccentric nor central; it is motionless and carried, floating, never pigeonholed, always atopic (escaping any topic), at once remainder and supplement.[43]

Morris's chosen mana-words – *projection, science, gift* – are all abstract, conceptual terms, but the words that I find particularly resonant through *The Gift*, *The Sword* and *Trilogy* are simpler, more prosaic words. These words convey images and material objects such as *bee, jewel, apple tree;* however, their repetition across the text generates more complex associations.[44]

The repetition and mobility of the image links H.D.'s mature work, both prose and poetry, with her earlier Imagism.[45] Imagism marks an early exploration in modernist poetry in which a small group of poets published under its banner initiated a revolution in style, aiming for 'direct treatment of the "thing" whether subjective or objective'.[46] Amy Lowell described the tenets of Imagism as follows:

> 1. To use the language of common speech, but to employ always the *exact* word, not the nearly-exact, nor the merely decorative word.
> 2. To create new rhythms – as the expression of new moods – and not to copy old moods. [...]
> 3. To allow absolute freedom in the choice of subject. [...]
> 4. To present an image (hence the name: 'Imagist'). We are not a school of painters, but we believe that poetry should render particulars exactly and not deal in vague generalities, however magnificent and sonorous. [...]

5. To produce poetry that is hard and clear, never blurred nor indefinite.
6. Finally, most of us believe that concentration is of the very essence in poetry.[47]

Imagism, then, marked 'a radical poetic reduction technique'.[48] However, confusion arises regarding the nature of the image itself. For Pound, the image was not a visual representation of an external object, but 'that which presents an intellectual and emotional complex in an instant of time'.[49] The image is 'a state of perception' rather than an object.[50] Imagism refers to a mode of presentation, a technique, rather than the content of that presentation, and the hallmarks of clarity and hardness are not always present; the poet 'may wish to convey a mood of indecision, in which case the poem should be indecisive'.[51] Dianne Chisholm points to the Imagists' emphasis on the productive imagination: 'It was not mimesis or the representative function of imagining which they emphasized but its creative and constitutive function, the capacity to present things that would otherwise remain unperceived or inconceivable'.[52] This resonates with Ricoeur's emphasis on creation of the new, rather than representation.

Although H.D.'s Imagist poems are an expression of Classicism, in terms of content, style and influence, Eileen Gregory argues that H.D.'s is a Romantic mode of Hellenism which owes as much to Walter Pater and other nineteenth-century decadents as to Sappho and Euripides.[53] Furthermore, Gregory links this Romantic Hellenism with Hermeticism.[54] The Hermeticism that we have explored through *Trilogy* finds expression in H.D.'s earlier work as well. H.D. explicitly aligns herself and her writing with Hermeticism, claiming that her first published lyric, 'Hermes of the Ways', initiated 'H.D. – Hermes – Hermeticism and all the rest of it'.[55]

Much recent criticism of H.D.'s early work has explored ways in which her Imagism cuts against the grain of earlier assessments of the movement. Freeing H.D. from the description 'crystalline' has been a major critical endeavour.[56] Her most popular and frequently cited poems demonstrate a dynamic energy that refuses to be confined. From the sea rose 'flung on the sand' to the 'whirl up, sea' of 'Oread', movement is at the heart of H.D.'s early poetry; the image may be clear, but it is not static.[57] Rachel Connor reads this movement as an invitation to the reader to engage in the production of meaning; 'Through an active relationship between author and reader – brought about by deliberate and careful juxtaposition of visual elements – the image is constructed as *process* through which the reader actively engages in the text's production.'[58] Likewise, the lyrics of *Sea Garden* and *The Gods* suggest ritualizing activity and a process of invoking the sacred.[59] I will return to the implications of process for embodiment later in this chapter. For now I wish to emphasize the dynamism of the image, which is a legacy of H.D.'s early work and joins with the broader scope of her mature work to enable her writing to maintain material particularity while exploring complex constellations of meaning.

Claire Buck argues that H.D.'s imagist poetry is characterized by 'an element of undecidability' due to the insecure attachment of images to meanings, narratives or references to the author.[60] This undecidability increases the dynamism of H.D.'s poetry in terms of the accrual of meanings, interpretations and subject positions. H.D. uses a word to create an image, or cluster of images, in a repetitive way so that meanings accrue and overlap within an increasingly dense language. Read through the lens of Ricoeur's and Cixous's poetics, we can see that difference inheres within that density in metaphor's openness and generation of multiple meanings. I suggest that these mana-words form a nexus for the material, the linguistic and the spiritual in H.D.'s writing. The words *bee*, *bee hive*, *beeswax* and *honey/comb* form an image cluster that appears repeatedly across H.D.'s oeuvre; the poems of *Sea Garden* use honey as an image that draws together the bitter and the sweet, indicating spiritual and erotic search, while in the final section of the late sequence, 'Winter Love' (1972), the bee represents the pain and hope of birth (H.D. 1983, pp. 8, 17, 28; H.D. 1972, p. 117). The image recurs in numerous contexts in *Trilogy*, *The Gift* and *The Sword*. Like Cixous's orange, bees and honey provide H.D. with a tactile, sweet, sticky, dynamic image. By tracing the appearances of these words and suggesting some of the various meanings that accrue across the texts, I will demonstrate the metaphorical density that contributes to the materiality of language.

Trilogy opens with a juxtaposition of the ruined sacred temple at Karnak with bombed London. The image of the 'Luxor bee' that 'continue[s] to prophesy/ from the stone papyrus' indicates the possibility for regeneration even in the midst of ruins, and unites image and word in the figure of the hieroglyphic carved in stone (*Walls* 1:5, 8–9).[61] By using an image that is stony, linguistic and pictorial, H.D. signals an important aspect of her metaphors; they are both natural and cultural. She deploys organic objects, such as honey, the bee and the pearl, that have gathered a weight of cultural meaning and reference. These culturally weighted images enable multiple meanings, both old and new, while continuing to foreground materiality. The honey/bee image cluster brings together Greek and Hebrew texts. The use of images from the natural world, particularly honey, to express syncretism between mythologies – Greek and Hebrew, Pagan and Christian – emerges in the earlier poem 'Sigil'. As the poet moves between worlds, she claims that past and present are bound up in each other: 'there is no old nor new:/wine, bread, grape and sweet/honey; Galilee, Delphi, to-day' (H.D. 1983, p. 411).[62] In the Hebrew Bible, honey is most frequently a reference for the Promised Land – 'a land flowing with milk and honey' – while also indicating the sensual delight of God's word, as well as the fulfilment of erotic desire.[63] The associations with sacred space, nourishment, language and eroticism will reappear in H.D.'s use of the image. Likewise, these images appear in Euripides and Sappho, important intertexts for H.D.[64]

Honey continues the image's tracing of the palimpsest of past and present, this time suggesting the sensual but ephemeral solace of previous spiritual experience in the face of current trauma. The poet declares 'we would feed forever/on the honey-comb/of your remembered greeting' (H.D. 1998b, *Walls* 29:8–13).[65] However, the poet's subsequent anger at war's destructiveness denies nostalgic retreat; memory is not nourishment enough. The honey of 'remembered greeting' sets the poet on a spiritual quest, discovering new life in the midst of this journey:

> resurrection is a bee-line,
>
> straight to the horde and plunder
> the treasure, the store-room,
>
> the honeycomb;
> resurrection is remuneration,
>
> food, shelter, fragrance
> of myrrh and balm. (*Rod* 7:2–8)

The bee becomes an image for the process of seeking; the honeycomb is the resource that fuels spiritual and cultural renewal. The honey that is physical, emotional, spiritual and creative nourishment echoes Cixous's orange. In *Trilogy*, resurrection is not so much the goal of the quest as the journey itself, both a movement and a sanctuary along the way. The honeycomb – food, shelter, fragrance – implies sensual renewal and solace, yet the beeline indicates the urgency and the speed of resurrection-as-flight. The previous chapter examined fragrance as the spiritual-material substance whose drift unites alchemical transformation and the scene of the London Blitz. In the context of the current chapter's interest in language, fragrance of myrrh here indicates the transformation mobilized by the movements of the bee/honey image traversing across *Trilogy*.

In *The Gift* and *The Sword* the metaphoric use of 'bee' and 'honey' connects spiritual renewal with creative practice and the poet's relationship to language.

In both *The Gift* and *The Sword* H.D. describes an imagined sanctuary as a beehive; she goes on to use honeycomb as a metaphor for regeneration located in the midst of community: 'if you are consoled or integrated, you help console and integrate the scattered remnant. [...] In saving oneself, one creates a shell [...] a minute coral-shell, one of a million, or a single wax-cell of the honey-comb' (2007, p. 67). Here the individual and the wider community are interdependent, but not undifferentiated. In *The Gift* she connects the beehive as sanctuary with her relationship to language. A foreign word, spoken by her grandmother, becomes a sacred space with the child as caretaker:

> [S]omething had come over me like the branches of a tree or the folds of a tent when she says *Wunden Eiland.* [...] The word is like a bee-hive, but there are no bees in it now. I am the last bee in the bee-hive, this is the game I play. The other bees have gone, that is why it is so quiet. Can one bee keep a bee-hive alive, I mean, can one person who knows that *Wunden Eiland* is a bee-hive, keep *Wunden Eiland* for the other bees, when they come back? (pp. 154–5)[66]

I will return to this passage and the significance of sanctuary and sacred space for H.D.'s work in the following chapter. Here, I wish to highlight the connection between language, creativity and the sacred in these examples. The child Hilda's visionary experience emerges from the sound of the word, she emphasizes that she doesn't know or care what it means; the sound itself carries the significance, as the voice of Clarice Lispector called Cixous back to writing. The beehive as the nexus of sound, sacred space and creativity is repeated at the end of *The Gift*, in H.D.'s audition of a Moravian choir singing, which sounds like the hum of bees (p. 222).

In *The Sword*, H.D. returns to the beehive and honey as a metaphor for resurrection, but this time in the context of creative practice. One of the vignettes involves the production of illuminated manuscripts. Blanchfleur suggests including a bee hive in the capital and Mother Beata agrees, making reference to Christ after the resurrection (Jesus eats fish and honeycomb) and the proverb that wisdom is sweeter than honey in the honeycomb (pp. 244–5).[67] Here we see the association of resurrection and the bee that H.D. adapts in *The Flowering of the Rod.* Moreover, Mother Beata's musings link resurrection with wisdom; both are characterized by the sweetness of honey. The illuminated manuscript indicates the identification of word and image, language and artefact, as the word itself becomes a work of art and bees become adornment.

Beeswax becomes the locus for divine immanence and human creativity in *The Gift.* In an extended reading of this image I argue that it forms the place where domestic, particular objects coincide with literary metaphor. H.D. describes the crafting of Christmas decorations by Hilda and her brothers as a spiritual activity that instantiates the Incarnation:

> God had made a Child and we children in return now made God; we created Him as He had created us, we created Him as children will, out of odds and ends; like magpies, we built him a nest of stray bits of silver-thread, shredded blue or rose or yellow coloured paper; we knew our power. We knew that God could not resist the fragrance of a burning beeswax candle! (p. 89)

H.D. suggests that the domestic creativity of children echoes divine creativity, conjuring a scene of divine immanence; God is seduced into being. H.D. argues elsewhere that children, artists and the devout have the gift of giving life to material objects (2007, p. 119). This is yet another reading of the gift that is both creative and spiritual. H.D. emphasizes the spiritual and creative life of children and considers their work to be as significant as that of the adult artist. In their engagement with material objects children, artists and devotees craft new worlds, thus participating in divine activity. H.D. reproduces this activity of creating out of scraps in the style of *The Gift*, patching together narrative fragments, multiple voices and temporalities.

H.D. uses the description of the Moravian Christmas to reflect on creativity. The festival is marked out from the everyday, yet is enmeshed in the ordinary both in terms of cyclical return and in the domestic activity that marks the event itself. She introduces an unknown 'thing' that depends upon ordinary objects to come into being. However, we soon discover that this mysterious 'thing' is not an object but an activity:

> It was not only the smell of the moss, it was not only the smell of the spiced ginger-dough that was waiting under a cloth in the biggest yellow bowl on the pantry-shelf, and yet it was all these; it was all these and the forms of the Christmas-cakes. [...] The 'thing' was that we were creating. (pp. 88–9)

The incantatory repetitions and specific sensory details serve to conjure this scene for the reader. The scene's evident construction foregrounds the author's presence, drawing together the creativity of writer and child and aligning the scene of writing (1940s London) with the Moravian Christmas decades earlier.

The material objects crafted by the children become God, yet, simultaneously, the objects make the children into God, endowing them with the power to create. The allure of beeswax and coloured paper reveals a religious intimacy and preoccupation with the stuff of the world. Elaine Scarry reads the Hebrew

Bible as, amongst other things, a history of the way in which crafted material objects 'confer on God a body'.[68] Scarry corroborates H.D.'s description of creativity: 'the Object [God] *is* their creator, for by making this Artifact they have recreated themselves, altered themselves profoundly and drastically.'[69] She argues that making things projects embodiment and its related sentience out into the external world. Unlike Scarry's examples – clothing which takes up the task of skin, a chair which supports the skeleton – H.D.'s 'nest' of beeswax and silver thread is emphatically un-useful and is situated in an interstice of cultural production. Hilda's creation of God out of odds and ends resonates with Walter Benjamin's assertion that children focus on the discarded remains of culture: 'They are irresistibly drawn by the detritus generated by building, gardening, housework, tailoring, or carpentry. [...] In using these things they [...] bring together, in the artefact produced in play, materials of widely differing kinds in a new, intuitive relationship.'[70]

H.D. puts the ancient practice of transformation – alchemy – into the hands of children. The patchwork of ordinary leftover threads and shreds form an idiosyncratic and subtle Hermetic gloss on the overt Moravianism in the text. The attention to the creative potential of domestic details resonates with the Hermetic regard for particularity: 'Because the universe is a forest of symbols, it is natural to wish to examine closely all that it contains. [...] [T]he Hermetist showed an extremely pronounced taste for the particular, for the hidden face and form in being and objects.'[71] For Hilda and her brothers, the hidden form of scraps of tissue, silver thread and fragrant beeswax is divine and their craft reveals God's face. The location of divinity within the human sphere, while retaining its mystery, resonates with Cixous's portrait of God discussed above.

I have lingered over the implications of Hilda's luring God into being with beeswax because I find this a key passage in understandings H.D.'s conception of creativity, transformation, spirituality and the everyday – themes that are explored in the previous instances of the bee/honey image. The appearances of this image in *Trilogy*, *The Gift* and *The Sword* play against and alongside H.D.'s earlier work, both poetry and prose, where the images 'bee' and 'honey' signify eroticism or Dionysian ecstasy, thus bringing the deployment of the bee/honey image cluster to the scene of embodiment.

In the essay *Notes on Thought and Vision*, a manifesto on aesthetics and visionary consciousness, honey indicates the dangerous pleasures of moving outside normative practice, whether spiritual, creative or erotic. H.D.'s meditations on creativity and embodiment lead her towards a vision of passionate, sensual ecstasy:

> Outside is a great vineyard and grapes and rioting and madness and dangers. It is very dangerous. An enormous moth detached himself from a bunch of yellow grapes [...] heavy with the sun and his soft belly swollen with the honey of the grapes [...]. He fell rather than flew. [...] I would have rescued him but I myself was dizzy with the heat and the fumes of the golden wine and I heard a great shout of laughter as I tried to steady my cup and I shouted in reply, he is drunk – he is drunk. So he was drunk. Outside is a great vineyard and rioting and madness and dangers. (pp. 41–2)

The passage evokes wild revelry, although H.D. also emphasizes the dangers and disorientation of such abandonment. She locates herself in this uncertain, Bacchanalian outside. The wild vineyard becomes the location for the coalescence of spirituality and eroticism as the grape and bead of honey signify female sexuality while the honey and wine engulf the poet in ecstasy. [72] In her pursuit of ecstasy H.D. is not seeking to transcend the body but to express embodiment in a new way. Like Cixous, she does not signify a contained and stable body but a body that is moving, fluid, fragmentary and strange: 'the goal of H.D.'s manifesto is not to make the body [...] strong but to abandon the body in ecstasy to alterity.'[73]

The body holds a place of primary importance in H.D.'s writing, although often approached in oblique ways. Kathleen Crown argues that *Notes* presents a complex view of embodiment: 'The *Notes*' modernist literary experimentation [...] acknowledges dualism while suggesting an alternate understanding of body and subjectivity as perpetually under construction, in process, and culturally permeable and vulnerable. The body made visible in *Notes* remains irreducibly material, other, and different.'[74] By linking the body with images in the natural world that signify growth, transformation and decay, H.D. presents a body that is constantly opening and changing. These particular images – flowers, shells, pearls, chrysalides – embed the spiritual in bodily experience, adding another dimension to the materiality of language in H.D.'s poetics. Throughout her writing, H.D. emphasizes both the sensory content of visionary experiences and the sensory experiences that lead to visions. This returns us once more to the alchemical jewel, which not only links language to material object but also connects the poetic image with the body. The jewel lives; it has a 'faint/heart-beat, pulse-beat' (1998b, *Angels* 14:8–9). Already the product of ritual and associated with divine names, here the jewel suggests that the sacred is located within the body. Language, spirituality and corporeality are layered in the one image.

For H.D., corporeality is interwoven with eroticism and spirituality. Connor argues that *Notes* disrupts the distinction between body and spirit and thus makes a space for an ecstasy that is corporeal, spiritual and aesthetic.[75] The sacred charge to the bee/honey image is more evident in H.D.'s homage to Sappho in her version of 'Fragment 113':

> not honey, not the deep
> plunge of soft belly
> and the clinging of the gold-edged
> pollen-dusted feet
> [...]
> not honey, not the south,
> not the tall stalk
> of red twin-lilies
> nor light branch of fruit tree. (1983, p. 131)

The multiple references to bees, honey, flowers, pollen and fruit indicate an erotic abundance that persists despite the repeated disavowals, the 'voluptuous denials of voluptuousness'.[76] Simultaneously, the repetition of 'not' suggests a tension between this soft, sticky sexuality and its renunciation.

The movement encoded in H.D.'s early imagist poems expresses a multivalent desire akin to Cixous's 'other bisexuality'. The movement between internal and external, seed and tree, lush garden and windy wilds in *Sea Garden* suggests a ritualized erotics which indicates that sexuality is a process in H.D.'s work and the self thus constructed 'moves from one (gendered) positionality to another'.[77] Thus sacred sexuality is queerly performed *in between*. H.D.'s heterodox poetics instigate a process of queering spirituality and aesthetics as well as sexuality. This process continues in *Trilogy*, from the textual alchemy that produces the erotic word/jewel, to the abundant swirls of Mary Magdalene's Pre-Raphaelite hair, which mark her as a femme fatale, to the uncontained drifting of fragrance.[78]

In the wartime texts, the experience of embodiment is frequently figured as traumatic.[79] As Amy Hollywood argues, attempts to transcend bodily trauma and loss lead to denial or repression and indicate a refusal to come to terms with mortality. She suggests that we need resources for 'thinking the body otherwise, as the site of possibility and limitation, pleasure and suffering, natality and death' and she reminds us that loss, as well as pleasure, is experienced in the body.[80] H.D.'s view of the body as mutable and multiple makes space for regeneration to be held alongside engagement with traumatic bodily experience. *Trilogy*, *The Gift* and *The Sword* all record bodily trauma and loss; from H.D.'s personal experiences of strain leading to physical and mental breakdown, to losses recorded in her family history, to the global wounds of atomic warfare. *The Gift* opens with the story of a young girl burning to death (one of H.D.'s great fears during the Blitz), while the first section of *Trilogy* compresses abjection with survival:

> the flesh? it was melted away,
> the heart burnt out, dead ember,
> tendons, muscles shattered, outer husk dismembered,
>
> yet the frame held. (*Walls* 1:46–9)[81]

The frame holds, survival is the central concern of H.D.'s Second World War texts, yet terror and dismemberment are never fully eradicated or forgotten. The irreducible presence of loss in H.D.'s writing correlates with the attention to the wound in Cixous's work. As an ongoing reminder of the material significance of loss, the wound provokes an engagement with history, while the orange indicates both the ecstatic plenitude of writing and the attention to the other that draws attention to both desire and trauma.

The complexity, ambiguity and dynamism of embodiment can be traced in the unfolding progression of another image, olfactory rather than visual or tactile. In *Trilogy*, pleasure and pain are held in the same resonant word: myrrh. The bitterness of the word, *marah*, which becomes the bitter jewel, is linked linguistically to myrrh, a substance associated with death and burial as well as incense and perfume. Yet myrrh is also associated with the beeline and honeycomb of resurrection. To return once more to fragrance, this sensual, illusive element holds together bodily experiences of beauty and bitterness, birth and death. Presented as fragmentary or whole, the site of ecstasy, desire and passion, as well as disruption, loss and grief, for H.D. the body is expressive of the multiplicity of human experience.

Conclusion

I have explored the image cluster of the bee/beehive/honey in order to demonstrate the richness of associations formed across H.D.'s texts in the exploration and deployment of minute details. The constellation of different forms and contexts for the image enables a Hermetic reading in which different contexts are drawn together through the web of associations: spirituality and sexuality, ecstasy and loss, desire and creativity. The movements of difference in Cixous's and H.D.'s writing illuminate the possibility for transformation within metaphoric language. From the oscillation and overlap of images, to the ambiguity of bodily experiences, Cixous and H.D. chart a continual unfolding of mystery, as the image both reveals and conceals the presence of the sacred within the text. The productive tension between materiality and alterity indicates a mysticism that refuses absolute distinctions: 'the passage of difference is also the path of the undecidable'.[82] Cixous's definition of divinity as 'what escapes us and makes us wonder' suggests a paradox to do with representation.[83] Cixous is concerned with tracing the path of a mystery that can never be fully known or represented. Her writing repeatedly returns to an aporia in attempts to say the unsayable. Yet in the details and ambiguities of images such as the orange and the bee we see that such mystery is not apart from everyday materiality and thus *can* be represented, if only partially. Cixous's encounter with the orange, the sticky residue of honey, the shattered survivors of *Trilogy*, and the erotic and mystical movements of Mary Magdalene's hair, all emphasize the insistence of the material within the most abstract of linguistic performances. If ritual highlights the performance of writing a material mysticism, then the path of the image through H.D.'s and Cixous's texts provides the representation of that mysticism.

Cixous's representation of writing as an attempt at a portrait of God, of divine escapability and authorial wonderment, provides a way of articulating H.D.'s writing as material mysticism. H.D. foregrounds spiritual engagement in her poetry and prose but, for all her explicit ruminations on creativity, spirituality and particular religious motifs, practices and figures, it remains a challenge to the critics to assess the implications of these meditations. Hermetic drift can be baffling. In Cixous's writing bafflement is reconfigured as wonder and an invitation to read again. Approaching H.D.'s texts with a Cixousian strategy supports my interpretation of her creative practice as a spiritual discipline. A Cixousian reading encourages engagement with the mysterious alterity at the heart of H.D.'s writing. It is this mystery that provides depth and dynamism to the image of the bee, the jewel, the beeswax and silver paper bricolage.

The alchemical energy of H.D.'s and Cixous's writing, the mobility of metaphors and wordplay further enable transformations of subjectivity. These in turn lead to new ways of apprehending and writing the world. The following chapter turns from explorations of writing as an activity and the objects within writing to the context of writing and how that context is engaged within texts. Ricoeur's understanding of metaphor as productive of alternative ways of being in the world provides a starting point for my discussion of writing as flight and sanctuary as mobilized by Cixous and H.D. There we see the context for the images of orange and bee when we look at the places of the garden and the bee hive and discover that these are locations for encouters with the sacred.

Notes

1 Corbin 1969, pp. 182–5; Faivre 1995, p. 65.
2 Tuveson 1982, p. 33.
3 Faivre 2000, p. 102.
4 Tuveson 1982, p. 25. For a systematic overview of scholarship on esotericism and Romanticism see Hanegraaff 1998.
5 Meakin 1995, p. 8.
6 Kearney 2004, p. 33.
7 Although language is a key concern of second- and third-wave feminism, earlier examples can be found, such as Elizabeth Cady Stanton's *Women's Bible* and the rhetoric of abolitionists such as Sojourner Truth.
8 Schneider 1998, p. 5. The relationship between image and symbol is ambiguous. I follow David Punter's distinction, that symbol has a broader 'cultural spread', i.e. it has more widely recognized associations and meanings; Punter 2007, p. 30. Writers may create new metaphors, but symbols have a history, although they may be used in new ways.
9 Bray 2004, pp. 73–4.
10 Oxford University Press 2010.
11 Baldick 2008, pp. 164–5.
12 Knowles and Moon 2006, p. 3.
13 Aristotle, quoted in Punter 2007, pp. 112–13.
14 Ricoeur 1991, p. 78.
15 Ricoeur 2003, p. 232.
16 Ricoeur 1991, pp. 78–9.
17 Ibid. pp. 80–1.
18 Cixous 1991, p. 24.
19 Ricoeur 1974, p. 110.
20 Walton 2007a, p. 56.
21 Kearney 2004, p. 38.
22 Ricoeur 1974, p. 109.
23 Ricoeur 1991, p. 85.
24 See Bray 2004, pp. 38–41; Lie 1999, pp. 2–7; Suleiman 1991, pp. x, xx.
25 Cixous 1991, p. 134.
26 Cixous 1979, p. 16.

27 Ibid. p. 40.
28 Ibid. p. 14.
29 Ibid. pp. 30–2.
30 Ibid. pp. 12–14.
31 Ibid. p. 96.
32 Ibid. pp. 32, 40.
33 Bray 2004, pp. 182–3.
34 Cixous 1991, pp. 129–30.
35 The understanding of the Second Commandment, the prohibition on creating images, has a complex and varied history in Judaism. It has generally been understood not to prohibit all images but only those that provoke idolatry. For an overview of the history of these debates, see Raphael 2009, pp. 19–42.
36 Cixous 1991, p. 106.
37 Augustine 1996, p. 130.
38 Samuel T. Coleridge, quoted in Piper 1962, p. 131.
39 Chisholm 1992, p. 64.
40 Morris 2003, p. 8.
41 Ibid. p. 89.
42 This concept emerges from Polynesian religions; Oxford University Press 2010.
43 Barthes 1977, p. 129.
44 Even a more abstract mana-word like 'spiral' is frequently paired with concrete images such as a shell, a labyrinth or an unfurling flower.
45 The dominant critical view of H.D.'s work for many years was largely determined by her early Imagist poems, which were judged excellent but minor. Her early work has posed a problem for feminist criticism; those critics interested in re-evaluating and reclaiming her work in the 1980s and early 1990s tended to privilege the later poetry over the early work, claiming that Imagism limited her and that the critical reception of her poetry overlooked the value of her later work because of its radical departure from her early lyrics; Friedman 1975, p. 801; Friedman 1981, pp. xi, 2–6. The past few decades have seen a renewed critical interest in H.D.'s early poetry as a number of critics have approached this work from new angles. These re-readings are organized around embodiment, subjectivity, poetic strategies and literary engagements; Buck 1991; Collecott 1999; Connor 2004; Gregory 1997; Stott 1997, pp. 27–46.
46 The term 'Imagist' was coined by Ezra Pound to describe the poetry of H.D. and Richard Aldington. The movement was fostered by Amy Lowell, who arranged for the publication of three Imagist anthologies between 1915 and 1917; Ayers 2004, p. 2; Hughes 1960, p. 34.
47 Lowell 1970, pp. 239–40.
48 Emig 1995, p. 106.

49 Pound 1954, p. 4. See also Beasley 2007, p. 39.
50 Emig 1995, p. 108.
51 Lowell 1970, pp. 244–5. See also Ayers 2004, p. 5.
52 Chisholm 1992, p. 52.
53 Gregory 1997, p. 2. See also Laity 1996.
54 Gregory 1997, pp. 41–2.
55 H.D., quoted in Chisholm 1992, p. 55.
56 Pearson 1972, p. v.
57 Thacker 2011, p. 57.
58 Connor 2004, p. 36.
59 Gregory 1997, p. 124.
60 Buck 1991, p. 29.
61 This image links H.D.'s experience of healing after the First World War – she visited Karnak with Bryher in 1923 and this is written in the dedication to *Walls* – with her experience of the Second World War.
62 Likewise, in the 'Luxor bee' H.D. links Egyptian and Christian mythology, foregrounding a syncretism that will continue throughout *Trilogy*.
63 Exodus 3.8; Psalms 19.10; Psalms 119.103; Song of Solomon 5.1.
64 See H.D.'s translation of Euripedes' *Hippolytus* and the epigraph from Sappho preceding her poem 'Fragment 113'; H.D. 1983, pp. 85, 131.
65 The greeting is from Jesus after the resurrection, an allusion to the end of the Gospel of John, which is also concerned with food, see John 21.9–13.
66 Hilda later learns that Wunden Eiland is the sacred site of the Moravian and Native American alliance and the place of the Moravian Hidden Church's rituals, as discussed in Chapter Three.
67 Mother Beata refers to Luke 24.42, where the resurrected Jesus eats fish and honeycomb, and Psalms 19.9–10.
68 Scarry 1985, p. 222.
69 Ibid. p. 311.
70 Benjamin 2006, pp. 52–3.
This mode of creativity also suggests the patchwork imagery that has been significant for numerous feminists, see hooks 2009, pp. 154–68; Kwok 2005, p. 46; Rich 1978, pp. 76–7.
71 Faivre 1995, pp. 57–8.
72 H.D. may have been inspired by the connection between Dionysus, honey and wine in Euripides' *Bacchae*, whose choruses she translated. The Maenads' ecstasy is expressed with reference to wine and honey; Euripides 1973, p. 216.
73 Crown 1995, p. 227.
74 Ibid. pp. 221–2.
75 Connor 2004, pp. 47–8.

76 Gregory 1997, p. 152.

77 Connor 2004, p. 50. Kathryn Simpson also reads H.D.'s early work as suggestive of mutable sexuality in her reading of pearls, jewels and seeds as signifiers of queer, woman-centred sexuality; 2004, pp. 38–42.

78 Laity 1996, pp. 179–81.

79 *Notes* was written shortly after the First World War, a time of intense bodily and mental trauma for H.D.; however, she does not address these experiences as directly in the manifesto as in the Second World War texts. After her psychoanalytic therapy in the 1930s H.D. returned to her First World War experiences more openly in the autobiographical novel *Bid Me to Live* (which she revised in the 1930s), as well as in *The Sword.*

80 Hollywood 2002, p. 186.

81 For further discussion of abject bodies in *Trilogy,* see Laity 1996, pp. 171–82.

82 Bray 2004, p. 187.

83 Cixous 1991, p. 129.

5

Writing as Sanctuary

While Chapter Three analysed sacred activity or ritual and Chapter Four addressed sacred objects or images, this chapter performs a shift in perspective by considering the context of these activities and objects, i.e. place or location. In so doing, it returns to the scene of war, recovery and creativity considered in Chapters One and Two. I have previously analysed transformation in H.D. through narratives of recovery and community, the activity of ritual and the dynamism of images; I now consider the context for this imaginative, literary creativity. This chapter is situated in the interstice between theoretical concerns and material particulars;[1] here I treat Cixous's work more extensively, turning to her autobiographical texts that focus on place, movement and identity, and reading them alongside H.D.'s work. This chapter attends to place in H.D.'s and Cixous's writing through an analysis of two spatial metaphors: garden and flight. The metaphors map onto the larger concerns of place and movement. Garden suggests stable, particular locations, while flight indicates movement in and between places. In tracing the contours of the garden and the trajectories of flight, the chapter moves from the imagined to the material and back again. Although gardens are settled, cultivated and grounded, while flight is mobile, unpredictable and airborne, Cixous and H.D. frequently bring the two metaphors together in unusual conjunctions.

The third term that enables an exploration of the relationship between garden and flight is sanctuary. Sanctuary's definition and location are rendered ambiguous and subject to startling transformations in Cixous's and H.D.'s writing. I am concerned here with two definitions of sanctuary: a holy place where the divine dwells; and a place of refuge.[2] Sanctuary is both the endpoint of flight and hidden within its trajectories; it is a goal and a way station. Moreover, it forms the connection between garden and flight as the gardens themselves are sanctuaries. However, this identification is ambiguous; for H.D. and Cixous gardens are sanctuaries in that they are places of sacred encounter, but they are not always safe refuges. In considering the relationship between origins, flight and creativity they configure writing itself as a sanctuary, thus bringing together imaginative concerns and material contexts. Michel de Certeau's writing on pilgrimage provides a useful model for imagining a sanctuary that encompasses both place and movement. De Certeau argues that, in the modern period, the pilgrim undergoes 'perpetual departure' in a pilgrimage whose goal has been effaced.[3] For de Certeau the pathways of this pilgrimage may be traced in writing; however, in Cixous's and H.D.'s work we see not merely the trace of a perpetual departure but the sacred places themselves, displaced into writing. The dwelling place of the stranger, mystery and all that escapes, writing becomes the sanctuary that is a place of healing, but one that is open to the movements of flight, theft and encounter.

Sometimes oppositional and sometimes harmonic, the two metaphors of garden and flight form a complex dialectic in Cixous's and H.D.'s work. Biblical texts posit the garden as the place of human origin (the Garden of Eden in Genesis) and divine encounter (God walks in the garden in the cool of the day; Mary Magdalene meets the risen Christ in the garden), while its loss has been seen as the original exile.[4] While Cixous and H.D. draw upon these Biblical tropes in their writing, they deconstruct traditional understandings of origin and exile. As children of immigrants who lived most of their adult lives away from their place of birth, both H.D. and Cixous complicate understandings of 'home'.[5] Places of past and present dwelling and the flights towards and away from them form a significant element of their creative projects. Their texts suggest a paradoxical understanding of creativity as rooted in the places of the past yet coming to fruition through movements away from those places, along with inevitable imaginary returns. Both writers locate the source of their creativity in the place of their birth.[6] Yet is it only through leaving these places that they come to writing.

This chapter considers both imagined spaces and material places, while continuing to assert that material places also function within the writer's imagination and that imagined spaces are inflected with traces of this materiality.[7] The imagined (or metaphorical) and the material are continually co-implicated. This is particularly evident in Cixous's and H.D.'s writing, as both authors frequently move from descriptions or invocations of material, real-world locations to imagined or interior (psychological) spaces, thus undermining distinctions between them. This reading emphasizes that locations are present in literary texts in highly mediated ways. Andrew Thacker emphasizes the importance of bringing considerations of literary form to discussions of space in modernist cultural practices. He argues that textual space and social space are co-implicated in literary production.[8]

In their avant-garde stylistics Cixous and H.D. represent space and movement in their writing. I have commented earlier that the connective stanza form of *Trilogy* reveals the influence of Hermeticism's analogical reasoning in H.D.'s work. I would now add that the chains of signifiers across *Trilogy*'s stanzas, yoked with the wide margins and spaces between the stanzas evident on the page, construct a space that is open but contains meaningful pathways. Turning to her prose, the dislocated but overlapping vignettes and illusive use of pronouns in *The Sword* suggest a fragmentation that echoes the fractured cities, landscapes and communities of the Second World War. Cixous's placement of concrete metaphors within more abstract theoretical writing and their subsequent permutations encode shifts of tone which in turn indicate a rapid back and forth movement. The expansiveness of her long sentences suggests the flight (an inherently spatial metaphor) of the woman writer as bird. Bi-lingual productions such as the des femmes edition of *Vivre l'orange / To Live the Orange*, where French and English literally face each other, highlight the importance of multiple languages to her theorizing about writing as relational.

In this chapter I consider how the metaphors of garden and flight illuminate place and movement in Cixous's and H.D.'s writing. After outlining my theoretical approach to place and movement, I discuss gardens and then flight in specific texts by Cixous and H.D. Finally, I turn to the dynamics provoked by the third term, sanctuary, and conclude by considering how the sacred movements of a pilgrimage without a goal yields a helpful model for understanding the significance of place for writing a material mysticism.

Place and movement in cultural criticism

Recent decades have seen a turn to space as a key concept in critical theory as well as the rise of interdisciplinary projects such as human geography (with its examination of the nexus of geography and sociology) and postcolonial studies (with its analysis of geopolitics). Such projects explore the convergence of place and culture and have fostered such concerns in other disciplines. Human geographers argue that 'place is best understood as a locus of meaning' and is thus a human construct as much as a natural one.[9] This is relevant for wild, so-called natural places as well as for the built environment. Simon Schama argues that there are few elements of the natural world that have not been significantly altered by human intervention (intentional or otherwise) and even wilderness areas, national parks, etc. are culturally implicated by their very designation.[10]

In modernist studies, the growing interest in the material context of modernism, along with the issues of the influence of imperialism on cultural production raised by postcolonial studies, has led to increasing attention to the locations and movements of modernism.[11] Modernist studies' attention to global locations suggests not a universalizing 'international' discourse that suppresses the provincial for the sake of the cosmopolitan, but, rather, attention to the movements and particularities of diverse modernisms, not transcending, but traversing locations.[12] In attending to particular places, the issues of movement and exchange are always already implicated. As Andrew Thacker argues, modernist literature repeatedly invokes the porous boundaries between places (especially public and private), the multiplicity of types of places (psychic and material), geographical conflict (particularly in the context of imperialism and the relationship between European imperial centres and colonial locations) and the movement of subjects through and within space (urban space, for example, is frequently described as space to be experienced by moving through it).[13] I will return to the question of movement shortly, but first I want to briefly consider the significance of space for theology.

The theoretical turn to spatial considerations is evident in theology's growing interest in sacred space. Religious scholars differ over whether to define sacred space as an 'irruption of the sacred into the world, breaking with the chaos of surrounding profane space' or an element in the human construction of meaningful space.[14] Louis Jacobs notes that sacred spaces, or holy places, are a vexed issue within monotheism, as they raise thorny questions about the possibilities of God being more present in one place than another, or degrees of sanctity between places. He goes on to suggest two definitions of sacred space: one is to see the divine as 'especially manifested' in a particular place, the other is to 'see the holy place as hallowed by experience and association'.[15] For the latter, the place is not inherently holy but is considered sacred 'due to the fact that it is believed to have been the scene of divine revelation or of sustained [...] worship'.[16] Although Jacobs is concerned with the Jewish tradition, his definitions have relevance for other theologies as well. In terms of Christianity, the second definition is more attractive to Protestant theologians intent on locating sacred space within the worshipping community.[17] Catholic theologians may be more inclined to consider places in the world, built and natural, as the scene of revelation. Thus Philip Sheldrake points to Duns Scotus's theology of particularity as a helpful guide to considering the religious significance of sacred places: 'for Scotus [...] God's life is so fruitful that it constantly and inherently seeks expression in the particularities of the created order.'[18] Some scholars interested in sacred space have turned their attention to the theological, social and aesthetic significance of European churches and cathedrals, while others have meditated on the sacredness of the (wild) landscape and its cultural representation.[19] Writers such as David Jasper, Belden C. Lane and Kathleen Norris have found harsh landscapes of desert, mountain and plains to reflect the radical otherness of God, while Rita Brock, Rebecca Parker and Terry Tempest Williams find the liminal zones of estuaries and marshes, with their rampant biodiversity, reflective of God's extravagant creativity.[20]

Consideration of sacred space often turns to pilgrimage as a practice of traversing geographical places that allows an exploration of both space and movement in religious terms. As a historical practice and a theological metaphor, pilgrimage demonstrates the folding together of material culture and abstract discourse. Christian theologians frequently turn to pilgrimage as a means of expressing the importance of the material world held in tension with a continual displacement of identity for those whose lives are aimed towards an eschatological beyond, a kingdom not of this earth: 'the pilgrim was a *hospes mundi*, a guest of the world.'[21] Thus the pilgrim is both at home and not at home on the earth. The pilgrim moves, yet the pilgrimage is consummated by reaching a particular place, a shrine or other sacred place. Margaret Visser's treatment of the church of Sant' Agnese fuori le Mura in Rome is notable because it treats the church not only as the endpoint of pilgrimage, but as the site of pilgrimage itself; her book focuses on the theological resonances of the pilgrim's journey through the space of the church.[22] Pilgrimage may be deployed as a spiritual metaphor in numerous ways. Philip Sheldrake argues that even mystics whose movements may be severely circumscribed utilize themes of 'journeys and perpetual departures'.[23] Pilgrimages, or spiritual journeys, may be interior events.

Discussions of place soon become complicated by the insistence of movement. From the prevalence of boundary erosion between places in modernist texts to the significance of pilgrimage to constructions of sacred space, movement intrudes on the arena of place from a variety of directions. Postcolonial studies provide an insistent foregrounding of movement in attending to issues of contested territory, migration, displacement, exile and diaspora. Postcolonial scholars have complicated issues of place, emplacement and identity. James Clifford shifts the anthropological opposition between 'cosmopolitan (travellers)' and 'local (natives)' and argues for a comparative cultural studies approach that examines 'travelling-in-dwelling' and 'dwelling-in-travelling.'[24] He argues that for many common assumptions of culture:

> Dwelling was understood to be the local ground of collective life, travel a supplement; roots always precede routes. But what would happen [...] if travel were untethered, seen as a complex and pervasive spectrum of human experiences? Practices of displacement might emerge as *constitutive* of cultural meanings rather than as their simple transfer or extension.[25]

Through this lens, Clifford sees 'heterogeneous modernity' where cultural centres and territories are sustained through contact with influences from elsewhere and continually traversed.[26] However, some scholars are wary of dismissing the space of 'home' too quickly (and indeed, in coining the phrase 'dwelling-in-travelling', Clifford is not so much dismissing 'home' as relocating it within a framework of movement).[27]

Postcolonial theologians such as Wonhee Anne Joh have emphasized roots *and* routes, arguing that the two terms complicate and illuminate each other, and suggesting their relevance for new theological endeavours:

> We might return to our origins, but the origins are forever changed and changing while we also change. [...] It is from these experiences of fragmentation [...] that I have come to realize that 'home' and 'elsewhere' are neither fixed, monolithic, nor unproblematic categories. As Sang Hyun Lee, a Korean American theologian, observes, this sense of homelessness might in turn be interpreted as a 'sacred journey.' This metaphor of 'journey' embodies both the remembering of our past roots and the forging of new routes.[28]

In Joh's formulation, 'home' becomes a place that is also a factor of movement, an interior space that participates in the sacred journey that is open to both past and future and their continually evolving relationship. In becoming part of a sacred journey, 'home' may be figured as a sanctuary-that-moves, an imagined space that yields healing and shelters new, creative gestures in its interaction with 'elsewhere'. As Kwok Pui-lan argues, attention to routes can provide a corrective to nostalgic desires for return to a pure origin that may flatten and distort difference: 'While such a desire may have the positive effect of resisting the fragmented and disjointed experience imposed by colonialism, it may also lead to the danger of reification of the past and the collapse of differences from within'.[29] This emphasis on difference has implications for identities constructed in the interstice between roots and routes. Joh draws upon Stuart Hall and Jacques Derrida to develop a dynamic concept of identity:

> The 'trace' of our 'origins' assumes *the supplement* necessary for living on the boundary, in the interstitial space, where sense of wandering and lostness

> prevail, but more importantly, where tantalizing memories of 'the trace' work effectively to fuel the vision needed to *move into* flourishing and sustaining life in between. Identity then is under continuous erasure even as it is reconstructed and reappropriated with close attunement to the 'trace' that works as an enlivening supplement.[30]

Joh is not advocating a teleological wandering oriented towards a return to origins but a revisioning of the possibilities for living 'in between' in ways that are oriented towards flourishing. It is this kind of interstitial flourishing and sustaining life-in-movement that I explore in relation to Cixous's and H.D.'s work.

Before turning to the specifics of their work, I wish to add a brief note on terminology. In her discussion of diasporic imagination, Kwok Pui-lan indicates the wide relevance of such discourse:

> Today, the term 'diaspora' shares a broader semantic domain that includes words like immigrant, expatriate, refugee, migrant worker, exile community, and ethnic and racial minorities. Diasporic discourse is currently appropriated by people who may not have experienced forced dispersion, who do not share the longing for a return to the homeland, or who may shuttle between the homeland and the host land in continuous commute. It connotes at once the experience of decentred and yet multiple-centred, displaced and yet constantly relocated, peoples who crisscross many borders.[31]

This appropriation may appear quite problematic when one considers H.D.'s and Cixous's economic, educational and racial privilege and the impact of this privilege on their ability to choose their modes of movement. Despite the depth of the semantic field indicated by Kwok, I am wary of using the terminology of exile or migrancy in this study. This chapter is primarily interested in writing that positions movement positively as a space of potential flourishing. This is not to suggest that issues of territory and migration are not difficult, traumatic and un-chosen for many people. However, I will primarily consider Cixous and H.D. in the context of expatriation or nomadism. Rosi Braidotti distinguishes nomadism from migrancy and exile, suggesting that nomads generally enjoy greater freedom of movement and choice.[32] However, the experience of expatriation is often fraught with complex psychological legacies:

> Expatriation, like love, is not only a condition that devastates and reconfigures the self; it is, like love, a trope, a figure with which we try to explain, to narrate profound psychological disruptions in terms of very measurable entities: a person, a place, an event, a moment, etc.[33]

Cixous most explicitly articulates expatriation, the experience of being foreign, in amorous terms, while psychological disruptions and physical dislocation are brought together in numerous texts by H.D.

Fragrant dust: Gardens in Oran

'In Oran, I had a very strong feeling of paradise, even while it was the war and my family was hit from all sides: by the concentration camps in the North, by Vichy in Algeria.'[34] These two images, paradise and unjust exclusion or destruction, are at the heart of Cixous's writing. The garden is an important trope in Cixous's work, allowing diverse explorations into Algeria, family, knowledge, sensuality, creativity. In speaking of her childhood in Algeria, Cixous invokes the garden, the Biblical image for paradise, yet this does not encode nostalgia for an imagined, lost, perfect childhood.[35] Her writing explores the complications, difficulties and losses of growing up Jewish in a French colony during the 1940s: 'North Africa was an arid and perfumed theatre, salt, jasmine, orange blossoms, where violent plays were staged. The scene was always war.'[36] Cixous does not consider the garden to be a site of pre-lapsarian perfection and innocence; rather, she chooses the inside of the fruit, to taste and to know. Moreover, the garden becomes the scene for an expulsion that occurs through the anti-Semitic politics of the Vichy government: 'The first garden out of which I was expelled was the "Cercle Militaire" in Oran. In 1940 we were thrown out as Jews.'[37] Cixous describes her experiences in this garden as a painful initiation to the dynamics of exclusion:

> My father was a military officer during the war (temporarily, because he was a doctor), so suddenly we were admitted to the only garden in Oran (Oran is a very desert city), that of the Officers' Club. But the place was a hotbed of anti-Semitism. I was three years old, I hadn't the slightest idea that I was Jewish. The other children started attacking me, and I didn't even know what it was to be Jewish, Catholic and so on.[38]

The garden is, of course, already marked by class and colonialism; it is because he is an officer in the French military that Georges Cixous and his family are admitted there in the first place. However, Cixous also claims that the political markers of nationalism, colonialism and anti-Semitism are insufficient to contain the burgeoning growth of the garden. She opposes the regimen of the formal garden with a wildly exuberant creativity: 'I skirted the walls of their French parks with my abundance, my drunken lands, my wild orchards.'[39] The wild orchard suggests the paradox of the garden, a space that is both wild and cultivated, the interstice of nature and culture that suggests that neither exists without the other.

In *To Live the Orange*, Cixous presents us with an abstract, imagined garden, one that is located both within the heart and between persons:

> [...] when we have not yet lost the gardens of Encounters [...] we conjure them up, stone after stone, each mountain, each orange, each stone of plant each fruit of sky each, and brooding before the heap of stars, planted before the flower of each face, we open ourselves up to things, we anticipate them, with words gathered on the carpet of the garden, with bouquets of words whose names we don't know, we do all that we can so that they will feel called upon, we water them with our regards [...] the seedings of earth and one by one, touched, they come towards us, and in their way of entering the garden by way of the breast, and of bearing themselves very gentle, very strong to encounter the heart, without detour, and of being there at the bottom of the garden in front of the heart, we sense that they are women, that we love [...]. To know them is to live.
>
> To learn everything by the light of things [...] letting roses grow in the garden of one's heart [...] understanding that space is the élan, in the breast the slow spaces of thoughts in full sunshine, [...] being garden and vigil, ground and roots, and thus waiting for everything, being the anticipation of each thing, the repose of the stone, the restiveness of the crocus on the eve of the first of march [...] we hear others living, everything calls and vibrates [...] telling us their names, giving us their names to say, to not forget. [...] But too often we forget. [...] Our tongues are deserted. We live there no more. We forget ourselves. And all of the gardens become phantoms.[40]

As I have previously discussed, Cixous argues that attending to the memory of atrocities is a necessary task for the writer. Yet her writing is far from bleak – she holds the responsibility of remembering alongside her delight in the presence of others. For Cixous the sweetness of fruit and the fragrance of flowers suggest an openness to the other that is not innocent. In this long description of the 'garden of Encounters', Cixous uses concrete, precise images – stones, flowers, sky, crocuses on the eve of the first of March – in a surrealist style. Stars are piled up like fruit stones, flowers are placed in the sky like stars and this strange vigil by the roots of trees becomes a metaphor for encounters with other women. These images are the markers of the intimacies of human communion experienced within the body, felt, touched and tasted. Moreover, the flowers, stones and oranges are also names, thus language and the sensual materiality of human encounter are brought together. Forgetting others is figured as a failure of imagination; others and the flowers and fruits of the garden go together. To forget entails a loss of creativity.

The aridity of the Algerian landscape is not something Cixous welcomes. She uses it as a metaphor for writer's block, 'dry silence', while the return of creativity is marked as succulent fruit: 'She [Clarice Lispector, as encountered through her writing] put the orange back into the deserted hands of my writing, and with her orange-colored accents she rubbed the eyes of my writing which were arid and covered with white films.'[41] However, the dry soil itself, the dust, functions alongside the fruits and flowers of the garden as a source of pleasure and delight. Cixous reverses the expected evaluation of dust. As she said in the interview quoted in the introduction, she considers the grain of dust to be a diamond, infinitely precious and beautiful: 'I believe that the stone is a diamond [...] What interests me is precisely to enable the celebration of the grain of dust.'[42]

The idea of 'native earth' is undermined in Cixous's writing. She loves the dust of Oran, not because she belongs there but because she does not, because she is foreign. It is not her own and she loves it not as a birthright but as a passion:

> In the smiling and happy little girl I was, I hid [...] a secret, restless, clandestine little girl, who knew well that in truth she had been born elsewhere. [...] [T]he physical feeling of being a frail mushroom [...] who only holds to the earth with hasty and frail roots. Another feeling in the shadows: the unshakeable certainty that 'the Arabs' were the true offspring of this dusty and perfumed soil. But when I walked barefoot with my brother on the hot trails of Oran, I felt the sole of my body caressed by the welcoming palms of the country's ancient dead.[43]

Here the dust itself participates in paradise, holding perfume as would flowers. In this essay, dust is an image that holds together life and death, foreignness and belonging. It is death, rather than birth that ties her to the land:

> I left my father there to mix his dust with that dust, a tribute paid to a borrowed land.
>
> To leave behind the grave of one's father: through dust I acquire a sort of invisible belonging to a land to which I am bound by my atoms without nationality. Because of the phantom of my father I cannot be patriated anywhere.[44]

Not only does her father's death confer belonging – albeit a precarious, 'sort of invisible belonging' – but it precludes subsequent possibilities for belonging anywhere else. Her father's dust mixes with Algeria's 'ancient dead' and therefore participates in the welcoming gesture towards the barefoot little girl from elsewhere who will always both belong and not belong to Oran.

H.D.'s garden in the city

Before the fruit comes the blossom and it is the blossom that is important to H.D. In considering the significance of gardens in H.D.'s poetry the most obvious point of entry is her first collection, *Sea Garden*, published in 1916. The poems of *Sea Garden* do not overtly address their historical context, the First World War, but, as Friedman points out, their implicit argument that 'poetry fostered faith' as the basis for post-war regeneration would be rendered explicit in *The Walls Do Not Fall*. Moreover, conflict and struggle pervade the volume; '[n]ever directly *about* it, *Sea Garden* is nonetheless *of* the Great War'.[45] Although my focus here is on H.D.'s Second World War writing, I will consider *Sea Garden* briefly before turning to the gardens in *Trilogy*. As we will see, both evoke places of sacred encounter.

The title of H.D.'s initial collection is the first indication that H.D.'s gardens are not traditional. *Sea Garden* emphasizes the liminal space where two differing environments meet: the boundary (which both separates and connects) between sea and shore. The poems play on the ambiguity of this unusual terrain. However, as Eileen Gregory points out, taken together the poems construct a particular landscape: 'desolate sandy beach strewn with broken shells, large promontories and rocky headlands; inland, a barren stretch of sparse but hardy vegetation beyond the beach, and low wooded hills nearby; deeper inland, the marshes and places of luxuriant or cultivated growth'.[46] *Sea Garden* erodes the boundary between cultivation and wilderness. The volume celebrates the orchard's pear tree, but also the wild poppy, whose 'stalk has caught root/among wet pebbles/and drift flung by the sea' (1983, p. 21). The sea garden is a space of contradiction – wilderness and cultivation, briny salt and sweet honey, flowers that are stony and brittle – in which the predominant characteristic is the wind.

Gregory argues that the island spaces of *Sea Garden* are influenced by Sappho's Lesbos, a sacred space consecrated to and by Aphrodite: 'The rich and dense fragrance of frankincense mingles with the delicate odors of flowers, and the murmur of cold water through graceful trees blends with the exquisite shadowing of roses. [...] Moreover, the "sacred grove" is the poem itself.'[47] The poems may be read as ritual incantations: 'The poems in *Sea Garden* are thrown out as bridges to the sacred.'[48] In Morris's reading, writing is envisioned as a movement through space. Through this process the divine is invited into a particular place. This understanding of the construction of sacred space within poetry is dynamic, hence the significance of the ever-moving wind in *Sea Garden*.

In her essay 'Wise Sappho' H.D. brings together wind and myrrh's fragrance to indicate a sensual wisdom at the meeting point of East and West: 'Wisdom [...] stood in the heavy Graeco-Asiatic sunlight, the wind from Asia, heavy with ardent myrrh and Persian spices, was yet tempered with a Western gale [...] its salt sting' (1982, p. 63). As in Cixous's garden writing, the senses, particularly smell, are central to *Sea Garden*. Fragrance indicates the inescapable materiality of places; the use of sensual and material images in evoking imagined or textual spaces establishes their interconnection with material places. Diana Collecott details the way H.D.'s engagement with the sensuality of Sappho and other Greek poets and her emphasis on their diversity of location and religion establishes an aesthetic that is 'centrifugal rather than centripetal, Asiatic rather than Attic [...] colourful, variegated'.[49] Thus fragrance also becomes a mode of challenging the racist and sexist modes of Hellenism that 'identified civilisation as *Attic* and barbarism as *Asiatic*' in its concern with aesthetic (and racial) purity.[50]

Fragrance also marks sacred space. Indeed, reading *Sea Garden*, with its debt to Sappho, alongside *Trilogy* indicates that fragrance can be read as a marker for the syncretism of paganism and Christianity. In *Sea Garden* the garden is the place of divine, rather than romantic, encounter, even if this encounter is erotically charged. *Sea Garden* as a whole presents a landscape that is the space of ritual and the poems suggest a ritual intent of initiation into its mysteries.[51] The final poem in the volume, 'Cities', suggests a return from this marginal space to an urban centre. This city is a crowded, wasted place, not unlike the city in Eliot's *The Wasteland*, lacking beauty and honey's sweetness. Gregory argues that the placement of the poem at the end of the volume indicates the urgency of the sea garden's rites: 'The city *necessitates* the sea garden [...] a place distinct from, yet within, the city – like old cells of honey in a new hive – where beauty is remembered'.[52]

Trilogy is another text in which we find gardens within the city, although here the distinction between urban and green space is more complex. In H.D.'s writing of the 1940s, the particularity and historicity of places is foregrounded. This is not the London of Clarissa Dalloway's or Miriam Henderson's distracted perambulations, but the wartime city of dangerous instability where the very atmosphere is treacherous. *The Walls Do Not Fall* is bracketed by evocations of the bombed city. It opens: 'An incident here and there,/and rails gone (for guns)/ from your (and my) old town square/[...]/ruin everywhere', and closes:

there is zrr-hiss,
lightening in a not-known

unregistered dimension
[...]
dust and power fill our lungs
our bodies blunder. (1:1–16, 43:3–8)

This opening volume of *Trilogy* is circular but it does not quite end up where it started – although the war still continues, a journey has been initiated that will lead away from the war-torn city: '*we are voyagers, discoverers/ of the not-known*' (43:27–8). The form of *Walls* suggest a spiral, a shape that appears again in the circling geese and opening flower of the final volume, *The Flowering of the Rod*, and will be crucial in H.D.'s post-war text *The Sword*. The spiral functions as a geometric, spatial version of H.D.'s palimpsest, which has been more often read in terms of time than of space.

H.D. employs the space of the garden in the city to explore survival, regeneration and vision. The liminal, sacred space between sea and land of *Sea Garden* reappears in *Walls:*

let us go down to the sea,

gather dry sea-weed,
heap drift-wood,

let us light a new fire
and in the fragrance

of burnt salt and sea-incense
chant new paeans to the new Sun

of regeneration. (17:8–15)

Here we do not have a garden as such, although 'fragrance' is reminiscent of one. In the second volume of *Trilogy*, *Tribute to the Angels*, a garden square, clearly located in London, becomes a sacred space. This is not a private suburban garden, but an urban space shared with numerous others.[53] The poet has a vision of a charred tree, 'burnt and stricken to the heart', that is also in flower (19:13). The burnt yet blossoming tree is an image of redemption, divinity and vision. H.D. brings together destruction and renewal and declares that divinity may be found in multiple places, not only in the blossom, but also in the charred remains. This is a vision in which the poet draws in her companions using the choric first person plural:

We are part of it;
we admit the transubstantiation,

not God merely in bread
but God in the other-half of the tree

that looked dead –
[…]
yet it was vision,
it was a sign,

it was the Angel which redeemed me,
it was the Holy Ghost –

a half-burnt-out apple-tree
blossoming. (23:1–14)

H.D. references the Christian Eucharist but also extends sacramentality to include the ordinary transformations of a tree in spring, thus bringing together Christian and pagan imagery. She locates redemption with the angels, the Holy Ghost and the burnt yet blossoming tree, suggesting that redemption is to be found in divine presence. Yet, for all its divinity, H.D. resists reading this vision as transcendent. She emphasizes the mundane, everyday aspect of this vision: 'it was an ordinary tree/in an old garden-square' (20:13–14). The boundary between private and public, already represented by the urban garden square surrounded by houses, becomes further destabilized as the square may well be surrounded by crumbling buildings and rubble. Divinity is hidden within the material.

In *Angels*, H.D. describes a transfigured city. The destruction of buildings allows the boundary between garden and city to be more readily transgressed. In the found spaces of destroyed buildings, plants grow. Thus we have an unusual construction of a garden that is more like the partially wild, partially cultivated space of *Sea Garden*, this time within the city:

the levelled wall

is purple as with purple spread
upon an altar,

[…]

where Uriel, we pause to give
thanks that we rise again from death and live. (7:6–12)

Unexpected flowers transform a fallen wall into an altar, a place of thanksgiving. Here, as elsewhere, H.D. emphasizes the necessity of hope.

We have seen how gardens – both the material gardens of Oran and London and the metaphorical, textual gardens of *Sea Garden* and *To Live the Orange* – are complicated places in Cixous's and H.D.'s writing. They are versions of the Garden of Eden that are locations for delight or exclusion, or spaces for ritual. In *Trilogy* H.D. revises the description of the city from *Sea Garden*. As squares open, the garden permeates the city, transforming its entirety into a sacred place:

> For Uriel, no temple
> but everywhere,
>
> the outer precincts and the square
> are fragrant. (*Angels* 18:1–4)

In this image of the city as a place of worship H.D. layers the paganism of *Sea Garden*'s homage to Sappho and Aphrodite (she mentions 'Love's sacred groves') with the Christian understanding of the sanctuary as the place for the celebration of the Eucharist (18:8). In *The Gift* and *The Sword* she develops a similar syncretism, suggesting that particular places are palimpsests of traditions:

> Mary, Maia, Miriam, Mut, Madre, Mère, Mother, pray for us, dark Mary, Mary, mère, mer; [...]This is Gaia, this is the beginning. This is the end. [...] There is, beneath the carved super-structure of every temple to God-the-father, the dark cave or grotto or inner hall or cella to Mary, mère, Mut, Mutter, pray for us. (1998a, pp. 113–14)[54]

This litany of names anticipates the more explicit alchemical process enacted by language in *Angels*. In both texts 'mère, Mother, Mary' enact a ritual that not only evokes the feminine divine, but also suggests that the ritual use of language is crucial to sanctifying space. I will return to the connections between language and sacred places, but first I wish to turn to the metaphor that complicates notions of place and emplacement: movement, or, more specifically, flight – the metaphor that denotes a way of being in space that disrupts settled or rooted self-understanding.

Cixous's Algeriance

As we have seen in her writing on the gardens of Oran, Cixous's understanding of her own emplacement is always complicated by a sense of her foreignness. This informs her approach to identity, language and writing more broadly. Language is intimately related to nationality and forms a complex constellation in Cixous's texts. Her attitude towards French nationality is different from her attitude to the French language: one she resists, the other she courts. For Cixous, being within French (the language) but not-French (the nationality) is a complex but compelling play of identity markers that provides a passport to literature.

Cixous follows Virginia Woolf's outsider when she declares: 'From 1955 on, I adopted an imaginary nationality which is literary nationality.'[55] The famous declaration, from a member of the fictional Society of Outsiders, 'as a woman I have no country' has been both celebrated and criticized by subsequent feminist thinkers.[56] Adrienne Rich has critiqued the statement for its false universalism, but Susan Stanford Friedman argues that Rich misreads Woolf.[57] Friedman contends that Woolf's manifesto is carefully situated within a critique of militarism and nationalism, and 'thus [it] implicitly advocates a transnational oppositional identity that replaces patriotism'.[58] Moreover, Woolf's texts can be read as 'ethnographies of travelling'.[59] Likewise, Cixous's claim to literary nationality does not indicate a refusal to engage with the politics of national identity (her criticism of French colonialism in North Africa is evidence of this engagement) but a choice to attend to the implications for personal belonging within literature and the traces of nationality, ethnicity and other differences that are evident within the literary realm. This may be seen in her literary criticism, where her work crosses numerous national lines (she considers literature from Ireland, France, Germany, Russia and Brazil), and in the fictional text *Manna: for the Mandelstams for the Mandelas* (1994), which ventures from Russia to South Africa in its exploration of the terrains of an exile that is not an ecstatic flight but one fraught with pain and loss.

Cixous's analysis of her family's journeys and national identity indicates the complexity and confusion generated by national boundaries:

> To be French, and not a single French person on the genealogical tree admittedly it is a fine miracle [...].
>
> The paradox of this passport: having it always closed me in a double-bind.
>
> On one hand 'I am French' is a lie or a legal fiction.

> On the other to say 'I am not French' is a breach of courtesy. And of the gratitude due for hospitality. The stormy, intermittent hospitality of the State and the Nation. But the infinite hospitality of the language.[60]

Her sense of 'luck' is such that she recognizes the value of the ability to move across boundaries, granted by the possession of a French passport. It was the possession of a French passport (due to the shifting French and German national boundary before and after the First World War) that enabled her grandmother and mother to emigrate to Algeria before the Second World War.[61] While Cixous acknowledges the privileges that come with her French passport, situating herself as a guest of both nation and language, she emphasizes that the delights of being French stem from France's position as a coastal nation which is constantly traversed by foreigners. Its boundaries are porous.

For Cixous, writing is always caught up with movement: 'Journeys, traversals, are the very stuff of all her writing'.[62] She is concerned with the speed of writing, detailing her efforts as a writer to catch a glimpse of language as it rushes past, but without holding it fast. Writing is also a message from elsewhere: 'A poem merely passes, coming from elsewhere then moving on. Signifying to us, in passing, at its passage, this elsewhere.'[63] The image of writing as messenger correlates with H.D.'s attention to Hermes, the messenger god. However, Cixous also suggests that movement and place are co-implicated. The mysterious elsewhere of writing's origin is a place that is not specific, but that indicates continual *dis*placement. 'Elsewhere' is a term that resonates across Cixous's texts, as we have seen in her writing on the dust of Oran. It is an/other space that serves to destabilize her belonging in Algeria, mirroring her own sense of herself as other:

> My way of thinking was born with the thought that I could have been born elsewhere, in one of the twenty countries where a living fragment of my maternal family had landed after it blew up on the Nazi minefield. [...] The strange molecule detached from the black skies of the north had landed in Africa.[64]

The sense of the precariousness of history's interaction with geography marks much of Cixous's work. Her family is described as merely a fragment, haunted by those who were lost in the concentration camps, whose roots will always be fragile. Lynn Penrod argues that 'the very concept of exile "from" is one, which, in Cixous's case, would be difficult to argue. Yet it is perhaps the very concept of "exile" in the fullest sense of its ambiguity and complexity that serves as the basic creative motor behind all her writing.'[65] While I am still uncomfortable with using the word exile in relation to Cixous's work, Penrod's argument is compelling. We have seen how, even in enigmatic texts like *To Live the Orange*, Oran is present not only in the locution 'Oran-je' (orange/Oran-I), but also in the play of aridity and sweetness within the text.[66] Cixous's relationship with (the memory of) places (Oran and Algiers), and movement from them, is clearly generative, whether termed exile, expatriation or nomadism. Cixous's departure from Algeria is both literal and metaphorical, a departure that marks the impossibility of her belonging to Algeria:

> When I was three [...] I knew that I was destined to leave. [...] I was in deferment and flight. [...] My own maternal family, the German one, had already detached itself from its earth (Strasbourg, Budapest, Osnabrück, Bratislava, etc.). The possibility of living without taking root was familiar to me. I never call that exile. Some people react to expulsion with the need to belong. For me, as for my mother, the world sufficed. [...] (In the family mode of dwelling there remained a nomad's simplicity: never any furniture. Always the backpack). I did not lose Algeria, because I never had it, and I never was it. I suffered that it was lost for itself, separated from itself by colonialization. If ever I identified it was with its rage at being wounded, amputated, humiliated. I always lived Algeria with impatience, as being bound to return to its own.[67]

Cixous lists the Eastern and Central European cities of her maternal family but never indicates that returning to Europe involves homecoming; rather, it is 'deferment and flight'. However, she also refuses to consider the loss of Algeria as an action that places her in exile because Algeria always already belonged to others. Thus she claims a rootless belonging, a nomadic mode of living: 'always the backpack'.

It is movement, departure, always-already departing that Cixous identifies with the process of writing:

> I went towards France, without having had the idea of arriving there. Once in France I was not there. I saw that I would never arrive in France. [...] [T]he chance of my genealogy and history arranged things in such a way that I would *stay passing*; in an originary way for me I am always passing by, in *passance*. I like the progressive form and the words that end in *-ance*. [...] To depart (so as) not to arrive from Algeria is also, incalculably, a way of not having broken with Algeria. [...] I want arriv*ance*, movement, unfinishing in my life. It is also out of departing that I write.[68]

She coins the term 'Algeriance' to signify this perpetual departure, the process of leaving that carries Algeria with her.[69] She undermines any stable definition of origin or emplacement; immigration is impossible and origin itself is located in movement. These movements are correlated with language and the formalities of grammar in Cixous's texts, 'the progressive form', but she also correlates them with the activity of writing itself: 'To fly/steal is woman's gesture, to steal into language to make it fly.'[70]

H.D.'s expatriatism: Spirals and beelines

As Bryony Randall has pointed out, few critics have devoted attention to the permutations of H.D.'s national identity when considering her writing.[71] H.D. began her expatriate nomadism in 1911 when she left the United States bound for Europe. In 1913 she married the Englishman Richard Aldington, and thus, according to the law of the time, became a British citizen. The marriage broke up during the First World War but the couple did not divorce until 1938. In 1959 she regained an American passport. Her daughter was then living in the United States and H.D. travelled there several times in the 1950s.[72] In the 1940s, indications of H.D.'s (inter)nationalism reveal a complex, even contradictory, picture. She was committed to remaining in London during the war, despite being urged by many friends to return to the United States. After the war, however, she returned to Switzerland and never lived in England again. She wrote her most English book, *By Avon River* (a poetic tribute to Shakespeare and a series of essays on English Renaissance poetry), in this period but the volume was begun as preparation for a series of lectures she planned to give in the United States as part of an attempt to heighten American sympathy for the British struggle against Hitler. Her prose from this period – *Tribute to Freud*, *The Gift*, *The Sword* and *The Mystery* – is concerned with forging connections between Pennsylvania and Europe. These details suggest the complexity of emplacement for expatriates. As her commitment to Europe remained, her self-awareness as American grew. Although passionately committed to England in the 1940s, H.D., like Virginia Woolf, eschewed nationalism.[73] I would suggest that this is one reason for the alternative histories in her writing of this period.

Susan Stanford Friedman coins the term 'expatriatism' to 'suggest more than the fact of expatriation in the commitment to and necessity of a self-imposed exile in the lives of H.D. and many other modernists.'[74] Friedman argues that for writers like H.D. expatriatism is not necessarily primarily about crossing national boundaries but is 'above all a flight from […] the norms of Victorian femininity that clashed with the demands of creativity'. She compares H.D.'s transatlantic flight to Virginia Woolf's flight across London to Bloomsbury and Emily Dickinson's commitment to a life of seclusion.[75] Friedman stresses the double meaning of flight, 'both fleeing from oppression and flying in freedom', and argues that the early poems of *Sea Garden* are poems of flight in that they celebrate a space of imaginative freedom in which H.D. evades the expectations of conventional femininity.[76]

What is most significant for my purposes is the quality of commitment and choice in the construction of expatriatism, although, as Friedman suggests, choice is a fraught term that easily elides the psychological and social pressures that may be at play in the attempt of women writers to find their literary voices (here the double meaning of flight is most helpful). Nevertheless, H.D. clearly did choose, in some way, to leave the United States as a young woman and to live the rest of her life in Europe. Her movements more closely approximate Braidotti's notion of nomadism than does Cixous's headlong, singular, ongoing flight.

H.D.'s routes across Europe and North Africa suggest a commitment to being 'elsewhere' rather than a sense of simply exchanging one passport for another. She lived in, or frequently visited: London, Cornwall, Switzerland, Berlin, Vienna and Lugano, while shorter trips to the Scillies, the Greek islands and Egypt provided significant emotional, spiritual experiences that would preoccupy her for years. Friedman argues that H.D.'s travels across Europe in the 1920s and early 1930s (her most peripatetic period) align a 'geographical homelessness' with 'spiritual exile' and were largely undertaken in search of healing.[77] Randall argues that H.D.'s expatriatism emerges through an ambivalent relationship to national identity that can be traced in her early autobiographical novels.[78]

H.D.'s nomadic wandering became more circumscribed in the late 1930s and thereafter; she settled into a routine of movement between domiciles in London and Switzerland before the war and Switzerland and Italy after the war. She may have experienced a certain spiritual grounding after her previous 'geographical homelessness', but her expatriatism remained a significant force in her writing life. I have considered the significance of specific places and imagined spaces to H.D.'s Second World War writing, from the material places of bombed London to more abstract dreamscapes. I would argue that, as with Cixous, H.D.'s own expatriatism is explored through the tropes of movement in her writing. As the wind is a signifier of incessant movement within *Sea Garden*, so movement is a crucial element of her later work.

In *By Avon River* (1949) H.D. turns from the myth and ritual that informed *Trilogy* to the scene of history, while in *The Sword* she brings the two together. In Chapter Three I considered the place of ritual in *The Sword* with its alignment with the drama of play and procession. I would also argue that the stories of different epochs – mapped onto Delia's personal history, dreams and spiritualist visions – bring the scene of history and the space of ritual together. In *The Sword* H.D. relocates *Trilogy*'s search for heaven to a preoccupation with the ground, sanctuaries and sacred remnants under the earth. The flight that is represented in *Trilogy*'s circling geese is not absent from *The Sword* but displaced onto a spiritual quest that is concerned with drawing together mythic and historical geographies. In her post-war work of the late 1940s H.D. is concerned with piecing together sacred remnants to create something new, and thus healing her own physical, psychic and spiritual wounds. She considers physical displacement to allow for temporal explorations, thus providing a justification for the temporal shifts that follow (2007, p. 64). H.D. uses the trope of movement to layer time and place. Of particular significance to this discussion is the use of spatial metaphors to figure the compression of time and place. Moreover, these metaphors are also aligned with the sacred, referencing the places of sanctuary and the movements of ritual: 'But in fifth-century Athens, the actual straight line was curved, in the foundation of the most famous temple of antiquity and of all time' (p. 95).

The curved line, the spiral or the zigzag (a line bent back on itself) are interrelated figures that draw together space and time in *Trilogy* and *The Sword.* These shapes are somewhat different but all share the feature of openness, and H.D. tends to use them in similar ways across numerous texts – in particular, to indicate movement. The zigzag, what H.D. would call a 'Z-line' or 'bee-line', is like the spiral in that it knits diverse places together. The spiral or the zigzag suggests the possibility of movement that is somewhat cyclical, allowing for numerous departures and returns, yet not static. The spiral's openness signals both change and a re-appropriation of the past. The spiral, or Z-line, indicates renewal, thus it is appropriate that H.D. unites this geometric image with the image of the bee. In *The Sword* the zigzag is explicitly tied to particular places, one that maps geography onto a historical palimpsest:

> We followed the Z or the bee-line in its zig-zag track or path across time. Time was conveniently pleated and the pleats lay flat under the chart or map that took us from London or Lausanne, to Lugano, to Knossos, to Athens, to Delphi … back to London, to Venice. (p. 214)

Here Delia's textual wandering aligns closely with H.D.'s own material, intellectual and spiritual travels (Knossos and Delphi were significant places for H.D. though she never visited them).

The 'bee-line' returns us to *Trilogy*, where the spiral is a recurring image for transformation. The extended metaphor of the chrysalis in *Walls* is linked to the spiral; H.D. describes withdrawal into a cocoon or shell as the 'time for you to begin a new spiral' (21:9). The zigzag as visionary space is indicated in a more mundane image, 'the turn of the stair', where the initiates pass each other and the Lady appears (*Walls* 13:17, *Angels* 15:14). The space of vision as a space of renewal is indicated in *Rod*:

> Resurrection is a bee-line,
>
> Straight to the horde and plunder,
> The treasure, the store-room,
>
> The honeycomb;
> Resurrection is remuneration,
>
> food, shelter, fragrance
> of myrrh and balm. (7:1–8)

Here the beeline becomes a flight to the sanctuary (figured elsewhere as a beehive), the place of refuge and ritual. The bee and the fragrance of myrrh evoke the garden that is also a ritual space. Thus the spiral/beeline indicates movement *and* place: the turn of the stair, a spiralled shell, circling geese, a route across a fractured world. The places described in *The Sword* are conflict zones and, although they are damaged, they are also the locations of spiritual power and vision. The beeline sutures the splits but does not erase them.

Writing as sanctuary: Sacred places

As we have seen, place and movement in H.D.'s and Cixous's texts form an intimate dialectic; each complicates and provokes the other, but they are thus brought into close proximity. Flight forms a crucial aspect of H.D.'s and Cixous's spatial poetics, while gardens are portrayed as the source and provocation for flights that enact a nomadism that carries with it the fragrance from dust, fruit and blossom. The nexus of place and movement, garden and flight, can be seen in H.D.'s and Cixous's deployment of sanctuary. If gardens are sanctuaries inasmuch as they are locations of ritual and divine encounter, sanctuary is also the final point of flight, its goal. However, as we have seen, H.D. and Cixous destabilize notions of origin and goal and this deconstructive practice is evident in their deployment of sanctuary as a third term that acts as a nexus of place and movement.

In deploying the beeline as an image for sacred movement and the beehive as a place of refuge, H.D. constructs an idiosyncratic notion of modern pilgrimage. Lodged in language and under the earth, sanctuary is both material and imagined, located both without and within. It is both a shelter and inspiration for creative practice and nurtures the transformations enabled by imagination. In *The Sword* H.D. draws together literal churches and more abstract, visionary space when she describes a dream space which is a refuge and place of healing: 'The bee-hive was at the very centre of the earth. [...] It was as big as Brunelesci's dome, opposite the Baptistery in Florence. [...] I didn't stay long in the bee-hive. I got well there' (p. 53). Here the bee of resurrection is alluded to in an imagined space that is holy and healing. This vision of a sanctuary that is fragile yet enduring as a sacred place underground links Delia's survival with the larger issues of post-war social and environmental recovery. Delia sees the devastation of the earth (both the bombed cities of Europe and the devastation of Japan wrought by the atomic bombs) as linked to a new consciousness which alters her previous vision. The optimism of *The Gift* and *Trilogy* gives way to a more wary and tentative hope that recognizes the bleakness of the post-war world and the challenges and real failures of any movement towards renewal. Her creative, spiritual practice is figured as hard work embedded in the beleaguered earth:

> I had felt the scar. The earth was furrowed with the irrational assaults that man had made upon her. She was always mother-earth. I felt that man was actually assaulting woman. [...] I have left the young men, the heroes who stemmed the tide, who broke the Steel Wall. They belong to the world of beauty. But I lived to see beauty die. [...] There is still something left, but it lives under the ground. It does not live in heaven. If we want to contact spiritual entities, we must drag them up from the earth. (p. 54)

In this strikingly gendered passage, Delia links her own rejection by Lord Howell (and by extension the estrangement of lovers throughout history) with the larger destruction of war. In setting up this gendered dynamic she chooses to align herself not with the RAF pilots, the heroes of war, but with the landscape itself. As such she becomes a witness to the devastation of life and land. Far from a traditional pastoral alignment of passive women with passive earth, this text calls for action beyond the silent witness of the destroyed cities. Delia is determined to be an active agent in nurturing the spiritual remnant. *The Sword* is not just an expression of grief (although it is that) but also a constructive response, 'dragging up' what is living from the ground.

In *The Gift* H.D. presents a more complex version of the beehive as sanctuary.

Here she explores a connection between a physical, historical place and an imagined space located in language:

> [S]omething had come over me like the branches of a tree or the folds of a tent when she says *Wunden Eiland*. [...] I want her to go on talking because if she stops, the word will stop. The word is like a bee-hive, but there are no bees in it now. I am the last bee in the bee-hive, this is the game I play. [...] [C]an one person who knows that *Wunden Eiland* is a bee-hive, keep *Wunden Eiland* for the other bees, when they come back? (pp. 1545)

The sound of the spoken words forms the sanctuary here. It is not a permanent place, but an imagined space located in the sound of Hilda's grandmother's voice speaking words in a language that Hilda does not know (German). The images used to describe this curious sensation suggest both rootedness (the sheltering branches of a tree) and nomadism (the shelter of a tent). H.D.'s wordplay links the Moravian tradition of wounds devotion with Hilda's developing imagination and vision; she thinks that 'Wunden' means wonderful because of its sound, but in fact the word means wounds. Hilda's sense of responsibility for keeping the beehive alive foreshadows *The Sword's* insistence on a sacred remnant that lingers in the beehive. This is a sanctuary that must be maintained. Rather than the space providing a shelter, as we see in *The Sword*, this space itself must be nurtured and protected. By placing a child in the role of witness and caretaker, *The Gift* indicates an orientation to the future and a disruption of generational hierarchies.

The wounded island is, of course, also Britain. In *Trilogy* and *The Gift*, H.D. extends the provisional sanctuary from London to the island and ultimately the entirety of the earth. At the end of *The Gift*, when she has her mystical audition of the litany of wounds, H.D. recognizes a broader understanding of sanctuary: 'Our earth is a wounded island as we swing around the sun' (p. 223). The Moravian devotion to Christ's wounds is reconfigured as attention to a war-torn world that remains a sacred place and site of healing, but one that must also be healed in return. It is this difficult task of healing that H.D. addresses in her post-war writing.

In her post-war historical novel, *The Mystery*, H.D. does not correlate sanctuary as closely with conflict she does in *The Gift* and *The Sword*. The novel is set in Prague in the late eighteenth century and revolutionary fervour and reaction provide background tension, but its focus is the mystical connection between the Moravian Elizabeth de Watteville and the magician and alchemist Louis Saint Germain. This novel returns to the Moravian emphasis of *The Gift*, and more explicitly ties together H.D.'s interest in Moravian history and spirituality with her esoteric concerns. In *The Mystery* H.D. uses spatial metaphors and the conjunction of persons and places to indicate the spiritual concerns of the novel.

Like much of H.D.'s prose, *The Mystery* is an enigmatic text that is difficult to interpret. Its style is markedly different from both *The Gift* and *The Sword*, which contain a plethora of details and meta-textual commentary on the possible meanings and implication of the narratives' events. The challenge to the reader, of *The Sword* especially, is sifting through the detail provided by the narrator. *The Mystery* poses the opposite challenge. It is a brief, spare text and the reader has to read between the lines to fill in the outlines of characters and events. The story is concerned with the remnant of the Knights Templar and the 'Church within the Church' of the Moravians, and the secrets of these groups elude the reader as much as the characters (p. 33).[79]

I do not have the space here to attempt a full exploration of the religious concerns of *The Mystery*. I wish to focus briefly on the Cathedral as a sanctuary and spiritual catalyst. For the purposes of this project, what is most striking about *The Mystery* is the connection it forges between Moravian Christianity and Hermeticism, and this connection's location in St Vitus's Cathedral in Prague. The building is a significant presence in the text. Like the dream sanctuaries of *The Sword*, the physical details of the Cathedral in *The Mystery* are not described at length. What is significant for H.D. is the spiritual resonances between the building and the characters. A place of Christian worship, the Cathedral is also the place where mysterious connections are manifest through spatial phenomenon. It is the meeting place of the magician, alchemist and member of the Knights Templar, Louis Saint-Germain, and Elizabeth de Watteville, the granddaughter of Count Zinzendorf, the Moravian leader.

Elizabeth is the spiritual sister of Anna von Pahlen and Morning Star in *The Gift* and *Trilogy's* enigmatic Lady. She possesses an inner wisdom and sensitivity to environment that resonates with the Cathedral. As she responds to the building, the place itself responds to her. It is not merely the background, setting or crucible but a more active presence: 'the place is seething with overtones' (p. 7). Elizabeth is also associated with the Virgin Mary (as is *Trilogy*'s Lady), an important figure in the background of *The Mystery* until the novel's close, where she is explicitly mentioned as the recipient of Saint Germain's prayers (p. 86). Here H.D. reconfigures the wounds of Christ yet again. I mentioned earlier how the eighteenth-century Moravians figured the wounds as domestic spaces of consolation and spiritual succour. These sanctuaries were then re-imagined by H.D. as a spiritual space within language guarded by the child Hilda. In *The Mystery*, Saint Germain is told that he 'worshipped the Wounds of Our Lord [...] as the *rosa mystica*' (p. 86). This is traditionally a title for Mary, and so the *rosa mystica* is Mary, Dante's mystic rose and Christ's wounds.[80] Thus Mary also acts as a sanctuary, demonstrating the capacity of this metaphor to shift in surprising ways.

Following Elizabeth's visit to light candles in the Cathedral, candles go out despite a lack of wind, doors open the wrong way and the entire Cathedral rotates. The cause of these mysterious events appears to be Elizabeth herself, as the space around her moves in response to the wisdom she contains. As Elizabeth disappears down the aptly named Street of the Alchemists, Moravian and Hermetic spirituality are brought together. Although it has now become a place of a mystery that Saint-Germain fears, he and Elizabeth both discover the Cathedral to be a place that shelters their own spiritual quests. Elizabeth declares, 'I feel I have found it, the answer, the Mystery, when I light the candles in the chapel of Saint Wenceslas' (p. 31). This mystery is never made entirely explicit by H.D.; she is more concerned with emphasizing the need of each generation to discover it anew. However, it is clear that a significant element of this mystery reprises the conclusions of *The Gift* and *The Sword*, the search for peaceful conflict resolution, healing and 'a world-unity without war' (p. 33). The importance for the renewal of wisdom in each generation is made clear by the repeated assertion, '*you must act out* the legend for yourself' (p. 46). This correlates with the Hermetic teaching that experience as well as knowledge is essential to gain wisdom.

The prominence of doorways, and the door that moves unexpectedly, echoes H.D.'s interest in liminal places in *Trilogy* and *Sea Garden*. Yet again the liminal space is one in which the sacred is manifest and questions raised that lead to spiritual insight. The differing traditions of Hermeticism and Moravian Christianity meet in the doorway of the Cathedral that leads to the Street of the Alchemists. The monk who acts as porter becomes a divine messenger who guides Saint Germain towards wisdom (p. 127). The differing spiritual traditions and their unusual connections are generative. In *The Mystery*'s Cathedral H.D. creates a sanctuary for spiritual exploration that enables new understanding to emerge. This resonates with Ricouer's understanding of metaphor as that which generates possible worlds. Like the door that moves in unexpected directions, *The Mystery* contains a double direction: it is set in the past but open to the future. Elizabeth and her brother are focused on the past, searching for clues to the history of the Moravians of the previous generations, but they are also oriented towards the future. They must work out the mystery in the present and pass on their wisdom to the generations to come.

H.D. understands the form and content of her creative work as being intimately connected. In 'H.D. by Delia Alton' she describes all of her prose works ranging from 1926 to 1948 as 'Chapter-houses, adjoining some vast Cathedral'. She goes on to declare that 'the Cathedral is the Dream', thus linking writing, visionary consciousness and sacred space. We see here yet another example of a spatial metaphor for writing. For H.D., *The Sword* embodied this vast Cathedral (pp. 204–5).[81] However, it is in *The Mystery* that this Cathedral of visionary consciousness and creative work is given a physical form.

The sanctuary that moves

In locating sanctuary in a language that escapes mastery by insisting on its foreignness to the speaker or auditor, these texts suggest that sanctuaries are as much a matter of routes as roots. The sanctuary-that-moves finds expression in the Jewish tabernacle, the repository of the Torah that travels with the people. In considering the relationship between settled location and movement within Judaism, Alana Vincent emphasizes that not only was the Torah given to a wandering people but, when King David suggested building the temple, the prophet Nathan has a vision in which 'the resistance of God to a fixed dwelling-place' is made clear.[82] Moreover, '*mishkan* [the Hebrew word for Tabernacle] shares the same root as *shekhinah*, the presence-of-God-dwelling-amongst-Israel.'[83] This suggests to me that, as the tabernacle is the shelter for the Torah and related to an understanding of God as dwelling-with, so God can be understood to reside within the language of Torah.

The relationship between sanctuary and language is also explored in Cixous's work. She presents a slippery construction of this relationship, a möbius strip that folds and unfolds into its own double:

> But god, I say, is the phantom of writing, it is her pretext and her promise. God is the name of all that has not yet been said. Without the word *Dieu* to shelter the infinite multiplicity of all that could be said the world would be reduced to its shell and I to my skin.[84]

The idea of sanctuary as located in language is initially reversed; here, the divine is a refuge for writing, for a language that is open to the future. However, God is also the other of writing, 'her pretext and her promise', the alterity within words and metaphors, 'what has not yet been said'. In this formulation writing becomes God's shelter and dwelling place.

In all the attention to Cixous's call to 'write the body' there has been little attention given to her construction of the body as a sacred text.[85] In 'Coming to Writing' she describes her body itself as a book:

> I am already text. History, love, violence, time, work, desire inscribe it in my body. [...] Vision: my breast as the Tabernacle. Open. My lungs like the scrolls of the Torah. But a Torah without end whose scrolls are imprinted and unfurled throughout time.[86]

The tabernacle is open; the reader is put in the position of the high priest entering the holy of holies. This 'Torah without end' resembles the 'hidden Torah' of Jewish mysticism that existed before the creation of the world and is identified with divine wisdom.[87] Cixous's declaration that her breast is an open tabernacle and her lungs, Torah, indicates that the divine dwells within bodily movement and is as close as breath. The word for breath and spirit is the same in Hebrew: *ruach*. In the beginning of Genesis, it is the *ruach* of God that hovers over the face of the deep and the *ruach* that God breathes into the clay to give it life.[88] Thus, in aligning her lungs with Torah, Cixous draws a connection between her own breathing and the divine spirit that speaks and breathes creation into being. Writing, materiality and divine movement are always already co-implicated.

We have seen how language becomes a sanctuary for both H.D. and Cixous and how particular words become a refuge that shelters creative activity and imagination. These refuges are not closed spaces but are open to the movements of writing towards the future. Language is often figured as a (fragile) home in the literature of exile.[89] In Cixous's work difference in language becomes the means of mapping the complexity of her family's movements across Europe and North Africa. Literary exiles or expatriates often figure their relationship to language in fraught terms – alienation from the 'mother tongue', or from their adopted languages, or both.[90] However, as I noted in the previous chapter, Cixous understands her relationship to language differently; she repeatedly returns to the numerous languages of her childhood as indicative of a lack of a singular mother tongue. This becomes a trope for her belief that she does not belong to, or 'have', a point of origin. But Cixous constructs this lack as plenitude – her lack of a singular origin yields a multiplicity of points of contact. In 'Coming to Writing' Cixous locates the source of her writing practice in her childhood experience of hearing multiple languages within an intimate environment:

> Blessing: my writing stems from two languages, at least. In my tongue the 'foreign' languages are my sources, my agitations. 'Foreign': the music in me from elsewhere; precious warning: don't forget that all is not here, rejoice in being only a particle, a seed of chance, there is no center of the world, arise, behold the innumerable, listen to the untranslatable. [...] Languages pass into my tongue, understand one another, call to one another, touch and alter one another, tenderly, timidly, sensually; blend their personal pronouns together, in the effervescence of differences.[91]

Here writing is the nexus of linguistic and geographic differences and movements. Space and language come together in writing. The 'elsewhere' that continues to re-appear in Cixous's writing is the site of creative sound that cannot be contained, while the 'untranslatable' that must be heard is reminiscent of H.D.'s '*Wunden Eiland*'. Here languages are personified and the sensuality of the writer's experience of speaking and hearing languages is projected onto the languages themselves, which grow and change in their interactions across difference.

Conclusion: Nomadic pilgrimage

The idea of a sanctuary that moves, the sanctuary of the beeline, suggests not only the Jewish tabernacle but also the sacred excursion of pilgrimage. Delia compares the geographical and historical layering of *The Sword* to a pilgrimage: 'I had visualised the pilgrimage or so-called path as winding up a mountain, spiral fashion' (p. 215). Here the spiral is again given a sacred inflection.[92] In considering the relevance of mysticism to the modern age, Michel de Certeau develops the idea of pilgrimage without a goal:

> [I]t seems that what for the most part still remains, in contemporary culture, is the movement of perpetual departure. [...] Unmoored from the 'origin' of which Hadewijch spoke, the traveller no longer has foundation nor goal. Given over to a nameless desire, he [sic] is the drunken boat. Henceforth this desire can no longer speak to someone. [...] It goes on walking, then, tracing itself out in silence, in writing.[93]

This nomadic pilgrimage of perpetual departure echoes Cixous's continual departure and non-arrival. As we have seen with the gardens of Oran and London, of *To Live the Orange*, *Sea Garden* and *Trilogy*, the traveller's foundation may be one she constructs in writing. In naming their desires, Cixous and H.D.

suggest that nomadic pilgrimage may not so much lack a goal, as resituate it, locating it in both the hands that write and the ground beneath the pilgrim's feet. Nomadism and expatriatism do not enact aimless wandering but rather, in their commitment to being elsewhere, follow purposeful creative trajectories.

De Certeau argues that in modernity the sacred is displaced from divine revelation to language: 'We find [...] a progression from a cosmos of divine messages (or "mysteries") to be understood, to itinerant practices which trace in language the indeterminate path of a mode of writing'.[94] H.D. complicates this model of progression because she does not abandon her commitment to apprehending mysteries, her Hermeticism, but places the unfolding of divine messages within an itinerant writing. Cixous's formulation of God as the 'pretext' and 'promise' for writing, paired with her claim that the woman writer is a thief, a bird, a fly-by-night, indicates a sacred space that is by definition open, and that moves with the trajectories of a writing that can never be captured or contained.[95] Thus divinity itself is place, a refuge for writing, for language open to the future. Writing becomes both God's dwelling place and an activity shaped within sacred space. The dialectic of garden and flight, approached through the metaphor of the sanctuary that moves, yields a creative practice that offers a way of being in the world that traverses material places (while continuing to attend to them), seeking divine encounter in myriad forms and gestures.

Notes

1 Brooker and Thacker suggest that a 'historical' turn has followed the 'linguistic' turn in literary studies and that interest in historicized spatiality and geography has followed on from historical materialism. However, linguistic theoretical approaches are not necessarily separate from historical and geographic concerns; 2005a, p. 1.

2 The two definitions merge in the medieval practice of granting fugitives immunity from arrest within a church; Oxford University Press 2010.

3 de Certeau 1992, p. 299.

4 Genesis 3.8; John 19.41–20.18; Bertrand 1995, p. 31; Buruma 2001, p. 34; Scott 2005, p. 133.

5 Although immigration was several generations removed from H.D.'s parents, part of her literary self-description involves constructing a genealogy that draws her closer to the early Moravian immigrants.

6 H.D. and Cixous situate the genesis of their creativity in their birthplaces in numerous texts. A non-exhaustive list would include: H.D. 1975; H.D. 1998a; Cixous 1991; Cixous and Calle-Gruber 1997; Cixous 1998b; Cixous 2006.

7 Scholars engaged in the spatial turn in cultural studies have defined the difference between space and place in different ways. In introducing his overview of different philosophical approaches to the terminology of space and place, Andrew Thacker argues that, generally, for geographical theorists space 'indicates a sense of movement, of history, of becoming, while *place* [...] impl[ies] a static sense of location, of being, or of dwelling'; 2003, p. 13. Avril Maddrell offers a contrasting definition that focuses on meaning: 'while "space" refers to an area or physical container, space becomes place through interaction and signification'; 2010, p. 124. My association of place with material locations and space with imagination and language is related to both of these definitions. 'Space' and 'place' are used loosely here, as the boundary between them is porous.

8 Thacker 2003, p. 4.

9 Smith 1987, p. 28.

10 Schama 1995, p. 7.

11 Critical studies of spatial modernism include: Bronfen 1999; Brooker and Thacker 2005b; Friedman 1998; Thacker 2003. The ongoing interest in this area is indicated by the high number of papers dealing with various 'transnational' modernisms at the Modernist Studies Association's Tenth annual conference in Montreal, November 2009. If the academic predilection for temporality is expressed by the ubiquitous prefix, 'post', then the prefix of the turn towards the spatial is 'trans'.

12 Friedman 1998, pp. 109–14.

13 The disruption of the boundary between inner and outer, private and public is sometimes enacted in violent destruction, as in the acts of war that blow open buildings, and sometimes in a more benign movement from household to street. Examples include Clarissa's movements through home and city in *Mrs Dalloway* and the porch as a place of community discourse and creativity that is vexed for black women in *Their Eyes Were Watching God*; ibid. pp. 128–9. Moreover, the danger of maintaining such boundaries too rigidly is amply shown in a text such as Charlotte Perkins Gilman's *Yellow Wallpaper*; Thacker 2003, pp. 6–7. Urban perambulation may be found in Virginia Woolf's 'Street Haunting' and *Mrs Dalloway*, Dorothy Richardson's *Pilgrimage*, and James Joyce's *Ulysses*, to name just a few examples; see also de Certeau 1984, pp. 91–110. The prototypical urban walker in modernism is the flâneur, or 'impassive stroller', who epitomizes the freedom to move about in public space; however, this is a problematic term for women, who have less freedom to loiter and wander unobserved; Pollock 1988, pp. 94–105.

14 Wenell 2007, p. 4.

15 Jacobs 2005, p. 51.

16 Ibid. p. 52.

17 See, for example, White 1995.

18 Sheldrake 2001, p. 23.

19 Brown 2004, pp. 245–349; McGinn 1995.

20 Brock and Parker 2008, pp. 411–20; Jasper 2004; Lane 1998; Norris 2001; Williams 2001.

21 Sheldrake 2001, p. 116. This is not to suggest that this is the only understanding of pilgrimage. As a practice that occurs in a wide variety of religious, historical and geographic contexts, it is important to remember that pilgrimage is 'a realm of competing discourses'; Eade and Sallnow 1991, p. 5.

22 Visser 2000.

23 Sheldrake 2001, p. 142.

24 Clifford 1997, p. 36.

25 Ibid. p. 3. Kwok Pui-lan argues that Clifford's emphasis on travel as a metaphor for diaspora can occlude the experience of women. She suggest an alternative metaphor, a storyteller who selects fragments to weave together; 2005, p. 46.

26 Clifford 1997, p. 3.

27 For further discussion of the importance of home and belonging, see Baker-Fletcher 1998, pp. 1–7, 37–46; hooks 2009, pp. 1–24.

28 Joh 2006, p. 9.

29 Kwok 2005, p. 39.

30 Joh 2006, p. 4.

31 Kwok 2005, p. 45.

32 Braidotti 1994, pp. 22–3. This is also problematic with respect to traditional tribal nomadism. Braidotti is constructing a contemporary theoretical (even utopian) concept that draws tropes from traditional nomadism (such as distinct patterns of movement) but is distinct from it.

33 Aciman 2000, p. 137.

34 Cixous and Calle-Gruber 1997, p. 196.

35 For a history of the understanding of the Garden of Eden in the Christian West, see Delumeau 1995.

36 Cixous 1998b, p. 208.

37 Ibid. p. 213.

38 Cixous, quoted in Suleiman 1991, pp. xviii–xix.

39 Cixous 1991, p. 46. This imagery is reminiscent of the dangerous 'Outside' in H.D.'s *Notes*, explored in the previous chapter.

40 Cixous 1979, pp. 70–4.

41 Ibid. pp. 12, 14.

42 Cixous 2008, p. 19.

43 Cixous 1998b, p. 205.

44 Ibid. p. 206.

45 Friedman 1990, pp. 60–2.

46 Gregory 1986, p. 536.

47 Ibid. p. 531.

48 Morris 2003, p. 98.

49 Collecott 1999, p. 115.

50 Ibid. pp. 114–16. For further discussion on racism within nineteenth- and early twentieth-century Classicism (in which the Greeks are reconstructed as Aryans), see Gere 2009, pp. 40–2, 112–16.

51 Gregory 1986, p. 538.

52 Ibid. p. 550.

53 London garden squares, developed between 1630 and 1680, were understood as public spaces, more visible than private gardens; Longstaffe-Gowan 2001, p. 183. For a discussion of suburban gardens as a private space for women who had difficulty finding privacy within the home, see Gan 2009.

54 In both *Trilogy* and *The Gift* H.D. references the chthonic matriarchal cults that some anthropologists (including Jane Harrison) believe to have preceded patriarchal religion. Here, she connects the Virgin Mary with ancient goddesses (the reiterated 'pray for us' echoes the end of the 'Hail Mary' prayer: 'Holy Mary, Mother of God, pray for us sinners, now and at the hour of our death'). H.D. indicates a womb-like space in her invocation of 'Mother' and 'the dark cave', yet this is not a regression to a pre-linguistic, undifferentiated state. By exhorting prayer at an altar in an inner hall she establishes ritual as a nexus of bodily experience, emotional life and culture. She simultaneously claims a place for female spirituality in patriarchal religion, replacing Zeus with Gaia. The association of Gaia with the beginning is very close to Jane Harrison's phrase 'Gaia the Earth was first', which is further evidence that H.D. was familiar with Harrison's work; Harrison 1903, p. 261. For a brief history of the 'Hail Mary' see De Marco 2003, pp. 616–17.

55 Cixous and Calle-Gruber 1997, p. 204.

56 Woolf 1966, p. 109.

57 Rich 1986, pp. 210–14. Rich conflates Woolf as narrator with her fictional speaker.

58 Friedman 1998, p. 118.

59 Ibid. p. 120.

60 Cixous 1998b, pp. 206–7.

61 Much of Cixous's extended family remained in Europe and many of her relatives perished in the Holocaust; Cixous and Calle-Gruber 1997, pp. 188–94.

62 Conley 1992, p. 58.

63 Cixous 1998a, p. 6.

64 Cixous 1998b, p. 204.

65 Penrod 2003, p. 136.

66 Cixous 1979, pp. 30–2.

67 Cixous 1998b, pp. 223–4.

68 Ibid. pp. 226–7.

69 Ibid. pp. 204, 30.

70 Cixous and Clément 1996, p. 96.

71 Randall 2009, pp. 191–2. A welcome reversal of this trend comes with the publication of Annette Debo's study on H.D. and nation, *The American H.D.*; 2012.

72 1950s; Guest 1984, pp. 56, 241; Hollenberg 1997, pp. 233, 35–6.

73 In 1933, she wrote: 'I still "see red" when people get foolishly patriotic, in the wrong way. I mean, all sorts of people, English and French and German and American equally. The thing is to keep out of War, but I have been flung into constant cycles of war-scares and war-talk and I hate it all'; H.D. 1933.

74 Friedman 1990, p. 394.

75 Ibid. p. 220.

76 Ibid. pp. 55–6.

77 Ibid. p. 221.

78 Randall 2009, p. 191.

79 Jane Augustine's introduction and substantial annotation provide excellent guidance to the reader and much useful detail on the wider framework of H.D.'s religious interests and research.

80 Dante's vision, like H.D.'s, emphasizes community; his mystic rose is the whole company of heaven in which each soul sees heaven differently and the unity of these unique perspectives forms the entirety of the heavenly vision. Jane Augustine's annotations on *The Mystery* explicate the numerous references to Dante in the text.

81 See also Augustine 2009, p. xxix.

82 Vincent 2010, p. 150. See 2 Samuel 7.5–7. Karen J. Wenell makes a similar point about the tabernacle's portability and origin in the wilderness; Wenell 2007, pp. 25–6.

83 Vincent 2010, p. 150. Further discussion of the significance of *shekinah* for Jewish Feminist Theology is found in Raphael 2003.

84 Cixous 1998b, p. 200.

85 Blyth and Sellers 2004, pp. 30–4; Bray 2004, pp. 28–37; Jones 1997, pp. 373–7; Shiach 1991, pp. 17–21. It is worth noting that Blyth and Sellers do make brief references to Cixous's Jewishness and note her interest in the Talmud as a model for reading, writing and interpretation; however, they do not mention her bodily metaphors in this context: pp. 75–6.

86 Cixous 1991, p. 52.

87 Handelman 1982, pp. 37–8; Plaskow 1990, p. 34.

88 I am grateful to my colleague, Alana Vincent, for reminding me of the connection between breath and spirit in the opening chapters of Genesis.

89 Borrowed languages may also become homes: 'Kafka did not often write about the country in which he was born, but he did write about the language – that is, the homeland – which he came to inhabit'; Manea 2008, p. 1.

90 For further engagement with the fraught issues of language, writing and exile, seeHartman 2008, pp. 135–7; Shreiber 1998, pp. 277–84; Suleiman 1993, p. 171.

91 Cixous 1991, p. 21.

92 A further connection between spirals and pilgrimage can be seen in the medieval labyrinths laid in cathedral floors. Their path functions as a spiral, circling into and out from the centre; walking them was meant to enact a contained form of pilgrimage; see Brown 2004, p. 227.

93 de Certeau 1992, p. 299.

94 de Certeau locates this shift in the mysticism of the early modern period; de Certeau 1986, p. 81.

95 Cixous 1998b, p. 200; Cixous 1997, pp. 356–7.

Conclusion

This book has argued that Cixous and H.D. write a material mysticism through their engagement with alterity, the sacred and the materiality of writing as a creative practice. Reading Cixous and H.D. together highlights the way they both attend to materiality, the sacred and writing as a creative practice. Cixous's and H.D.'s apprehension of the sacred is mystical in its search to move beyond the knowable, to trace the space of alterity in their writing. Their attention to materiality, to the domestic and the mundane, does not imply a domesticated God; rather, in their texts, the domestic and the mundane are made strange and divinity dwells within this alterity.[1] The context of the Second World War, and Cixous's and H.D.'s creative responses to it, have been important for this book. I now turn to an analysis of a poem of H.D.'s from 1943 which allows further exploration H.D.'s religious and creative sensibilities during wartime.

Ancient Wisdom

In 1943 Edith and Osbert Sitwell organized a gala poetry reading in London to promote the arts during war time.[2] H.D. read a poem proclaiming the endurance of Ancient Wisdom, personified as a woman dressed in a blue cloak.[3] 'Ancient Wisdom Speaks' anticipates many of the themes and images of *Trilogy*. Like *Trilogy* this poem is syncretist, drawing upon Jewish, Christian and pagan motifs. Ancient Wisdom herself correlates with the Lady of *Trilogy*, who is related to Holy Wisdom as well as Isis, the 'veiled Goddess', and the Bona Dea (Roman goddess of healing and fertility) (*Angels* 36:2, 37:12, 38:8).[4] The blue that characterizes Ancient Wisdom in H.D.'s poem also suggests the Virgin Mary, whose colour is blue, while the 'snow on your [Wisdom's] sleeve and hood' correlates with Our Lady of the Snow, who is invoked in *Tribute to the Angels* (1983, p. 482, 1998b, *Angels* 36:2, 31:12). Ancient Wisdom personifies the Hermetic ancient wisdom of *The Walls Do Not Fall* while also demonstrating openness to the future in the guise of the Lady with her blank book (*Walls* 15:9, *Angels* 38:11–12).

While H.D.'s religious syncretism leads to Hermetic interpretations of

Moravian Christianity and spiritualism, her work can be read in the Wisdom tradition. The clues provided by the intertextual connections between 'Ancient Wisdom Speaks' and *Trilogy* provide an initial answer to the question of Ancient Wisdom's identity. Additional sources may be found in the biblical Wisdom traditions as well as in Hermeticism's interest in ancient wisdom.[5] In the book of Proverbs, Wisdom (Hokmah in Hebrew, Sophia in Greek) is personified as a woman who participates in creation, calls for justice and unites domestic and public spheres:

> Does not wisdom call,
> and does not understanding raise her voice?
> On the heights, beside the way,
> at the crossroads she takes her stand;
> beside the gates in front of the town,
> at the entrance of the portals she cries out:
> [...]
> Hear, for I will speak noble things,
> and from my lips will come what is right;
> [...]
> I walk in the way of righteousness,
> along the paths of justice,
> [...]
> when he [the Lord] marked out the foundations of the earth,
> then I was beside him, like a master worker. [6]

In Proverbs Wisdom takes on actions elsewhere associated with God.[7] Silvia Schroer argues that 'Personified Wisdom is a figure who creates connections and connectedness. She joins transcendence to the female, God to human experience, theology to everyday reality, the woman teacher to the teaching, the creatrix to the principle of creation.'[8] This activity of creating connections is reminiscent of Hermeticism's view of the universe as a web of connections and H.D.'s stylistic emphasis on connectedness and unfolding analogies. A similar correlation to Hermeticism's view of the divine as ceaselessly unfolding within the world may be found in the work of Russian Orthodox theologian Sergei Bulgakov, who describes Sophia, Holy Wisdom, as God's creative activity.[9]

However, the emphasis on connectedness should not occlude the presence of difference in discourse on Wisdom. In Proverbs the figure of Wisdom, the wise (and good) woman, is contrasted with the 'strange' or 'foreign' (and transgressive) woman who is portrayed as dangerous and threatening in her otherness: 'You will be saved from the loose woman/from the adulteress with her smooth words/who forsakes the partner of her youth/and forgets her sacred covenant'.[10] However, Claudia Camp points out that, although Wisdom and the Strange Woman appear to be contrasted, in fact some of their descriptions are the same: both are found 'in the street' and 'in the marketplace', encounters with them involve 'embracing' and 'grasping', both invite followers to their homes and offer food and drink.[11] Furthermore, both the Strange Woman and Wisdom are connected to YHWH. His deeds are described as 'strange' and his work is 'alien', the same words Proverbs uses for the Strange Woman. Similarly, both Wisdom and YHWH give strength and reward the faithful with 'beautiful' or 'glorious' crowns.[12] Thus the divine becomes another locus of connection between wisdom and otherness. Camp goes on to argue that the Strange Woman is inseparable from Wisdom and is herself a prophetic reminder of the significance of difference within Wisdom.[13] Difference, as we saw in Chapter Four, is crucial to creativity. In her writing on encounter Cixous explores a similar dynamic of connection and difference, suggesting that the way through this paradox is openness towards alterity so that difference is not annihilated, nor are connections severed.

Hokmah shares many qualities with the Egyptian Ma'at (the goddess of truth who also represents world order, plenitude and justice) and Isis (in late antiquity Isis assumed many of Ma'at's attributes, including presiding over world order, justice and healing).[14] Moreover, Hellenist thinkers such as Philo and the Gnostics frequently merged Isis and Sophia.[15] In Hellenic Egypt Isis becomes closely associated with Hermes/Thoth and thus is associated with Hermeticism.[16] Isis is credited with inventing written language, as is Hermes, while Hokmah is associated with sacred language (Torah is 'the earthly manifestation of Wisdom'), and Sophia with the Word (Logos) of John's Gospel.[17] This association of Wisdom with sacred language and textuality resonates with H.D.'s association of goddesses and words in the alchemical ritual and the Lady who carries a book. Surprisingly, rather than seeking knowledge in the mythology of the past she claims that the Lady's book is *not* 'the tome of the ancient wisdom', as we might expect from a Hermeticist. Instead, the Lady's book holds 'the blank pages/of the unwritten volume of the new' (1998b, *Angels* 38:10–12). Here H.D. extends the role of Wisdom to the contemporary poet and reader. Ancient Wisdom speaks with many voices; she is Hokmah, Sophia, Isis, Mary, Ma'at and *Trilogy*'s Lady; she is Hebrew, Greek and Egyptian; she is ancient and contemporary. She is a figure who embodies H.D.'s syncretism.

In H.D.'s lyric poem 'Ancient Wisdom Speaks', the blue-clad Wisdom stands on a mountain, above a river, watching the turning seasons and witnessing the desolation of war-torn cities; the ancient cities of Nineveh and Tyre are named, while the contemporary London scene is implied. H.D. asserts the endurance of Wisdom as a consolation:

> she knew our fear,
> and yet she did not falter
> nor cast herself in anguish by the river:
>
> but she stood,
> the sun on her hair
> or the snow on her blue hood:
>
> winter and summer,
> summer and winter
> … again … again …
>
> never forgetting
> but remembering
> our peculiar desolation. (pp. 483–4)

Wisdom is a steadfast witness through the turning seasons; she is able to witness individual suffering but is not overcome by it.

Beyond the consolation of her presence and the promise of her endurance, Wisdom's message is appropriate for its setting in the Sitwells' gala and anticipates a central concern of *Trilogy*: the question of the validity of poetry in wartime (and, by extension, creative work more broadly) (*Walls* 8:3–34). In 'Ancient Wisdom Speaks' H.D.'s aesthetic manifesto is more direct than the slowly unfolding argument of *Trilogy*. The poet suggests that all would have been lost if Wisdom did not 'stand waiting,/not forgetting/[…]/if you had not said over and over,/[…]/repeatedly, this prayer' (p. 482). Here Wisdom takes on the role of witness; she sees the trauma of war and holds those who suffer in remembrance and the litany of her prayers. Along with witness and remembrance, Wisdom claims that beauty endures despite destruction:

> remember these (you said)
> who when the earth-quake shook their city,
> when angry blast and fire
>
> broke open their frail door,
> did not forget
> beauty. (p. 482)

The command to remember beauty (and to remember those who have held to it in previous times of destruction and loss) is here given the weight of a sacred charge. It is not goodness or duty that saves, but beauty. The devotion to beauty marks H.D.'s work from her early days of *Sea Garden* with its sacred wild gardens and *Notes on Thought and Vision* with its extended meditation on aesthetics and creativity. However, in her work from the 1940s the nexus of aesthetics, the sacred and creative practice, finds a fuller, more explicit expression. Divinity is to be found within beauty and beauty itself appears in the most surprising of places – even in a pile of rubble in a bombed-out London square.

The context for Wisdom's repeated prayer is the coming of spring. She repeats the words as the snow melts and flows down the mountain, where she watches it 'become/blossom of apple, quince and the wild-pear' (p. 482). Here H.D. links Wisdom's call to remember beauty with trees in blossom, just as the Lady in *Trilogy* is associated with the half-burnt, half-blossoming apple tree and Hokmah is 'a tree of life to those who lay hold of her' in Proverbs.[18] H.D. aligns beauty with life, suggesting the divine life breathing through the world of Hermeticism. Beauty contributes to the endurance and renewal of the desolate community and thus is a creative as well as an aesthetic quality.

The poem closes with Wisdom speaking words of comfort, assuring the desolate of her enduring presence. Her devotees are both vanquished and yet still responsive:

> your ashes,
> sainted ones,
> your chastened hearts,
> your empty frames,
> your very bones,
> still serve
> to praise my name. (p. 484)

Here H.D. suggests a mingling of sacred and profane, bodily reality and transcendence. Anguish, loss and death are not vanquished, yet while they remain Wisdom also endures and witnesses the renewal that may take place despite, even within, destruction. For H.D., saints are those who have cleaved to Wisdom and her call to attend to beauty. In 'Ancient Wisdom Speaks' – as in the primary texts of this volume, *Trilogy*, *The Gift* and *The Sword Went Out to Sea* – we see the richness of H.D.'s visionary, religious imagination and the imagery she uses to deploy it. In presenting 'Ancient Wisdom Speaks' at the Sitwells' gala, H.D. aligns the poem with the creative arts and asserts their importance for the public sphere. While the significance of poetry is implied within the poem, material mysticism is more explicit in Wisdom's evocation of the returning spring, the snow turned to blossom and the witness to Wisdom that resides within the physical remains of destruction.

Wisdom continues to be an important figure in H.D.'s late work. While this book has focused on the nexus of spirituality and creativity in H.D.'s writing from the Second World War, I wish to briefly consider the role of Wisdom in H.D.'s late work and her connection to Hermeticism in order to demonstrate the relevance of H.D.'s work from this period to her subsequent writing. The title of the posthumously published *Hermetic Definition* (1972) is a clear indication that Hermeticism continued to preoccupy H.D. beyond the period examined in this volume. The correspondence of the title with H.D.'s own initials suggests that she sees her role as the interpretation of hermetic mysteries. However, she is tentative in this volume; in 'Sagesse' (another word for wisdom), she describes herself as 'aspiring yet questioning/my right to mention even one of the seventy-two regents/of the great Temple' (9:8–10).[19] The poetic sequences in *Hermetic Definition* are littered with questions marks, as if H.D.'s understanding of divine mysteries must be expressed through circumlocution and gesture, rather than assertion. Yet she is also confident in the importance of the interrelationship between the small and the great, wondering if 'the vast cycle require[s] this space, this place,/this corner of this room, to prove the might/of the infinitely great to protect/the most minute, the almost invisible spark' ('Sagesse' 9:12–15). Here the poet's room correlates to the celestial spheres, a mundane place becoming a place of sacred encounter. The room is transformed into a temple – 'fragrant with enchantment' – by the presence of flowers left by 'the German, *Germain*' (7:13, 8:1).[20]

In 'Sagesse' H.D. attends to angels as guardians of time and the connection between sacred time and mundane places. The poem begins with a picture of a Scops owl, an avatar for divine Wisdom. At first glance this owl seems a peculiar representation of Wisdom, he (and it is a he) is both fierce and faintly ridiculous. Yet the owl is a trickster figure and thus serves as a link between Wisdom and the trickster Hermes. In the day he is 'a fool, a clown', yet 'when darkness comes' he will be the object of devotion where 'there is only faint light from the braziers/and the ghostly trail of incense, and cries of recognition/and of gladness in the fragrant air' (2:9--18). As we know from *Trilogy*, fragrance denotes a ritual space and marks the presence of the sacred. As she often does, H.D. gives a description of ritual as mysterious and fragmentary, enticing the reader but not making clear exactly where we are invited or what this worship may involve. 'Sagesse' moves back and forth from sacred to mundane space with a disorienting lack of transition or explanation; this juxtaposition suggests the interpenetration of the two and the impossibility of completely separating them.

The wise trickster owl witnesses this juxtaposition as H.D. signifies his divine status: 'May those who file before you feel/something of what you are – that God is kept within/the narrow confines of a cage, a pen' (2:1–3). Here H.D. links the owl with the divine and also with writing, another indication that the owl is linked with Wisdom and Hermes, the inventors of writing. The connection between divinity and writing is slipped in, almost casually, and only returned to later in the poem. When H.D. returns to writing, she comments on her own efforts, whose intensity leave her 'shivering but inert' (12, 16:2). As in *The Sword*, H.D. indicates that writing may be a difficult but necessary task.

Like *The Gift*, 'Sagesse' portrays a precocious child who visits the owl and sees with greater clarity than the adults around her (who are caught up in distressing memories of the Blitz as the war makes its presence felt even in this late poem). The child recognizes the mystery and wonder of the owl and is 'touched by the majesty, the lifted wings' (2:5). The child as visionary prefigures the poet who will bring this vision to writing. We also see a child in 'Winter Love', a late poetic sequence that is a coda to *Helen in Egypt* (1963) but published in *Hermetic Definition*. Here Wisdom (named *Sage Femme*) is a midwife who delivers the child, Hope. This is a wild child, who is unknown and other yet compels hope and love, rather like the bundle of myrrh in *The Flowering of the Rod*, whose fragrance drifts where the wind blows and cannot be contained. The image of birthing is often used as a metaphor for creative production, with the child likened to the work of art. Here Wisdom is neither the poet/mother nor child/poem but the one who assists the process, guiding the child into life. However, this is not a cosy image or an easy birth. H.D./Helen calls *Sage Femme* cruel and resists being drawn away from rest, invisibility and hopelessness. The child requires sustenance and the poet knows that 'terrible the weight of honey and of milk' (28:21). However, the poet embraces the child and her demands, even though this return to life will ultimately end in death: 'come, come, O *Espérance,/Espérance*, O golden bee,/take life afresh and if you must,/so slay me' (28:30–3). Here we have a more explicit rendering of the cost of renewal than H.D. acknowledges in *Trilogy*. Wisdom's gifts are not only plenitude, delight and beauty but also the witness of suffering, the pain, work and letting go of motherhood and the knowledge of death.

Feminist revisioning, imagination and modernism

Wisdom embodies creative activity; presiding over the creation and ongoing working of the world, she acts as witness, prophesies beauty, reveals difference. 'Ancient Wisdom Speaks' performs a revisioning of the Wisdom tradition by emphasizing the connections between pagan, Jewish and Christian traditions as well as providing a strong and beautiful feminine divine figure. In her seminal essay, 'When We Dead Awaken', Adrienne Rich defines 're-vision' as 'the act of looking back, of seeing with fresh eyes, of entering an old text from a new critical direction'. She argues that it is a crucial activity; 'for women [it is] more than a chapter in cultural history: it is an act of survival'.[21] H.D.'s work, then, provides a creative resource for the feminist project of excavating a useable tradition. In writing themselves into religious and literary traditions, feminists have relied on the imagination to enable a revisioning practice that transforms the old into new modes and models, both within and beyond historic traditions.

Alicia Ostriker reads H.D. in the tradition of feminist revisioning, while also considering her a visionary poet. Within this critical tradition, both Ostriker and Eileen Gregory situate H.D. as inheritor of the Romantic tradition of the visionary imagination, as I have previously noted. Ostriker offers a reading strategy for approaching H.D., in which the reader is also figured as a wild, unorthodox visionary: 'How do we read the late H.D.? With the wind in our hair, a gleam in our eyes, and a sense of headlong forward motion.'[22] In her feminist revisions, H.D. engages with the Romantic tradition, shaping it to her own ends and developing her own vehicles for expression.

This book has explored the presence of the wild, strange and divine imagination through the analysis of Hermeticism in H.D.'s work and its correlation with the writing practice of both H.D. and Hélène Cixous; this view of imagination can also be seen in Romanticism. In the Romantic worldview, the creative, or productive, imagination – with perhaps its most extreme exponent in Blake – shapes the world, and places the poet in the role of prophet and priest.[23] For Blake, imagination is the basis of all art and vision; it is the gift or even the divine person of the Holy Ghost.[24] Blake's imagination involves an opening of world boundaries.[25] Peter Otto draws upon Blake's conflation of the divine and the imagination to argue that Blake understands imagination as that which disrupts boundaries and thus creates openness to the other:

> [T]he major prophecies are an attempt to describe the way in which the created world [...] can open itself to others. [...] [T]he Imagination is first glimpsed

> not in the fabrication of a world, but at the point at which our worlds are cast off.[26]

In this vision of creativity and imagination, the shaping of the world leads to crossing boundaries between worlds and moving towards the limits of the possible. Worlds are cast off as alterity calls the poet towards transformation.

This reading raises the issue of imagination in modernist writing. The resources of a sacred alterity are not reserved for the Romantic poets alone. Modernist studies tends to leave questions of imagination and the sacred to romanticists; however, there is a stream of Romanticism within modernism.[27] Moreover, Paul Ricoeur's work on imagination as that which enables the completion of metaphor and as generative of possible worlds indicates that imagination may be a crucial category for modernism. Its experimentation, avant-garde aesthetics and interest in new creative forms can be read as gestures towards possible worlds and new ways of being in the world. This valorization of 'process, the new, and the ever-changing' and the 'commitment to imaginative vitality' is particularly romantic.[28] Michael Levenson argues that tension between the 'search for novelty' and the 'recollection of precursors [...] creates an abiding instability, a sense of modernity as inescapable but undecidable'.[29] For H.D. and Cixous this undecidability indicates a spiritual haunting, a presence that is never fully delineated but always hinted at, invoked or described in startling ways. It is an invitation for creative work that also remains undecidable but concerned with possibility.

H.D.'s and Cixous's engagement with the intersection of difference, creative practice and materiality raises the question of where the traces of sacred alterity and material mysticism are to be found in other modernist texts. Writers such as Rosamond Lehmann, Rebecca West, Mary Butts and Dorothy Richardson occupy an uneasy place in the modernist canon. Likewise, their writing includes marginal religious discourses like those explored in H.D.'s work. Literary criticism has much to gain from attending to the religious imagination in modernist texts and its interaction with aesthetic, ethical and political concerns. This exploration has begun in scholarship such as Hobson's work on the role of angels as signifiers for the modernist utopian imagination. As Hobson argues, angels as untimely, awkward figures that persist past the point of expected obsolescence are well placed to indicate an imaginative project that also appears to have had its day, to have failed to deliver on its promises. Yet angels persist in the literature of late modernism, as does utopian imaginative interventions. For writers like H.D., this imaginative project is inherently spiritual, but it is a spirituality that looks to earth, rather than the heavens: 'crouch[ing] near the grass and near to the earth that made us' (H.D., 1998a, p. 50).

Attention to the avant-garde stylistics of H.D. and Cixous enables an exploration of poetic form and spirituality, and of creative, playful engagements with language and divine difference. As we have seen, God as a sanctuary for the not-yet written opens up a creative space for imagining difference. This space of imagining is hospitable to interdisciplinary projects such as this one. In attending to writing as a spiritual practice, the reading practice developed over the course of this book allows what is mysterious within language to emerge. Likewise, the material mysticism elaborated here suggests that mystery inheres in materiality and divinity emerges from, and exceeds, the diversity of the material world: from a beeswax candle to an orange; from stone hieroglyphics to a medium's table; from expansive journeys across continents and oceans to the minute movements of breath. In bringing together the familiar and the strange, indeed, in making the familiar strange and the strange familiar, H.D.'s and Cixous's writing crafts a hospitable place in which we might encounter alterity, both within and outwith ourselves. In gesturing to the unknown and the elsewhere, this writing invites us to imagine differently.

Notes

1 In her analysis of the work of Elizabeth Smart, Heather Walton uses the term 'domestic sublime' to describe a feminine religious writing in which ordinary objects are 'transform[ed] [...] into strange and holy shapes'; 2007b, p. 180.

2 Rather oddly, T. S. Eliot chose to read a section of *The Wasteland* which concludes, 'London Bridge is falling down'; Bryher 1972, p. 84.

3 The first three (of four) sections appeared as 'Ancient Wisdom Speaks to the Mountain' in the *Times Literary Supplement* on 8 May 1943; Martz 1983, p. 621.

4 H.D. alludes to the Lady's syncretist connections to the Byzantine figure of Holy Wisdom and pagan goddesses in a letter to Norman Pearson: 'I distinctly link the LADY up with Venus-Annael, with the Moon, with the pre-Christian Roman Bona Dea, with the Byzantine Greek church Santa Sophia and the SS of the Sanctus Spiritus'; Hollenberg 1997, p. 45. H.D. would have seen the Byzantine church, the Hagia Sophia in Constantinople, when she travelled there with Bryher in the 1920s; Bryher? 1922; Guest 1984, p. 156. The authorship of 'Bryher's note-book' is unclear: the page is typed, including the title, but it is held with other autobiographical papers in the H.D. Papers, so it may have been written, or typed, by H.D., or jointly composed.

5 For an introduction and overview of Biblical Wisdom literature see Hunter 2006.

6 Proverbs 8.1–30. Later in Proverbs, Wisdom is figured as a host, who builds her house, lays her table and invites others to dine; Proverbs 9.1–5.

7 Camp 1996, p. 87.

8 Schroer 2000, p. 37. For further feminist analysis of Biblical Wisdom literature, see Brenner 1995; Brenner and Fontaine 1998.

9 Bulgakov 1993, p. 31.

10 Proverbs 2.16–17. Camp notes that the Hebrew words that are usually translated into English as 'loose woman/adulteress' more literally mean 'stranger' or 'foreigner'. However, the correlation between foreignness and religious and sexual infidelity is a frequent trope in the Biblical literature; 1996, pp. 92–3.

11 Ibid. p. 94.

12 Ibid. pp. 103–4.

13 Ibid. pp. 107–9.

14 Assmann 2001, pp. 3, 73, 240; Hunter 2006, pp. 99–101; Schroer 2000, pp. 17, 105; Seligman 1971, p. 42; Witt 1997, pp. 106–7. Hokmah is also associated with another Middle-Eastern goddess, the Ugaritic Asherah, 'She who treads on the sea'; Hunter 2006, p. 102.

15 Fiorenza 1994, p. 136; Witt 1997, p. 194. *Paganism in our Christianity* (a book H.D. owned and marked; her copy is held in the Beinecke Rare Book and Manuscript Library) argues that Isis and Mary were united, both referred to as Queen of Heaven and the object of women's devotion; Weigall 1928, pp. 126–7.

16 Witt 1997, p. 108.

17 Ibid.; Camp 1996, pp. 96–7; Ruether 2005, p. 128; Fiorenza 1994, pp. 138, 48–9. Ruether also points out that the early Christian understanding of Jesus as embodiment of Wisdom draws upon the milieu of later Jewish wisdom writing; 2005, p. 128.

18 3.18.

19 The 72 regents are the angels that guard time: days, hours and minutes.

20 '[T]he German' correlates to the figure of Saint-Germain in *The Mystery*.

21 Rich 1979, p. 35.

22 Ostriker 1983, p. 29.

23 Jasper 1985, pp. 10–11; Engell 1981, p. 238.

24 Damon 1965, p. 195.

25 Otto 1991, p. 8.

26 Ibid., pp. 12, 14.

27 Eileen Gregory aligns H.D.'s work with the Romantic Hellenism of Pater, Wilde and Swinburne, thus complicating the usual opposition (advanced by writers such as T. E. Hulme, Eliot, Pound and others) between Romanticism and modernist classicism; Gregory 1997, pp. 1–4, 11–28, 75–84; Hulme 1998, pp. 178–85.

Cassandra Laity also links H.D. to Romanticism via the decadents, while Michael O'Neil traces the influence of Romantic poets on twentieth-century poets; Laity 1996; O'Neill 2007.

28 Ibid. p. 8.

29 Levenson 2011, p. 2.

Bibliography

Aciman, A. (2000) *False Papers: Essays on Exile and Memory*, New York: Farrar, Straus and Giroux.

Anderson, E. (2012, in press) 'Burnt and blossoming: materiality mysticism in *Trilogy* and *Four Quartets*'. *Christianity and Literature*, 62:1, 303–24.

Anon. (1908–26) Mysticism. In Hastings, J. (ed.) *Encyclopaedia of Religion and Ethics*. Edinburgh: T & T Clark.

—(2000–9) 'The comprehensive report on the Brethren's negotiations in Bethlehem and Gnadenhütten with the Nanticokes and Shawnee Nations from April 1752 and also on the pact made with both nations at that time in Gnadenhütten, on the same visit to Bethlehem in July 1752 etc.' In Talarico, J. (ed.) *Bethlehem Digital History Project*. Bethlehem, PA: Bethlehem Digital History Project, Available online at http://bdhp.moravian.edu/personal_papers/journals/detailed12.html [accessed 17 October, 2010].

Armstrong, T. (2005) *Modernism: A Cultural History*, Cambridge: Polity Press.

Assmann, J. (2001) *The Search for God in Ancient Egypt*, Ithaca, NY and London: Cornell University Press.

Atwood, C. (2004) *Community of the Cross: Moravian Piety in Colonial Bethlehem*, University Park: The Pennsylvania State University Press.

—(2005) '*The Passion of the Christ* and Christian devotion from a Moravian perspective'. *Covenant Quarterly*, 63:2, 16–28.

Augustine, J. (1996) 'Preliminary comments on the meaning of H.D.'s *The Sword Went Out to Sea*'. *Sagetrieb*, 15:1–2, 121–32.

—(1998) 'Introduction'. *The Gift by H.D.: the complete text*, Gainsville, FL: University Press of Florida, 1–28.

—(2009) 'Introduction'. In Augustine, J. (ed.) *The Mystery*, Gainesville: University of Florida Press, xxiii–xxxii.

Ayers, D. (2004) *Modernism: A Short Introduction*, Oxford: Blackwell Publishing.

Baker-Fletcher, K. (1998) *Sisters of Dust, Sisters of Spirit*, Minneapolis, MA: Fortress Press.

Baldick, C. (2008) *Oxford dictionary of literary terms*, Oxford: Oxford University Press.

Barthes, R. (1977) *Roland Barthes*, London and Basingstoke: Macmillan.

Beasley, R. (2007) *Theorists of Modern Poetry: T. S. Eliot, T. E. Hulme, Ezra Pound*, London and New York: Routledge.

Bell, C. (1997) *Ritual: Perspectives and Dimensions*, Oxford: Oxford University Press.

—(1998) 'Performance'. In Taylor, M. C. (ed.) *Critical Terms for Religious Studies*. Chicago: The University of Chicago Press, 205–24.

Benjamin, W. (2006) *One-Way Street and Other Writings*, London and New York: Verso.

Berkowitz, C. A. (2003) 'Paradise reconsidered: Hélène Cixous'. In Joy, M., O'Grady, K. and Poxon, J. L. (eds) *Religion in French Feminist Thought*. London: Routledge, 176–88.

Bertrand, D. (1995) 'Order and chaos in paradise: colonial and "postcolonial" constructions of religious identity through the Robinson Crusoe story'. *Religion and Literature*, 27:3, 29–51.

Bettelheim, B. (1986) *Surviving the Holocaust*, London: Collins.

Blyth, I. and Sellers, S. (2004) *Hélène Cixous: Live Theory*, New York and London: Continuum.

Boughn, M. and Coleman, V. (2011) 'Introduction'. In Duncan, R. *The H.D. Book*, Berkeley: University of California Press, 1–30.

Braidotti, R. (1994) *Nomadic Subjects: Embodiment and Sexual Difference in Contemporary Femininst Theory*, New York: Columbia University Press.

Braude, A. (1989) *Radical spirits: spiritualism and women's rights in nineteenth-century America*, Boston: Beacon Press.

Bray, A. (2004) *Hélène Cixous: Writing and Sexual Difference*, Basingstoke: Palgrave Macmillan.

Brenner, A. (ed.) (1995) *A Feminist Companion to Wisdom Literature*, Sheffield: Sheffield Academic Press.

Brenner, A. and Fontaine, C. (eds) (1998) *Wisdom and Psalms: A Feminist Companion to the Bible (second series)*, Sheffield: Sheffield Academic Press.

Brock, R. N. and Parker, R. A. (2001) *Proverbs of Ashes: Violence, Redemptive Suffering and the Search for What Saves Us*, Boston: Beacon Press.

—(2008) *Saving Paradise: How Christianity Traded Love of this World for Crucifixion and Empire*, Boston: Beacon Press.

van den Broek, R. (1998) 'Gnosticism and Hermeticism in antiquity'. In van den Broek, R. and Hanegraaff, W. (eds) *Gnosis and Hermeticism from Antiquity to Modern Times*, Albany: State University of New York Press, 1–20.

Bronfen, E. (1999) *Dorothy Richardson's Art of Memory: Space, Identity, Text*, Manchester: Manchester University Press.

Brooker, P. and Thacker, A. (2005a) 'Introduction: locating the modern'. In Brooker, P. and Thacker, A. (eds) *Geographies of Modernism: Literatures, Cultures, Spaces*, London and New York: Routledge, 1–5.

—(eds) (2005b) *Geographies of Modernism: Literatures, Cultures, Spaces*, London and New York: Routledge.

Brown, D. (2004) *God and Enchantment of Place: Reclaiming Human Experience*, Oxford: Oxford University Press.

Bryher (1972) *The Days of Mars: A Memoir 1940–1946*, London: Calder and Boyars.

—(1922) Autobiographical Notes: Bryher's Note-book, 1922 [typescript]. H.D. Papers, Yale Collection of American Literature, New Haven, CT: Beinecke Rare Book and Manuscript Library, Yale University.

Buck, C. (1991) *H.D. and Freud: Bisexuality and Feminine Discourse*, New York: Harvester Wheatsheaf.

Bulgakov, S. (1993) *Sophia: the wisdom of God*, Hudson, NY: Lindisfarne Press.

Buruma, I. (2001) 'Creativity in exile'. *New Republic*, February 12, 33–8.

Bush, D. (1957) *Mythology and the Romantic Tradition in English Poetry*, New York: Pageant Book Company.

Bynum, C. W. (2002) 'The blood of Christ in the later Middle Ages'. *Church History*, 71:4, 685–714.

Camp, C. V. (1996) 'Woman Wisdom and the strange woman: where is power to be found?' In Beal, T. K. and Gunn, D. M. (eds) *Reading Bibles, Writing Bodies: Identity and the Book*, London and New York: Routledge, 85–112.

Carpentier, M. C. (1998) *Ritual, Myth, and the Modernist Text: The Influence of Jane Ellen Harrison on Joyce, Eliot, and Woolf*, Amsterdam: Gordon and Breach.

Caruth, C. (1996) *Unclaimed Experience: Trauma, Narrative, and History*, Baltimore and London: The Johns Hopkins University Press.

Celan, P. (1978) 'The Meridian'. *Chicago Review*, 29:3, 29–40.

de Certeau, M. (1984) *The Practice of Everyday Life*, Berkeley: University of California Press.

—(1986) *Heterologies: Discourse on the Other*, Manchester: Manchester University Press.

—(1992) *The Mystic Fable: Volume One, the Sixteenth and Seventeenth Centuries*, Chicago and London: University of Chicago Press.

Chisholm, D. (1992) *H.D.'s Freudian Poetics: Psychoanalysis in Translation*, Ithaca, NY and London: Cornell University Press.

Chopp, R. (2001) 'Theology and the poetics of testimony'. In Brown, D., Daveney, S. G. and Tanner, K. (eds) *Converging on Culture: Theologians in Dialogue with Cultural Analysis and Criticism*, Oxford: Oxford University Press, 56–70.

Cixous, H. (1979) *Vivre l'orange / To live the Orange*, Paris, Des Femmes.

—(1991) *'Coming to writing' and Other Essays*, London: Harvard University Press.

—(1992) *Readings: The Poetics of Blanchot, Joyce, Kafka, Kleist, Lispector, and Tsvetayeva*, New York: Harvester Wheatsheaf.

—(1997) 'The laugh of the Medusa'. In Price Herndl, D. and Warhol, R. R. (eds) *Feminisms: An Anthology of Literary Theory and Criticism*, Basingstoke: Macmillan, 347–62.

—(1998a) *First Days of the Year*, Minneapolis and London: University of Minnesota Press.

—(1998b) *Stigmata: Escaping Texts*, London and New York: Routledge.

—(2006) *Reveries of the Wild Woman: Primal Scenes*, Evanston, IL: Northwestern University Press.

—(2007) *Insister of Jacques Derrida*, Stanford, CA: Stanford University Press.

—(2008) *White Ink: Interviews on Sex, Text and Politics*, Stocksfield: Acumen.

Cixous, H. and Calle-Gruber, M. (1997) *Rootprints: Memory and Life Writing*, London and New York: Routledge.

Cixous, H. and Clément, C. (1996) *The Newly Born Woman*, London: I. B. Tauris Publishers.

Clifford, J. (1997) *Routes: Travel and Translation in the Late Twentieth Century*, Cambridge, MA and London: Harvard University Press.

Collecott, D. (1999) *H.D. and Sapphic Modernism, 1910–1950*, Cambridge and New York: Cambridge University Press.

Conley, V. A. (1992) *Hélène Cixous*, Toronto and Buffalo, NY: University of Toronto Press.

Connor, R. (2004) *H.D. and the Image*, Manchester and New York: Manchester University Press.

Copenhaver, B. P. (1992) 'Introduction'. In Copenhaver, B. P. (ed.) *Hermetica: The Greek* Corpus Hermeticum *and the Latin* Asclepius *in a New English Translation*, Cambridge: Cambridge University Press, xiii–lxi.

Corbin, H. (1969) *Creative Imagination in the Sūfism of Ibn 'Arabī*, London: Routledge and Kegan Paul.

Cottom, D. (1991) *Abyss of Reason: Cultural Movements, Revelations, and Betrayals*, Oxford: Oxford University Press.

Crown, K. (1995) 'H.D.'s jellyfish manifesto and the visible body of modernism'. *Sagetrieb*, 14:1–2, 217–41.

Damon, S. F. (1965) *A Blake Dictionary: The Ideas and Symbols of William Blake*, Providence, RI: Brown University Press.

Davis, C. (2007) *Haunted Subjects: Deconstruction, Psychoanalysis and the Return of the Dead*, Basingstoke: Palgrave Macmillan.

De Marco, A. A. (2003) Hail Mary. In Carson, T. and Cerrito, J. (eds) *New Catholic Encyclopedia*, 2nd edn, Detroit and New York: Gale, 616–17.

Debo, A. (2012) *The American H.D.*, Iowa City: University of Iowa Press.

Delumeau, J. (1995) *History of Paradise: The Garden of Eden in Myth and Tradition*, New York: Continuum.

Derrida, J. (1981) *Positions*, London: The Athlone Press.

—(1997) *Of Grammatology*, Baltimore and London: The Johns Hopkins University Press.

—(2001) *The Work of Mourning*, Chicago: University of Chicago Press.

Detloff, M. (2009) *The Persistence of Modernism: Loss and Mourning in the Twentieth Century*, Cambridge and New York: Cambridge University Press.

Dillon, S. (2007) *The Palimpsest: Literature, Criticism, Theory*, London, Continuum.

Duncan, R. (2011) *The H.D. Book*, Berkeley: University of California Press.

Duplessis, R. B. (1986) *H.D.: The Career of that Struggle*, Sussex: The Harvester Press.

Dupré, L. and Moore, P. (2005) Mysticism. In Jones, L. (ed.) *Encyclopedia of Religion*, 2nd edn, Detroit and New York: Thomson Gale.

Eade, J. and Sallnow, M. J. (1991) 'Introduction'. In Eade, J. and Sallnow, M. J. (eds) *Contesting the Sacred: The Anthropology of Christian Pilgrimage*, London and New York: Routledge, 1–29.

Ebeling, F. (2007) *The Secret History of Hermes Trismegistus: Hermeticism from Ancient to Modern Times*, Ithaca, NY and London: Cornell University Press.

Eco, U. (1990) *The Limits of Interpretation*, Bloomington, IN: Indiana University Press

Eliot, T. S. (1951) *Selected Essays*, London: Faber & Faber.

Emig, R. (1995) *Modernism in Poetry: Motivations, Structures and Limits*, London and New York: Longman.

Engell, J. (1981) *The Creative Imagination: Enlightenment to Romanticism*, Cambridge, MA and London: Harvard University Press.

Euripides (1973) *The Bacchae and Other Plays*, London: Penguin Books.

Faivre, A. (1995) *The Eternal Hermes*, Grand Rapids, MI: Phanes Press.

—(1998) 'Renaissance Hermeticism and the concept of western esotericism'. In van den Broek, R. and Hanegraaff, W. J. (eds) *Gnosis and Hermeticism from Antiquity to Modern Times*, Albany: State University of New York Press, 109–23.

—(2000) *Theosophy, Imagination, Tradition: Studies in Western Esotericism*, Albany: State University of New York Press.

Faull, K. M. (2004) 'Christ's other self: gender, the body and religion in the eighteenth-century Moravian Church'. *Covenant Quarterly*, 62:4, 28–41.

Felman, S. and Laub, D. (1992) *Testimony: Crises of Witnessing in Literature, Psychoanalysis, and History*, London and New York: Routledge.

Fiorenza, E. S. (1994) *Jesus: Miriam's child, Sophia's prophet: Critical Issues in Feminist Christology*, New York: Continuum.

Fogleman, A. S. (2007) *Jesus is Female: Moravians and the Challenge of Radical Religion in Early America*, Philadelphia: University of Pennsylvania Press.

Fowden, G. (1986) *The Egyptian Hermes: A Historical Approach to the Late Pagan Mind*, Cambridge: Cambridge University Press.

Freud, S. (2005) 'Mourning and melancholia'. *On Murder, Mourning and Melancholia*, London: Penguin, 201–18.

Friedman, S. S. (1975) 'Who buried H.D.? a poet, her critics, and her place in "the literary tradition"'. *College English*, 36:7, 801–14.

—(1981) *Psyche Reborn: The Emergence of H.D.*, Bloomington: Indiana University Press.

—(1990) *Penelope's Web: Gender, Modernity, H.D.'s Fiction*, Cambridge: Cambridge University Press.

—(1998) *Mappings: Feminism and the Cultural Geographies of Encounter*, Princeton: NJ, Princeton University Press.

—(ed.) (2002) *Analyzing Freud: Letters of H.D., Bryher and their Circle,* New York: New Directions.

Gan, W. (2009) *Women, Privacy and Modernity in Early Twentieth-Century British Writing*, Basingstoke: Palgrave Macmillan.

Gere, C. (2009) *Knossos and the Prophets of Modernism*, Chicago and London: University of Chicago Press.

Gollin, G. L. (1967) *Moravians in two worlds: a study of changing communities*, New York: Columbia University Press.

Graham, S. H. S. (2002) '"We have a secret. We are alive": H.D.'s *Trilogy* as a response to war'. *Texas Studies in Literature and Language*, 44:2, 161–210.

—(2007) 'Falling walls: trauma and testimony in H.D.'s *Trilogy*'. *English*, 56: Autumn, 299–319.

Gregory, E. (1986) 'Rose cut in rock: Sappho and H. D.'s *Sea Garden*'. *Contemporary Literature*, 27:4.

—(1997) *H.D. and Hellenism: Classic Lines*, Cambridge: Cambridge University Press.

Gubar, S. (1978) 'The echoing spell of H.D.'s *Trilogy*'. *Contemporary Literature*, 19:2, 196–218.

Guest, B. (1984) *Herself Defined: The Poet H.D. and Her World*, Garden City, New York, Doubleday and Company, Inc.

H.D. (1933) Letter to Viola Jordan, 9 January, 1933 [typescript], Viola Jordan Baxter Papers, Yale Collection of American Literature, New Haven, CT: Beinecke Rare Book and Manuscript Library: Yale University.

—(1938) Letter to Bryher, 2 March, 1938 [typescript], Bryher Papers, Yale Collection of American Literature, New Haven, CT: Beinecke Rare Book and Manuscript Library: Yale University.

—(1941) Letter to Viola Jordan, 10 November, 1941 [typescript], Viola Baxter Jordan Papers, Yale Collection of American Literature, New Haven, CT: Beinecke Rare Book and Manuscript Library: Yale University.

—(1945a) Letter to Bryher, 23 September, 1945 [typescript], Bryher Papers, Yale Collection of American Literature, New Haven, CT: Beinecke Rare Book and Manuscript Library: Yale University.

—(1945b) Letter to Viola Jordan, 25 March, 1945 [typescript], Viola Baxter Jordan Papers, Yale Collection of American Literature, New Haven, CT: Beinecke Rare Book and Manuscript Library: Yale University.

—(1946) Letter to Bryher, 6 October, 1946 [typescript], Bryher Papers, Yale Collection of American Literature, New Haven, CT: Beinecke Rare Book and Manuscript Library: Yale University.

—(1951) The Mystery – Zinzendorf notes [manuscript], H.D. Papers, Yale Collection of American Literature, New Haven, CT: Beinecke Rare Book and Manuscript Library: Yale University.

—(1960) Academy of Arts and Letters Acceptance Speech [typescript], H.D. Papers, Yale American Literature Collection, New Haven, CT: Beinecke Rare Book and Manuscript Library: Yale University.

—(1972) *Hermetic Definition*, Oxford: Carcanet Press.

—(1975) *Tribute to Freud*, New York: McGraw-Hill.

—(1982) *Notes on Thought and Vision and The Wise Sappho*, San Francisco: City Lights Books.

—(1983) *Collected Poems 1912–1944*, New York: New Directions.

—(1986) 'H.D. by *Delia Alton*'. *Iowa Review*, 16:3, 180–221.

—(1998a) *The Gift by H.D.: The Complete Text*, Gainesville, FL: University Press of Florida.

—(1998b) *Trilogy: The Walls Do Not Fall, Tribute to the Angels, The Flowering of the Rod*, New York: New Directions.

—(2007) *The Sword Went Out to Sea: (Synthesis of a Dream), by Delia Alton*, Gainesville, FL: University Press of Florida.

—(2009a) *Majic Ring*, Gainesville, FL: University Press of Florida.

—(2009b) *The Mystery*, Gainesville, FL: University Press of Florida.

—(2012a) *Magic Mirror, Compassionate Friendship, and Thorn Thicket: A Tribute to Erich Heydt*, Victoria: ELS Editions.

—(2012b) *Narthex and Other Stories*, Toronto: BookThug.

Handelman, S. A. (1982) *The Slayers of Moses: The Emergence of Rabbinic Interpretation in Modern Literary Theory*, Albany: State University of New York Press.

Hanegraaff, W. J. (1998) 'Romanticism and the esoteric connection'. In van den Broek, R. and Hanegraaff, W. J. (eds) *Gnosis and Hermeticism from Antiquity to Modern Times*, Albany: State University of New York Press, 237–68.

Harrison, J. E. (1903) *Prolegomena to the Study of Greek Religion*, Cambridge: Cambridge University Press.

—(1912) *Themis: A Study of the Social Origins of Greek Religion*, Cambridge: Cambridge University Press.

—(1913) *Ancient Art and Ritual*, London: Williams and Norgate.

Hartman, G. (2008) 'A displaced scholar's tale: the Jewish factor'. In Rosenfeld, A. H. (ed.) *The Writer Uprooted: Contemporary Jewish Exile Literature*, Bloomington: Indiana University Press, 133–60.

Henke, S. (2000) 'H.D.: psychoanalytic self-imaging'. In Henke, S. (ed.) *Shattered Subjects*, Basingstoke: Palgrave Macmillan, 25–53.

Hickman, M. (2012) '"Uncanonically seated": H.D. and literary canons'. In Christodoulides, N. and MacKay, P. (eds) *The Cambridge Companion to H.D.*, Cambridge: Cambridge University Press, 9–22.

Hobson, S. (2011) *Angels of Modernism: Religion, Culture, Aesthetics 1910–1960*, Basingstoke: Palgrave Macmillan.

Hogue, C. and Vandivere, J. (2007) 'Introduction'. *The Sword Went Out to Sea: (Synthesis of a Dream), by Delia Alton*, Gainesville, FL: University Press of Florida, xv–liii.

Holdsworth, K. (2007) 'Two literary questions'. *What's in Kelvin's Head*, Glasgow. Available online at http://www.thurible.net/20070702/two-literary-questions/ [accessed 17 October, 2010].

Hollenberg, D. K. (ed.) (1997) *Between History and Poetry: The Letters of H.D. and Norman Holmes Pearson*, Iowa City: University of Iowa Press.

Hollywood, A. (1995) *The Soul as Virgin Wife: Mechthild of Magdeburg, Marguerite Porete and Meister Eckhart*, Notre Dame and London: University of Notre Dame Press.

—(2002) *Sensible Ecstasy: Mysticism, Sexual Difference, and the Demands of History*, Chicago and London: The University of Chicago Press.

—(2003a) 'Mysticism, death and desire in the work of Hélène Cixous and Catherine Clément'. In Joy, M., O'Grady, K. and Poxon, J. L. (eds) *Religion and French Feminist Thought: Critical Perspectives*, London and New York: Routledge, 145–61.

—(2003b) 'Towards a feminist philosophy of ritual and bodily practice'. In Goodchild, P. (ed.) *Difference in Philosophy of Religion*, Aldershot: Ashgate, 73–83.

hooks, b. (2009) *Belonging: A Culture of Place*, New York and London, Routledge.

Hornung, E. (2001) *The Secret Lore of Egypt: Its Impact on the West*, Ithaca, NY and London: Cornell University Press.

Hughes, G. (1960) *Imagism and the Imagists: A Study in Modern Poetry*, London: Bowes and Bowes.

Hulme, T. E. (1998) 'From "Romanticism and Classicism"'. In Goldman, J., Kolocotroni, V. and Taxidou, O. (eds) *Modernism: An Anthology of Sources and Documents*, Edinburgh: Edinburgh University Press, 178–85.

Hunter, A. (2006) *Wisdom Literature*, London: SCM Press.

Hutton, J. E. (1909) *A History of the Moravian Church*, London: Moravian Publication Office.

Hyde, L. (1998) *Trickster Makes this World*, New York: Farrar, Straus and Giroux.

Jacobs, L. (2005) *Judaism and Theology: Essays on the Jewish Religion*, London: Vallentine Mitchell.

James, M. (2007) 'Ritual, drama and social body in the late medieval English town'. In Coldewey, J. C. (ed.) *Medieval Drama: Critical Concepts in Literary and Cultural Studies Vol. II: English Cycle Plays: Studies Past and Present*, London and New York: Routledge, 70–97.

Jantzen, G. (1995) *Power, Gender and Christian Mysticism*, Cambridge: Cambridge University Press.

Jasper, D. (1985) *Coleridge as Poet and Religious Thinker*, Allison Park, PA: Pickwick Publications.

—(2004) *The Sacred Desert: Religion, Literature, Art, and Culture*, Oxford: Blackwell Publishing.

Joh, W. A. (2006) *Heart of the Cross: A Postcolonial Christology*, Louisville and London: Westminster John Knox Press.

Jones, A. R. (1997) 'Writing the body: toward an understanding of l'écriture féminine'. In Herndl, D. P. and Warhol, R. R. (eds) *Feminisms: An Anthology of Literary Theory and Criticism*, Basingstoke: Macmillan, 370–83.

Kaiser, S. (1997) 'Four cases of Delaware Indian land loss and the Moravian Church'. *Religion and Identity in the Americas*. Möckmühl: Anton Saurwein, 135–52.

Kapferer, B. (2005) 'Sorcery and the beautiful: a discourse on the aesthetics of ritual'. In Hobart, A. and Kapferer, B. (eds) *Aesthetics in Performance: Formations of Symbolic Construction and Experience*, New York and Oxford: Berghahn Books, 129–60.

Kearney, R. (2004) *On Paul Ricoeur: The Owl of Minerva*, Aldershot: Ashgate.

Kidwell, C. S., Noley, H. and Tinker, G. E. T. (2001) *A Native American Theology*, Maryknoll, NY: Orbis Books.

Kinkle, G. S. (1990) *Our Dear Mother the Spirit: An Investigation of Count Zinzendorf's Theology and Praxis*, London: University Press of America.

Kloepfer, D. K. (1989) *The Unspeakable Mother: forbidden discourse in Jean Rhys and H.D.*, Ithaca, NY and London: Cornell University Press.

Knowles, M. and Moon, R. (2006) *Introducing Metaphor*, London and New York: Routledge.

Kwok, P. (2005) *Postcolonial Imagination & Feminist Theology*, London: SCM Press.

Laity, C. (1996) *H.D. and the Victorian Fin de Siècle: Gender, Modernism, Decadence*, Cambridge: Cambridge University Press.

Lane, B. C. (1998) *The Solace of Fierce Landscapes: Exploring Desert and Mountain Spirituality*, Oxford: Oxford University Press.

Levenson, M. (2011) *Modernism*, New Haven and London: Yale University Press.

Lewis, P. (2010) *Religious Experience and the Modernist Novel*, Cambridge: Cambridge University Press.

Lie, S. (1999) 'Life makes text from my body: a reading of Hélène Cixous' *La Venue à l'écriture*'. In Jacobus, L. A. and Barreca, R. (eds) *Hélène Cixous: Critical Impressions*, Amsterdam: Gordon and Breach, 1–22.

Linden, S. J. (2003a) 'Introduction'. In Linden, S. J. (ed.) *The Alchemy Reader: From Hermes Trismegistus to Isaac Newton*, Cambridge: Cambridge University Press, 1–23.

—(ed.) (2003b) *The Alchemy Reader: From Hermes Trismegistus to Isaac Newton*, Cambridge: Cambridge University Press.

Lochrie, K. (1991) 'The language of transgression: body, flesh and word in mystical discourse'. In Frantzen, A. J. (ed.) *Speaking Two Languages: Traditional Disciplines and Contemporary Theory in Medieval Studies*, Albany: State University of New York Press, 115–40.

Longstaffe-Gowan, T. (2001) *The London Town Garden: 1740–1840*, New Haven, CT and London: Yale University Press.

Lowell, A. (1970) *Tendencies in Modern American Poetry*, New York: Haskell House Publishers.

Lucy, N. (2004) *A Derrida Dictionary*, Oxford: Blackwell.

MacKay, M. (2007) *Modernism and World War II*, Cambridge: Cambridge University Press.

Maddrell, A. (2010) 'Memory, mourning and landscape in the Scottish mountains: discourses of wilderness, gender and entitlement in online and media debates on mountainside memorials'. In Anderson, E., Maddrell, A., McLoughlin, K. and Vincent, A. (eds) *Memory, Mourning and Landscape*, Amsterdam and New York: Rodopi, 123–45.

Manea, N. (2008) 'Nomadic language'. In Rosenfeld, A. H. (ed.) *The Writer Uprooted: Contemporary Jewish Exile Literature*. Bloomington: Indiana University Press, 1–26.

Martz, L. L. (1983) 'Notes'. In H.D. *Collected Poems 1912–1944*. New York: New Directions, 613–24.

Materer, T. (1995) *Modernist Alchemy: Poetry and the Occult*, Ithaca, NY and London: Cornell University Press.

McGinn, B. (1992) *The Foundations of Mysticism*, London: SCM Press.

—(1995) 'From admirable tabernacle to house of God: some theological reflections on medieval architectural integration'. In Brush, K., Draper, P. and Raguin, V. C. (eds) *Artistic Integration in Gothic Buildings*, Toronto: University of Toronto Press, 41–56.

McIntosh, M. A. (1998) *Mystical Theology: The Integrity of Spirituality and Theology*, Oxford: Blackwell.

McKnight, S. A. (1989) *Sacralizing the Secular: The Renaissance Origins of Modernity*, Baton Rouge and London: Louisiana State University Press.

Meakin, D. (1995) *Hermetic Fictions: Alchemy and Irony in the Novel*, Keele: Keele University Press.

Merezhkovsky, D. (1936) *The Secret of the West*, London: Jonathan Cape.

Miles, M. R. (2005) *The Word Made Flesh: A History of Christian Thought*, Oxford: Blackwell.

Moi, T. (1985) *Sexual/Textual Politics: Feminist Literary Theory*, New York and London: Routledge.

Moravian Church in North America (1891) *Offices of Worship and Hymns*, Bethlehem, PA: Moravian Publication Office.

—(1908) *The Liturgy and the Offices of Worship and Hymns of the American Province of the Unitas Fratrum, or The Moravian Church*, Bethlehem, PA: Moravian Publication Office.

Morris, A. (1986) 'H.D.'s "H.D. by *Delia Alton*"'. *Iowa Review*, 16:3, 174–8.

—(1990) 'Signaling: feminism, politics, and mysticism in H.D.'s war trilogy'. *Sagetrieb*, 9:3, 121–33.

—(2003) *How to Live / What to Do: H.D.'s Cultural Poetics*, Urbana and Chicago: University of Illinois Press.

Normington, K. (2007) *Modern Mysteries: Contemporary Productions of Medieval English Cycle Dramas*, Cambridge: D. S. Brewer.

Norris, K. (2001) *Dakota: A Spiritual Geography*, New York: Houghton Mifflin.

O'Neill, M. (2007) *The All-Sustaining Air: Romantic Legacies and Renewals in British, American, and Irish Poetry Since 1900*, Oxford: Oxford University Press.

Olmstead, E. P. (1991) *Blackcoats among the Delaware: David Zeisberger on the Ohio Frontier*, Kent, OH and London: The Kent State University Press.

Ostriker, A. (1983) *Writing Like a Woman*, Ann Arbor, The University of Michigan Press.

—(1990) 'No rule of procedure: the open poetics of H.D.' In Friedman, S. S. and Duplessis, R. B. (eds) *Signets: Reading H.D.*, Madison and London: The University of Wisconsin Press, 336–51.

Otto, P. (1991) *Constructive Vision and Visionary Deconstruction: Los, Eternity, and the Productions of Time in the Later Poetry of William Blake*, Oxford: Oxford University Press.

Owen, A. (1989) *The Darkened Room: Women, Power and Spiritualism in Late Victorian England*, London: Virago.

—(2004) *The Place of Enchantment: British Occultism and the Culture of the Modern*, Chicago and London: The University of Chicago Press.

Oxford University Press (2010) *Oxford English Dictionary*, Oxford: Oxford University Press. Available online at www.oed.com [accessed 17 October, 2010].

Pearson, N. H. (1972) 'Foreword', *Hermetic Definition*, Oxford: Carcanet Press, v–viii.

Pencak, W. A. and Richter, D. K. (2004) 'Introduction'. In Pencak, W. A. and Richter, D. K. (eds) *Friends and Enemies in Penn's Woods: Indians, Colonists, and the Racial Construction of Pennsylvania*, University Park: The Pennsylvania University Press, ix–xxi.

Penrod, L. (2003) 'Algeriance, exile and Hélène Cixous'. *College Literature*, 30:1, 135–45.

Piper, H. W. (1962) *The Active Universe: Pantheism and the Concept of Imagination in the English Romantic Poets*, London: The Athlone Press.

Plaskow, J. (1990) *Standing Again at Sinai: Judaism from a Feminist Perspective*, New York: Harper Collins.

Pollock, G. (1988) *Vision and Difference: Feminism, Femininity and the Histories of Art*, London and New York: Routledge.

Pondrom, C. N. (1987) '*Trilogy* and *Four Quartets*: contrapuntal visions of spiritual quest'. *Agenda*, 25:3–4, 155–65.

Pound, E. (1954) 'A retrospect'. In Eliot, T. S. (ed.) *Literary Essays of Ezra Pound*, London: Faber & Faber, 3–14.

Prosser, E. (1961) *Drama and Religion in the English Mystery Plays*, Stanford, CA: Stanford University Press.

Punter, D. (2007) *Metaphor*, London and New York: Routledge.

Rainey, L. (1998) *Institutions of Modernism: Literary Elites and Public Culture*, New Haven and London: Yale University Press.

Randall, B. (2007) *Modernism, Daily Time and Everyday Life*, Cambridge: Cambridge University Press.

—(2009) '"Funny, but no hybrid": H.D., tea and expatriate identity'. *Symbiosis*, 13:2, 189–210.

Raphael, M. (2003) *The Female Face of God in Auschwitz: A Jewish Feminist Theology of the Holocaust*, London and New York: Routledge.

—(2009) *Judaism and the Visual Image: A Jewish Theology of Art*, London: Continuum.

Reid, C. E. (2010) 'H.D. and the archaeology of religion'. *Journal of Cultural and Religious Theory*, 10:2, 1–5.

Renshaw, S. (2009) *The Subject of Love: Hélène Cixous and the Feminine Divine*, Manchester and New York: Manchester University Press.

Rich, A. (1978) *The Dream of a Common Language: Poems 1974–1977*, London and New York: W. W. Norton & Company.

—(1979) *On Lies, Secrets, and Silence: Selected Prose 1966–1978*, New York: W. W. Norton & Company.

—(1986) *Blood, Bread and Poetry: Selected Prose 1979–1985*, London and New York: W. W. Norton & Company.

Ricoeur, P. (1974) 'Metaphor and the main problem of hermeneutics'. *New Literary History*, 6:1, On Metaphor, 95–110.

—(1991) *A Ricoeur Reader: Reflection and Imagination*, Hemel Hempstead: Harvester Wheatsheaf.

—(2003) *The Rule of Metaphor: The Creation of Meaning in Language*, London: Routledge.

Ruether, R. R. (2005) *Goddesses and the Divine Feminine: A Western Religious History*, Berkeley, Los Angeles and London: University of California Press.

Scarry, E. (1985) *The Body in Pain*, Oxford: Oxford University Press.

Schama, S. (1995) *Landscape and Memory*, London: HarperCollins.

Schechner, R. (1988) *Performance Theory*, New York: Routledge.

Schmidt, L. E. (2000) *Hearing Things: Religion, Illusion and the American Englightenment*, Cambridge, MA and London: Harvard University Press.

—(2003) 'The making of modern "mysticism"'. *Journal of the American Academy of Religion*, 71:2, 273–302.

Schneider, L. C. (1998) *Re-imagining the Divine: Confronting the Backlash against Feminist Theology*, Cleveland, OH: The Pilgrim Press.

Schroer, S. (2000) *Wisdom has Built her House: Studies on the Figure of Sophia in the Bible*, Collegeville, MN: The Liturgical Press.

Schutt, A. C. (2004) 'Female relationships and intercultural bonds in Moravian Indian missions'. In Richter, D. K. and Pencak, W. A. (eds) *Friends and Enemies in Penn's Woods: Indians, Colonists, and the Racial Construction of Pennsylvania*, University Park: The University of Pennsylvania Press, 87–103.

—(2007) *Peoples of the River Valleys: The Odyssey of the Delaware Indians*, Philadelphia: University of Pennsylvania Press.

Schwarz, A. (2000) *Kabbalah and Alchemy: An Essay on Common Archetypes*, Northvale, NJ and Jerusalem: Jason Aronson Inc.

de Schweinitz, E. (1885) *The History of the Church Known as the Unitas Fratrum or the Unity of the Brethren, Founded by the Followers of John Hus, the Bohemian Reformer and Martyr*, Bethlehem, PA: Moravian Publication Office.

Scott, B. K. (ed.) (1990) *The Gender of Modernism: A Critical Anthology*, Bloomington: Indiana University Press.

—(2007) *Gender in modernism: New Geographies, Complex Intersections*, Urbana: University of Illinois Press.

Scott, J. M. (2005) *On Earth as in Heaven: The Restoration of Sacred Time and Sacred Space in the Book of Jubilees*, Leiden: Brill.

Seligman, K. (1971) *Magic, Supernaturalism and Religion*, New York, Random House.

Sheldrake, P. (2001) *Spaces for the Sacred: Place, Memory and Identity*, London: SCM Press.

Shiach, M. (1991) *Helene Cixous: A Politics of Writing*, New York and London: Routledge.

Shreiber, M. Y. (1998) 'The end of exile: Jewish identity and its diasporic poetics'. *PMLA*, 113:2, 273–87.

Simpson, K. (2004) 'Pearl-diving: inscriptions of desire and creativity in H.D. and Woolf'. *Journal of Modern Literature*, 27:4, 37–58.

Sitwell, E. (194-) Letter to H.D. [manuscript], H.D. Papers, Yale Collection of American Literature, New Haven, CT: Beinecke Rare Book and Manuscript Library, Yale University.

Smith, J. Z. (1987) *To Take Place: Toward Theory in Ritual*, Chicago and London: University of Chicago Press.

Stott, R. (1997) 'Posting signs on the bog: fixing and unfixing H.D., Imagiste'. *Journal of Gay, Lesbian and Bisexual Identity*, 2:1, 27–46.

Suleiman, S. R. (1991) 'Writing past the wall: or the passion according to H.C.' In

Jenson, D. (ed.) *'Coming to Writing' and Other Essays*, Cambridge, MA and London: Harvard University Press, vii–xxii.

—(1993) *Budapest Diary: In Search of the Motherbook*, Lincoln and London: University of Nebraska Press.

Sword, H. (1995) 'H.D.'s *Majic Ring*'. *Tulsa Studies in Women's Literature*, 14:2, 347–62.

—(2002) *Ghostwriting Modernism*, Ithaca, NY and London: Cornell University Press.

Tate, T. (1998) *Modernism, History and the First World War*, Manchester and New York: Manchester University Press.

Thacker, A. (2003) *Moving through Modernity: Space and Geography in Modernism*, Manchester: Manchester University Press.

—(2011) *The Imagist Poets*, Tavistock, Northcote House Publishers.

Thurschwell, P. (2001) *Literature, Technology and Magical Thinking, 1880–1920*, Cambridge: Cambridge University Press.

Tooker, E. (ed.) (1979) *Native North American Spirituality of the Eastern Woodlands: Sacred Myths, Dreams, Visions, Speeches, Healing Formulas, Rituals and Ceremonials*, London: SPCK.

Trigilio, T. (2000) *'Strange Prophecies Anew': Rereading Apocalypse in Blake, H.D., and Ginsberg*, London: Associated University Presses.

Tripp, D. H. (1978) 'Protestantism and the Eucharist'. In Jones, C., Wainwright, G. and Yarnold, E., SJ (eds) *The Study of Liturgy*, London: SPCK, 248–63.

Tryphonopoulos, D. (2009) 'Introduction'. In Tryphonopoulos, D. (ed.) *Majic Ring*, Gainesville: University Press of Florida, xxi–xxxix.

—(1992) *The Celestial Tradition: A Study of Ezra Pound's The Cantos*, Waterloo, ON: Wilfred Laurier University Press.

Turner, V. (1975) *Dramas, Fields, and Metaphors: Symbolic Action in Human Society*, Ithaca, NY: Cornell University Press.

Tuveson, E. L. (1982) *The Avatars of Thrice Great Hermes*, London: Associated University Presses.

Vetter, L. (2010) *Modernist Writings and Religio-scientific Discourse: H.D., Loy and Toomer*, Basingstoke: Palgrave Macmillan.

Vincent, A. M. (2010) 'Seder and imagined landscapes'. In Anderson, E., Maddrell, A., McLoughlin, K. and Vincent, A. M. (eds) *Memory, Mourning and Landscape*, Amsterdam and New York: Rodopi, 147–63.

Visser, M. (2000) *The Geometry of Love: Space, Time, Mystery and Meaning in an Ordinary Church*, London: Penguin.

Vogt, P. (1998) 'A voice for themselves: women as participants in congregational discourse in the eighteenth-century Moravian movement'. In Kienzle, B. M. and Walker, P. J. (eds) *Women Preachers and Prophets through Two Millenia of Christianity*, Berkeley, Los Angeles and London: University of California Press, 227–47.

Walton, H. (2007a) *Imagining Theology: Women, Writing and God*, London: T & T Clark.

—(2007b) *Literature, Theology and Feminism*, Manchester: Manchester University Press.

Weigall, A. (1928) *The Paganism in our Christianity*, London: Hutchinson.

Wenell, K. J. (2007) *Jesus and Land: Sacred and Social Space in Second Temple Judaism*, London: T & T Clark.

White, S. (1995) 'The theology of sacred space'. In Brown, D. and Loades, A. (eds) *The Sense of the Sacremental: Movement and Measure in Art and Music, Place and Time*, London: SPCK, 31–43.

Williams, T. T. (2001) *Refuge: An Unnatural History of Family and Place*, New York: Random House.

Witt, R. E. (1997) *Isis in the Ancient World*, Baltimore and London: The Johns Hopkins University Press.

Wolters, C. (ed.) (1966) *Julian of Norwich: Revelations of Divine Love*, London: Penguin.

Woolf, V. (1966) *Three Guineas*, New York: Harcourt.

Yaeger, P. (1988) *Honey-mad Women: Emancipatory Strategies in Women's Writing*, New York: Columbia University Press.

—(1997) 'Consuming trauma; or, the pleasures of merely circulating'. *Journal X*, 1:2, 225–51.

Zilboorg, C. (ed.) (2003) *Richard Aldington and H.D.: Their Lives in Letters 1918–61*, Manchester: Manchester University Press.

Index

Lightning Source UK Ltd.
Milton Keynes UK
UKOW06f1147120315

247746UK00001B/142/P

9 781474 222839